THE GREEN BUNDLE

THE GREEN BUNDLE

Pairing the Market with the Planet

Magali A. Delmas with David Colgan

STANFORD BUSINESS BOOKS

An Imprint of Stanford University Press • Stanford, California

Stanford University Press
Stanford, California

Special discounts for bulk quantities of Stanford Business Books are available
to corporations, professional associations, and other organizations. For details
and discount information, contact the special sales department of Stanford
University Press. Tel: (650) 725-0820, Fax: (650) 725-3457.

Printed in the United States of America on acid-free, archival-quality paper

Library of Congress Cataloging-in-Publication Data

Names: Delmas, Magali A., author. | Colgan, David, 1979- author.
Title: The green bundle : pairing the market with the planet / Magali A.
    Delmas with David Colgan.
Description: Stanford, California : Stanford Business Books, an imprint of
    Stanford University Press, 2018. | Includes bibliographical references and
    index.
Identifiers: LCCN 2017054456 (print) | LCCN 2017057473 (ebook) |
    ISBN 9781503606425 (e-book) | ISBN 9781503600867 (cloth : alk. paper) |
    ISBN 9781503606418 (pbk. : alk. paper) | ISBN 9781503606425 (ebook)
Subjects: LCSH: Green marketing. | Green products. | Consumer behavior—
    Environmental aspects.
Classification: LCC HF5413 (ebook) | LCC HF5413 .D45 2018 (print) |
    DDC 658.8/02—dc23
LC record available at https://lccn.loc.gov/2017054456

Cover design: Tandem Creative
Typeset by Motto Publishing Services in 11.75/16 New Baskerville

CONTENTS

ACKNOWLEDGMENTS

This book is a team effort. I have many people to thank.

Over the years, in the course of my research, I have had the pleasure to interact with executives at some of the world's greatest businesses. I could not mention all of them here, but I would like to thank a few of those who inspired this book. They include Deirdre Wallace and John Strozdas at the Ambrose Collection, Lisa Colicchio and David Pogue at CBRE, Jim Fetzer at Ceago, Jack Dell'Accio at Essentia, Gay Browne at Greenopia, Chris Mann at Guayaki, William Hayward at Hayward Lumber, Jacob Atalla and Dan Bridleman at KB Homes, Brad Sparks at KPMG, Caryl Levine at Lotus Food, Jennifer Dubuisson at Mattel, Adam Lowry at Method, Yvon Chouinard and Elisa Loughman at Patagonia, Megan Rast and John Rego at Sony Pictures Entertainment, Roberto Munoz at Tesco, and Jana Hartline and Ryan McMullan at Toyota. Some of their stories are reported in this book.

This book derives most directly from research I have conducted in the past decade with colleagues. I thank my brilliant coauthors, who have helped develop my thinking on green bundle information strategies. These include Omar Asensio, Michaela Balzarova, Vanessa Burbano, Chien-Ming Chen, Victor Chen, Charles Corbett, Vered Doctori-Blass, Dror Etzion, Miriam Fischlein, Olivier Gergaud, Noah Goldstein, Laura Grant, Mathew Kahn, William Kaiser, Aanchal Kohli, Neil Lessem, Jinghui Lim, Stephen Locke, Maria Montes-Sancho,

Ivan Montiel, Suresh Muthulingham, Nicholas Nairn-Birch, Sanja Pekovic, Jay Shimshack, Amarjeet Singh, Mike Toffel, and Stephanie Vezich. Our collaborative work is referenced in this book.

I have also benefited greatly from the thinking and writing of many colleagues and researchers in the areas of corporate sustainability, strategy, marketing, and behavioral economics. I was fortunate to receive excellent comments on the research for this book from my colleagues at the Alliance for Research in Corporate Sustainability (ARCS), and the Organization and the Natural Environment division of the Academy of Management.

I particularly want to express my gratitude to Alberto Aragon Correa, Robert Lalasz, Alfred Marcus, Peter Kareiva, Jorge Rivera, and David Vogel. They encouraged me to write this book and provided excellent advice during various phases of this journey.

I thank my colleagues and the staff at the UCLA Institute of the Environment and Sustainability for their support, and I thank Morgan Barnes, Paul Barton, Louise Huang, Patrick Jurkiewicz, and Nate Tsang for their research assistance.

I also want to express my appreciation for the comprehensive and thoughtful comments of the reviewers at the Stanford University Press as well as for the outstanding encouragement and advice from my editor, Margo Beth Fleming.

Finally, I am profoundly indebted to my family. I thank my wonderful husband, Romain Wacziarg, for his support, and I thank my three amazing children for their patience.

INTRODUCTION

A FEW YEARS AGO, I was shopping for a bottle of wine to take to a friend's dinner party. It had to be high quality and sustainable—such would be expected of me as a professor at the UCLA Institute of the Environment and Sustainability. The owner of my local wine store suggested Frog's Leap, saying that "it has a rating above ninety on Wine Enthusiast, and it is made with organically grown grapes. It's a win-win."

I looked at the bottle and asked, "How do you know it's certified? There is no organic label." He said he knew the winery owner personally, so I took a chance and bought the wine. At home, a cursory Google search uncovered that the vineyard was indeed certified organic. I also came across an interview with John Williams, founder of Frog's Leap. He said there was no advantage to marketing the company's wine as organic but that the company was pursuing sustainability anyway because it led to higher-quality wine.[1] I later found quotes from other organic-certified winery owners declaring that they would not put "organic" on their labels because it confuses the public. As an environmental economist, I was intrigued.

As I researched wineries further, I discovered that only one-third of those with organic certification labeled their bottles as such. This was puzzling, since consumer surveys indicate that more than 70 percent of people actively seek responsible products wherever possible. Why would wineries go through costly organic certification without promoting it to their customers?

They discovered that selling sustainability is more complicated than it seems. Consumers come in many forms, and the context of the purchase matters. With wine, it may be that a relatively new term such as *organic* undercuts the legitimacy and legacy of vintages and vineyards. Or perhaps consumers see a trade-off in quality, despite organic wines being rated higher by experts. Maybe they aren't concerned about health benefits when they're drinking alcohol. Whatever the case, many winemakers found that an environmental benefit such as "certified organic" didn't resonate with their target audience. It affected their bottom line, and that has implications for the health of our planet.

Something similar happened to Nike in 2005 when it launched Considered, its first line of environmentally friendly shoes. The company had high hopes for its walking boot, which was made with brown hemp fibers. It looked earthy, obviously communicating that the shoe was sustainable. But critics panned the line, calling the $110 shoes "Air Hobbits" because of their forest-dweller appearance, and took Nike to task for releasing a design that detracted from its high-tech image. The boots also sold poorly, and they were off shelves within a year.[2] After the debacle, Nike decided to go green quietly instead and to stop communicating about the sustainability of its products. The Air Hobbit's big mistake was overlooking performance.

Both cases illustrate a central reality of the modern green

marketplace: it is complicated, and it is interwoven with human psychology and the history of industry and advertising. As a result, companies trying to sell sustainability have frequently missed the mark with broad-based appeals to a general sense of environmentalism.

Both cases also show that there is opportunity for businesses to take advantage of the growing but largely untapped consumer market for environmentally sound goods and services. This book provides strategies to understand specific audiences and what moves them in order to tap this market.

It almost goes without saying that the sum of our individual and household behaviors has a massive impact on the environment. Increasing awareness of environmental issues has led to a rise in conscious consumption, a movement consisting of those who seek ways to make positive decisions about what to buy and look for solutions to consumerism's negative impacts. But it remains challenging for citizens to relate their personal behavior to large-scale problems such as climate change, pollution, biodiversity loss, and natural-resource depletion.

In theory, markets can provide effective solutions by helping those who care about the environment act responsibly through personal choices. When consumers are armed with information about the impact of environmental products, each purchase becomes a vote for the planet, and this can be incredibly powerful in driving firms toward sustainability. With advances in science and information technologies, it is possible that in ten years we will live in a world of green transparency—that is, we will know almost everything about how our lives impact the environment. We could receive a detailed weekly carbon-footprint report based on commuting, eating, and housing choices. With that information, we can make each consumer choice a better one for the environment. This, in turn, would drive a sustainability revolution for entire corporate sectors. In this future, Walmart sells only organic because its consumers demand it. The number-one seafood offering in grocery stores and restaurants is sustainably farmed fish, spurring a recovery in ocean fish stocks. The popularity of high-carbon products such as beef would decline in favor of alternatives that involve fewer greenhouse-gas emissions.

There is evidence this vision will become reality. Markets fueled by sustainability information have expanded rapidly over the last decade. Lifestyles of Health and Sustainability (LOHAS) is a multibillion-dollar market of consumers focused on the well-being of the environment, themselves, and other people. Consumer demand for organic food has grown by double digits nearly every year since the 1990s, while the overall food market grew only by single digits.[3] From 2006 to 2011, the green-building segment grew 1,700 percent, whereas the overall construction market *contracted* 17 percent.[4] More companies now communicate about the greenness of their products and practices to take advantage of these markets: green advertising has increased almost tenfold in the last twenty years, and has nearly tripled since 2006.[5]

This rapid development has attracted many firms, but few have been able to harvest the fruits of green markets. Some hold a naive view of green consumers and fail to get the response they hoped. Others provide inaccurate claims about the greenness of their products, hampering the development of the sustainable market by damaging consumer trust. Many green-information strategies have failed by overlooking the essential components of such strategies. Most executives know they need to address the challenge of sustainability, but they are unsure how to reach their customer base.

"More information" is an incomplete answer. It has to be the right information presented in the right way. Consumers face a dizzying array of green choices at supermarkets and other stores. They are confused by the state of green-product information or even distrust it.

With the rise of social media, consumers wield unprecedented power to demand that companies align with their values. They can publicly access a wealth of information and rate the performance of firms. And, often in concert with activists, they can hold companies accountable for poor environmental records. This ability is cultivating smarter consumers who get information through a multitude of channels and quickly turn their backs on firms that lie. Well-designed information strategies create the opportunity to engage these consumers in a more positive way.

The bottom line? Token marketing campaigns are no longer enough. A coat of green paint that hides a brown reality no longer works. In an increasingly open, digital world in which honesty and authenticity are paramount, businesses need to keep up with growing demands for ethical behavior and transparency in their own operations and supply chain.

This book offers a way to cut through the noise and realize the potential of sustainable business. With insight from sustainable business and from behavioral economics, this book provides evidence-based approaches to overcoming barriers and participating effectively in green markets.

Successful strategies demand a holistic approach. A company must not only demonstrate a commitment to sustainability on multiple organizational levels but also ensure that sustainability measures come with benefits or attributes consumers will pay for. In the case of Nike, the "green look" of the shoe was not valued. With organic wine, firms failed to effectively communicate the personal benefits a consumer could expect, including better taste.

"Dark green" consumers, those willing to accept trade-offs for the environment, remain a small minority. Most people will not buy environmentally friendly goods if there is any perceived sacrifice in quality. Many are convenient environmentalists: they say they are willing to buy green, but their actions tell another tale. These people are reachable, but businesses must appeal to something more than pure altruism—they must combine altruism with personal benefits.

Information strategies that target altruism alone reach only the small minority of truly passionate green consumers. With what we call the "green bundle"—natural or implicit cobenefits of environmental goods and services—companies can strategically appeal to both the altruistic and egoistic values of consumers. Broadly, green bundle cobenefits include the following: quality, status, health, money, and emotion. Messaging that pairs sustainability with these private benefits creates a win-win for consumers. They are not only doing right by the world but also doing right by themselves. In a sense, they get to have their cake and eat it too—benefiting psychologically from altruism and benefiting in a more tangible sense from added value.

In this book, we describe the elements of effective information strategies that will help managers guide consumers along the difficult path from knowledge to consumption. We evaluate the attractiveness of information strategies for sustainability based on the form of the communication as well as the content of the message.

First, as noted, products need to provide benefits beyond environmental ones to reach the vast majority of consumers. They must be developed in a way that connects sustainability to other positive attributes that people often value more. Second, environmental claims need to be easily understood and credible. Green bundle strategies differ from the traditional communication techniques used for conventional products. They include the goal—explicit or implied—that a consumer is doing something to better the environment in addition to promoting her individual well-being. Brand credibility is important for conventional products, but it is even more important for green products. We describe ways of preventing greenwashing while providing accountability and transparency.

This book intends to speak to managers, policy makers, activists, and students—anyone who wants to use market forces to lead organizations down a sustainable path. We describe the elements of effective information campaigns based on case studies from different industries. The explosion of sustainable markets presents a huge opportunity, but it cannot be taken advantage of haphazardly. This book offers a thoughtful approach to capitalizing on these markets in a way that ensures future success.

In chapter 1, we lay out the context for this book. We describe how consumers have changed in the last decade, becoming not just more conscious about the environment but also more sophisticated, more suspicious about green messages, more convenience oriented, and less likely to put in extra effort to go green. In chapter 2, we introduce the framework of the green bundle, whereby configurations of environmental and private benefits with clear and authentic messaging can be designed to appeal to a majority of consumers, creating a tipping point in green consumption. We describe the psychological mechanisms that lead consumers to be attentive to green messages and motivate them to make the leap to green consumption.

Chapters 3 through 7 describe the green bundle—a series of strategic paths based on the cobenefits of environmental products and services. In chapter 3, we start with quality, highlighting how performance, functionality, durability, comfort, and convenience can all be bundled with sustainability. In chapter 4, we describe how status can be a powerful tool to compel green behavior in the marketplace. In chapter 5, we explain how the realization of the connection between environmental damage and poor health triggers stark modifications in consumption patterns. Chapter 6 addresses the complex relationship between money and sustainability; it also addresses how the context in which premiums or savings are framed is particularly important in convincing consumers to buy green. Chapter 7 emphasizes how storytelling can generate emotional responses that deeply engage consumers and amplify the cobenefits of green products. In chapter 8, we talk about how to avoid the pitfalls of greenwashing, which can foil sustainable-marketing strategies. Finally, in chapter 9, we discuss the signaling elements of the green bundle and provide strategies for sending clear and authentic messages to consumers. We conclude with a summary of the context in which bundle strategies are the most effective.

Returning to the example of organic wine, it's clear that none of these approaches are simple to execute, but we will provide clear and understandable ways to do so. With communications, sometimes less is more; with wine, it may be best to promote the quality benefit of better taste without heralding its sustainability. The message would still be there, but it would be subtle and perhaps more effective.

Given our history, it may seem incredulous that we can get the forces of business and the environment to go hand in hand in a way that benefits the planet, consumers, and bottom lines at the same time. And yet this is clearly the direction things are headed. With innovations and the rising power of green markets, these unlikely bedfellows are in it for the long haul. And with global environmental problems ever more pressing, we need these forces to work together as fast as possible. This book shows how to make that happen.

Chapter 1

WHAT SUSTAINABILITY HAS COME TO MEAN

THE GREEN MARKETPLACE is as imperfect as it is aspirational. Well-intentioned companies miss the mark when courting consumers. Customers have proven to be capricious, with stated preferences that contradict their willingness to buy green. And even the meaning of "green" has evolved over the past fifty years. We increasingly use the term *sustainability* to address not only nature and wilderness but also social-justice issues. Technology has unleashed an explosion of information, which (somewhat paradoxically) has left many people confused about what sustainability really looks like in practice.

The 1970s Granola Consumer

The cultural upheaval of the 1960s planted the seeds—activism and a back-to-earth ethos—that would become the 1970s green consumer. A stereotypical image may spring to mind: a Birkenstock-shod Berkeley resident whose dedication to nature included a lot of sacrifice. There were rough, recycled paper towels; messy, labor-intensive cloth diapers; and, of course, granola.

At least in part, this stereotype belies reality. Green consumers were emerging in cities and towns across the United States, and their concerns were very real. In the late 1960s, a series of well-publicized environmental crises focused the nation's attention on negative impacts of industrialization and on the need to control pollution. Consider the following examples.

On January 28, 1969, the idyllic coast of Santa Barbara turned pitch-black. An offshore-drilling rig operated by Unocal, then known as Union Oil, suffered a massive blowout. Three million gallons of oil flowed into the ocean, creating a thirty-five-mile-long slick. At the time, it was the worst spill in the nation's history. Oil-soaked birds washed onto blackened beaches by the thousands, as did corpses of dolphins and seals.

Six months later, another incident two thousand miles away highlighted the precarious relationship between industry and nature.[1] On the morning of June 22, 1969, the Cuyahoga River, which runs through the heart of blue-collar Cleveland, Ohio, into Lake Erie, burst into flames. *Time* magazine published dramatic photos of the burning river, describing it as so polluted by industrial waste and sewage that it "oozes rather than flows."

The two disasters terrified the public with visible consequences of toxic waste, pollution, and contamination while prompting policy makers to pass important legislation. The 1970s saw the passing of the National Environmental Policy Act, the Safe Drinking Water Act, and the Endangered Species Act as well as the creation of the Environmental Protection Agency (EPA) and Occupational Safety and Health Administration (OSHA). The Natural Resources Defense Council (NRDC) was formed, and the first Earth Day was celebrated in 1970.

A small group of individuals responded to the crises by using their consumption behavior as a tool to fight pollution and waste. For these people, consumption became part of activism.[2] They engaged in consumer boycotts to influence firms' environmental behavior by urging individual consumers to refrain from making selected purchases in the marketplace.[3] These boycotts were viewed as marketplace means to influence market ends.

A tuna boycott persuaded major canned-tuna producers to consider alternative fishing methods that did not harm dolphins. This boycott, which started in the 1970s, called attention to the incidental but widespread killing of dolphins associated with the fishing of yellowfin tuna. Eight environmental organizations, with a combined total of roughly two million members, were involved in the boycott. They sent approximately 150,000 letters to tuna-canning companies protesting the incidental killing of dolphins.[4] In St. Louis, they picketed Ralston Purina, producer of Chicken of the Sea tuna. In Long Beach, demonstrators picketed in front of J. H. Heinz Company—the parent company of StarKist Seafood Company, the largest producer of canned tuna in the world. Demonstrators carried signs saying, "Sorry Charlie—StarKist Kills Dolphins," and they chanted, "Save the dolphins, boycott Heinz!" On September 6, 1989, protesters demonstrated outside the hotel in which Heinz was holding its annual shareholder meeting. Two people climbed a building and unfurled a banner that read, "Heinz, Stop Killing Dolphins," and another interrupted the proceedings.[5]

The boycotts and protests worked. In 1990, the three largest tuna companies in the world—Heinz's StarKist, Bumblebee, and Chicken of the Sea—agreed to stop purchasing, processing, and selling tuna caught by the intentional chasing and netting of dolphins. Heinz chairman Anthony J. F. O'Reilly indicated that the company's decision was in response to ongoing and growing consumer pressure.[6]

Not all boycotts are effective, of course, but there is evidence of the impact they have on firms and their actions.[7] For example, in an event study of the performance of the stock prices of forty companies that were the target of a boycott between 1969 and 1991, there was a significant decrease in company share prices following boycotts compared with companies that were not subject to a boycott.[8]

For these activist consumers, consumption was a political act: they avoided specific products for political, ethical, or environmental reasons to change market practices.[9] They used their "purchase votes" to favor firms with preferred environmental impacts. Boycott participation was a forceful response to the perception that a firm had engaged in some egregious act.[10] While these consumers hoped they could make a difference, they also constrained their consumption and sacrificed personal benefits.

Boycotts represent a social dilemma. They put individuals at odds with their group, forcing them to choose between selfish or collective interests.[11] Boycotts differ from personal decisions to withhold consumption of a good; they constitute an organized and collective but nonmandatory (that is, no formal sanctions can be imposed on noncompliers) refusal to consume a good.[12] In this sense, the dynamics underlying an individual's decision to participate in a boycott are similar to those underlying the decision of many to participate in labor movements such as strikes. Individual suffering is necessary to promote collective interests.

Despite this emerging awareness of the power of consumption as a tool to influence corporations, few products in the 1970s and the 1980s were marketed in a way that would be considered green today. But some businesses were beginning to appeal to a consumer segment that rejected mainstream brands. Food cooperatives selling organic, natural products began to flourish. The committed green consumers fueling these operations understood that they were part of something new and that they might have to leave a few comforts of modernity behind. They were willing to go to specialized stores and pay steep premiums. They researched the origins and impacts of their purchases. But there was a long way to go before these markets became mainstream. The USDA organic label did not emerge until 2002.

Today's Excuse Makers

If the sacrifice-driven consumers of the 1970s met today's green consumers, they might feel as though they followed Alice down the rabbit hole. Driven by numerous factors other than conservation, the lives of modern green consumers are much more convenient and high-tech. A dozen electric Teslas pull into Whole Foods after self-navigating the quickest ways through rush-hour traffic. Comfortably nestled in headphones, consumers in TOMS shoes emerge to gather supplies for dinner. Aisle after aisle of sustainable products greet them. They're more expensive, but they're healthier—and who can put a price on that? Driven by a government ban on single-use plastic bags, they've switched to reusable cloth ones. It would be a minor faux pas to ask for paper at the checkout. But some do, recycling them later. After dinner, they read news on their mobile device and turn the thermostat down from bed using the Nest phone app.

Sure, they are another extreme—not unlike the 1970s bohemians. But there's truth in this depiction too. Today's green consumer is bound by convenience. Journalist David Brooks calls this new crop "bobos," short for "bourgeois bohemians," referring to the relative affluence needed to maintain such a lifestyle. And, much like the first generation of green consumers, bobos are a product of their environment.

Look around, and you will see: green seems to be everywhere, and markets for sustainable goods and services have rapidly expanded during the last decade. The organic food market is a good example. Over the ten-year period from 2006 to 2016, it grew 213 percent, from $15 billion in 2006 to $47 billion in 2016, while the overall food-retail market grew just 30 percent.[13] Today's consumer has access to a veritable mountain of environmental-product information. It can be overwhelming at times. Most grocery stores carry eco-labeled products, and there are currently more than 460 different eco-labels.[14] The green market also includes products that contribute to improving social justice. Fair-trade coffee, for example, emphasizes transparency and equity in international trade. And not all eco-labels come on products that fit on shelves or in stock rooms. Green buildings are also on the rise—and they're getting labeled too. LEED, or Leadership in Energy and Environmental Design, is the most widely used third-party verification for green buildings, with around 1.85 million square feet being certified daily in 2016.[15] From 2006 to 2011, the market for green buildings grew 1,700 percent, while the overall construction market shrank by 17 percent.[16]

To take advantage of these expanding markets, companies increasingly tout green products and practices. Green advertising has nearly tripled since 2006 and has increased tenfold in the last twenty years.[17] Walmart alone spends $500 million annually on the development and implementation of green technologies.[18] Meanwhile, General Electric will reportedly invest $10 billion in its own green product line over the next five years,[19] and General Motors is estimated to be spending upwards of \$2.5 billion a year on research and development for alternative-energy vehicles.[20]

Technology and the internet have made information about these products more accessible than ever before. Websites and smartphone applications inform purchasing choices based on environmental criteria. One example is the Good Guide, which uses scientific research to provide reviews for over 250,000 products based on the health, environmental, and ethical impacts of those products.[21] Another is the Monterey Aquarium Seafood Watch, which provides recommendations aimed at helping consumers select seafood that has been fished or farmed in ways that have less impact on the environment.[22] While these third-party tools are useful, there is no central, go-to location for all sustainable-product information. The responsibility for finding and sorting out the information remains with the consumer.

Although consumers are more aware of environmental issues than ever before, awareness is not action. It's important to understand the difference between the two. For three decades, people have repeatedly claimed in surveys and opinion polls that they are willing to change their behavior to reduce environmental impacts. A majority have said that they have concern for the environment and make shopping decisions at least some of the time based on that.[23]

To understand these claims further, we conducted a survey of US consumers, using opinion scales rooted in the field of psychology, to assess their awareness and concern about environmental issues. The New Economic Paradigm (NEP) scale asks questions to gauge the "pro-environmental orientation" of respondents by focusing on three dimensions of belief: the balance of nature, limits to growth, and human domination over nature. [24] The altruism scale (ALT), however, asks questions aimed at measuring how such beliefs influence personal behavior.

The results are telling.[25] In the NEP survey, a majority of the respondents were concerned about the environment. Seventy-four percent agreed with the statement that "if things continue on their present course, we will soon experience a major catastrophe," and 71 percent agreed that "the balance of nature is very delicate and easily upset." Responses to the ALT questions showed that a substantial majority (80 percent) of respondents believe that "personal action" and "contributions to community organizations" can improve the well-being of others.

These concerns were more likely to be expressed by millennials, who have been exposed to environmental issues throughout their childhood education.[26] Multitudes of college students now enroll in environmental-science courses and take part in on-campus sustainability initiatives. For this generation, climate change is tangible. Seventy-one percent say energy policy should focus on developing "alternative sources of energy such as wind, solar and hydrogen technology." Only a quarter believe it should focus on "expanding exploration and production of oil, coal, and natural gas."[27]

Generally speaking, all of this environmental concern should lead to environmentally friendly behavior.[28] But this is not always the case. Despite what the surveys say, heightened awareness of environmental problems is not associated with significant changes in consumption. And despite major investments and green-marketing efforts, the vast majority of consumers do not buy environmentally sustainable products, which represent a small fraction of global markets to begin with.[29] Estimates report that the market share for green products is less than 4 percent worldwide.[30] Some have even argued that the ethical, or green, consumer is just a myth.[31]

A more thorough understanding of the relationship between concern and behavior is necessary for marketers and
public-policy makers to reduce the attitude-behavior gap. To
begin with, it is important to understand that green consumers come in different variations. Numerous scholars have attempted, often using colorful labels, to categorize consumers' attitudes toward the environment.[32] Walter Coddington
proposed categories ranging from "true blue greens"—consumers who vocally support ecological concerns and whose
purchasing behavior mimics those concerns—to "sprouts,"
"grousers," and "basic browns," consumers who didn't believe individuals could contribute to solving environmental
problems and were thus the least likely to buy green products.[33] The Natural Marketing Institute described five segments of consumers, who are on a continuum from those
most engaged with the issues related to health and sustainability (the LOHAS [Lifestyles of Health and Sustainability]
consumers) to those who are not engaged (the unconcerned
consumers). In between are the naturalites, who make the
most of their purchase decisions based on benefits to their
personal health; the drifters, who are motivated by the latest
trends, including sustainability; and the conventionals, who
are driven by practicality and frugality rather than pure environmental benefits.[34] Another study by Ogilvy and Mather, a
New York–based ad firm, proposed the following categories:
activists, who are likely to buy green products and services;
realists, who are worried about the environment but skeptical about the green bandwagon; complacents, who see the solution as somebody else's problem; and alienated, those who
are unaware of green issues or see them as transient. Others
depict green consumers in yet other ways: on a continuum
from committed to complacent;[35] as committed, mainstream,
occasional, or non-environmentalists;[36] as vocal activists, con-

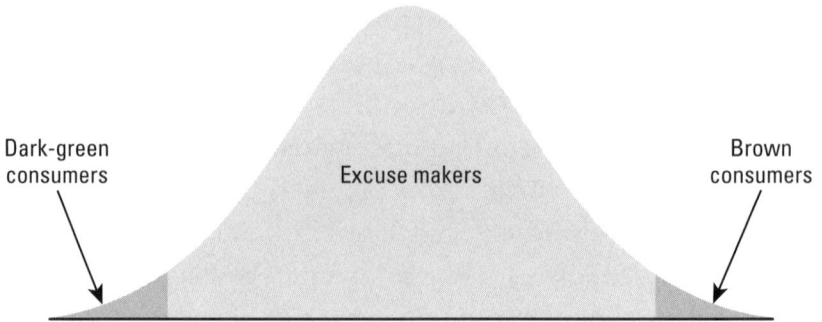

FIGURE 1.1. The Green Consumer Bell Curve

veniently conscious, or onlookers;[37] and as addicts, aspirants, or avoiders.[38]

For clarity and simplification, we condensed this universe of categories into three main groups (see figure 1.1).

1. **Dark-green consumers**—those who actively support ecological concerns and whose purchasing behavior mimics those concerns.

2. **Excuse makers**—those who express a limited willingness to pay for environmental features and stress other product attributes that are more important to them, such as convenience, comfort, and low maintenance.

3. **Brown consumers**—those who believe individuals cannot positively contribute to solving environmental problems and thus are the least likely to buy green products.

As in the early days of the modern environmental movement, dark-green consumers represent a small minority. An optimistic estimate found that the "true-blue greens" represent 11 percent of total consumers, but a more recent study found that "committed" green shoppers constitute a mere 2 percent of this group.[39] This segment is more likely to be female and married and have at least one child living at home.[40]

In surveys, dark-green consumers say that today's ecological problems are severe, corporations do not act responsibly toward the environment, and behaving in an ecologically favorable way is important and not inconvenient. These buyers value security and warm relationships with others and often consider ecological issues when making purchases.[41] They are resource conservers, health fanatics, animal lovers, and outdoors enthusiasts.[42] They might also be younger.[43] They are the green marketer's dream.

But businesses seeking to broaden the reach of eco-friendly products and services ask, How can we get consumers beyond the dark-green category to purchase? Can excuse makers be reached? How easy to purchase must our products be? How can we translate aspirations into action? To answer these questions, we need to understand the excuses that lie beyond the dark green.

Few people admit to lacking the motivation to purchase environmentally friendly products, but they offer plenty of other reasons why they can't buy green. As shown in figure 1.2, our survey results revealed five primary reasons: high cost, lack of information, difficulty finding products, lack of trust about

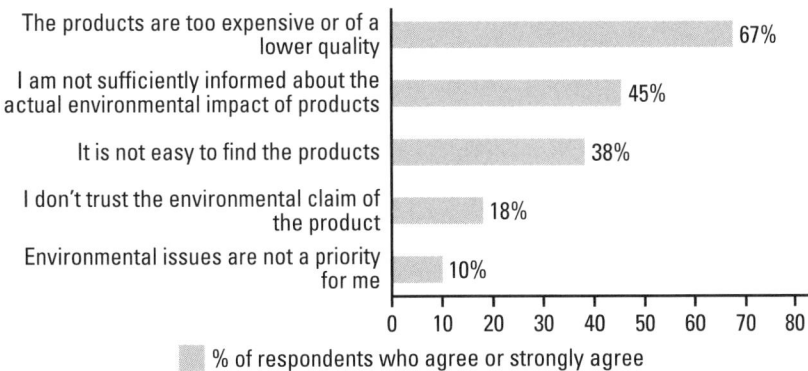

FIGURE 1.2.   Reasons to Avoid Environmentally Friendly Products

environmental claims, and lack of interest in environmental issues.[44]

What does each of these really mean? Let's break it down. First, there's the high price, low quality component. Sixty-seven percent of respondents reported not purchasing products because they were too expensive or lower in quality. The excuse may be partly left over from a bygone era—think about recycled, scratchy toilet paper or the first generation of green cleaning products. It reflects consumers' low tolerance for sacrifice. In 2010, Frito-Lay launched 100 percent recyclable packaging[45] for SunChips, a multigrain snack brand.[46] The packaging was excessively noisy, and sales plummeted.

Second, one must consider the unaware or confused. Forty-five percent reported not buying green products because they weren't sufficiently informed about the products' environmental impacts. Specific benefits can be hard to understand, and labels often make things worse by using vague terms such as *natural, eco-friendly*, or *good for the planet*. As an example, the EU Ecolabel has increasingly become the target of criticism for its high complexity, high costs, and poor consumer recognition. The label, which was developed by the European Commission and represents more than 36,000 different products and services,[47] has been boycotted by several high-profile firms[48]—a loss for consumers and companies alike.

Whereas labels may be loaded with imprecise information, 38 percent of survey respondents said environmentally friendly products were difficult to find. On the one hand, this excuse is dubious. As we have mentioned, large retailers such as Walmart have now embraced the movement and stock a variety of green products, often devoting entire sections of stores to them. Even AutoZone, a car-parts retailer, touts products with environmental benefits.[49] On the other hand, some products can take effort to find when first launched. It was difficult for Home Depot to stock enough wood certified by the Forest Stewardship Council (FSC) when their stores first offered it in 1994. It took until 2011 for the company to announce that all framing lumber would be FSC-certified at the company's forty-one San Francisco Bay–area stores.[50] That means the supply chain took a full thirteen years to mature enough to provide a stable supply.[51] Plus, as we have noted, green products still represent a small percentage of the total market, so they can't be everywhere. It's a catch-22—customers don't buy green products because they can't find them, and suppliers don't offer them because there's not enough demand.

Other respondents see green options, but they don't trust them, which is the result of cases of greenwashing that have emerged over the last few years. Greenwashing is the act of misleading consumers about the environmental practices of a company (firm-level greenwashing) or the environmental benefits of a product or service (product-level greenwashing).[52] Volkswagen's false claims about clean diesel have received international, front-page exposure as a blatant example of this practice. Indiscriminate eco-labeling further confounds the situation. According to a recent review of the twenty existing eco-labels in the US fish-farming industry, most people do not distinguish sustainable practices from conventional ones—or even from below-average operations.[53]

These cases build on a long history of dishonesty in advertising. Claims that cigarettes, excessive meat consumption, and the pesticide DDT have health benefits are early examples of this legacy. In a broader sense, the credibility of business has been continuously undermined since at least the start of the twenty-first century. Consider that major scandals at Enron, WorldCom, Tyco, and Xerox had all hit front pages by mid-2002.[54] In the past several years, significant greenwashing cases have come to light in lawsuits against Dole,[55] Fiji Water,[56] and Kimberly-Clark.[57]

These unfortunate traditions are part of our public consciousness and, for many, represent a starting point in how advertising is perceived.[58] Millennials appear particularly sensitive to it—they trust advertisements less than older generations and are turned off by communications that lack authenticity.[59]

Finally, there are the folks who lack an interest in environmental issues. As the survey shows, few are willing to acknowledge this indifference. But as we will explain, this is probably the single most significant barrier to green purchasing. Luckily for companies and the environment, though, excuse makers make up the vast majority of consumers, and they can almost certainly be reached.

Messaging Matters

How companies reach people is just as important as the motivations that drive buyers on the consuming end. Sometimes consumers just don't understand. And unsuccessful communication strategies often to blame. After initiating a campaign with the World Wildlife Fund "to raise awareness and funds to help create a safe haven for the polar bear—an Arctic refuge," Coca-Cola rolled out a series of white cans stamped with polar bears. They soon had to give them up, however. The cans looked too much like Diet Coke cans, which was especially problematic for diabetic customers.[60] The green message led to consumer confusion in a way the company hadn't anticipated. In the end, it's unclear whether anyone picked up on the environmental message. With so many products out there, people often don't understand what specific environmental problem or effort packaging refers to.

Another example is that of eco-friendly wine, which confuses people—and not just in the fun way. There are two main eco-labels in the US wine industry: Organic certification follows the US National Organic Program farming standard. It prohibits additives or alterations to natural seeds, plants, and animals, including pesticides, chemicals, and genetic modification. Biodynamic farming also prohibits synthetic pesticides and fertilizers. While organic farming focuses on human health, biodynamic farming emphasizes a self-sufficient, healthy ecosystem. With similar approaches but different goals, these two labels leave wine lovers scratching their heads.[61]

That's not to say that multiple labels are always a problem. The reputation of one label can sometimes build off others. In a survey, positive perception of individual wine eco-labels increased with familiarity of other eco-labels within the industry. Respondents who were unfamiliar with organic and biodynamic wines tended to view them negatively. But connoisseurs with a positive perception of certified-organic wine also had a positive perception of the biodynamic certification. Even among those familiar with organic wine, though, the vast majority had not heard of the biodynamic label.[62]

The term *biodynamic* may be too technical for most. Before being presented with any information about biodynamic farming practices, individuals were asked to provide one word to describe "wine from biodynamically grown grapes." Examples of the words they used fell into the following categories: *artificial, bioengineered, nonsensical,* and finally, *sustainable.* Only 17 percent associated biodynamic wine with sustainability. And those other terms run precisely against the grain (or grape) of what winemakers aim to convey.[63]

Clearly, well-meaning companies are often talking past their customers or sending information into a void. In just four decades, green has gone from a grassroots movement to a global cacophony. So, where does that leave us?

Green Isn't the New Black

The bottom line is that we have a long way to go. We have to meet people where they are and deal with the fact that environmental and social performance is complex. Our concerns include climate change, water usage, loss of biodiversity, and the prevention of toxic pollution, to name just a handful. Likewise, corporate philanthropy is just one element of social performance; there are many others, such as diversity in the workplace and employee benefits. Knowing where we stand— what sustainability has come to mean and where consumers and companies get lost—is a start.

Consumers are more aware than ever of environmental issues, and they openly state their concern about the fate of our planet. Few walk the talk by purchasing green products. As a result, green consumers still represent a tiny minority of the consumer population. The vast majority of consumers are convenient environmentalists. They come up with many excuses for not purchasing green products. These include a confusion about what green means, a distrust of environmental claims, and the perception that green products are of lower quality or too expensive. Some of them even acknowledge that they do not care too much about the environment. Knowing what stops consumers from purchasing green products allows us to understand the gap between environmental consciousness and green purchasing behavior.

In order to address this gap, we need to eliminate or reduce the obstacles between green intention and action. In the next chapter, we will talk about several ways to do so.

Chapter 2

THE GREEN BUNDLE

IT HAS BEEN CALLED the "green paradox."[1] Demand for eco-friendly products does not match growing environmental concern among consumers.[2] There is a gap between what people say about the environment and what they do in the marketplace.[3]

Research shows that most consumers are aware of the discrepancy between their green aspirations and their green behavior.[4] One noted problem is a lack of knowledge about how to act more sustainably. In our survey, 67 percent of respondents said they were not sufficiently informed about the actual environmental impact of products. People demand accurate claims, reject greenwashing, and require full transparency, and they also want better clarity about the effectiveness of their green purchase.

They also want to know what's in it for them. The green bundle contains five distinct paths for promoting personal advantages while remaining sustainable, using benefits that often come naturally with environmental goods: quality, status, health, money, and emotion.

Bridging the Gap

Current environmental-information strategies have failed to reach a broader set of consumers because they are based on two incorrect assumptions. The first assumption is that information is the main—if not only—problem to address. The thinking is that once consumers learn about the negative environmental impact of a product, they will change their consumption behavior. In other words, once you solve the information asymmetry, you will fill the gap between intention and action. This is an oversimplification that misses the motivation factor inherent in effective information strategies. The second false assumption is that altruistic values always conflict with the egoistic values of consumption, so the two cannot be bundled. This assumes there is always a trade-off between the value a consumer derives from a product and its environmental benefits. Therefore, businesses can rely only on the minority of consumers who are willing to sacrifice value for the public good. Before explaining the concept of the green bundle in more depth, let us debunk these assumptions, which are based on psychological concepts that can be useful when part of a broader strategy.

The first derives from the theory of planned behavior, one of the most influential models in psychology. This theory fueled the myth that consumer education is the main solution to get more people to buy green. It links beliefs to behavior and has been used to explain variations in sustainable behavior.[5] It suggests that people are much more likely to decide to engage in certain behaviors when they feel they can do so successfully. To act, consumers need to have a positive attitude toward sustainability, and people around them must consider that behavior desirable. They also need to feel their behavior can contribute to the solution of the problem. According to this theory, the stronger the intention to engage in environmental behavior, the more likely it is that people will behave environmentally.

The theory of planned behavior is built on a core cognitive progression: (1) beliefs determine attitudes, (2) attitudes lead to intentions, and (3) intentions inform behavior.[6] The natural conclusion to take from this model is that consumers need more explanation. Businesses and nongovernmental organizations need to better describe the magnitude of environmental problems and be clearer about the solutions. This would, in turn, lead more people to care about the environment and drive more consumers to purchase green products.

The usefulness of the theory to explain environmental intentions has been demonstrated in dozens of studies, but the studies are often based on surveys, and they fail to explain green behavior. For example, a recent systematic review of 237 independent prospective tests found that the theory accounted for only 19.3 percent of variability in health behavior, with intention being the strongest predictor.[7] It was also discovered that the theory is considerably less predictive of behavior when studies used long-term rather than short-term design, when participants were not university students, and when outcome measures were taken objectively rather than as a self-report.[8] Some scholars contended that it is "time to retire the theory of planned behavior."[9] Because the theory focuses exclusively on rational reasoning, it excludes unconscious influences on behavior[10] and the role of emotions beyond anticipated affective outcomes.[11] Moreover, the static explanatory nature of it does not help to understand the effects of behavior on cognitions and future behavior.[12]

Still, this line of reasoning is not sufficient to explain the gap.[13] Intentions are not a reliable proxy for consumption behavior. Yes, consumers need to be aware of the environmental problem, and yes, they will not act without thinking they can make a difference. But awareness and understanding are not enough. As Method's cofounder Adam Lowry states, "I fundamentally believe that if you build something and ask people to buy it for the sole reason it's green, you'll ultimately fail."[14] People need the desire to act on their intentions.[15] Environmental information is often not sufficient to motivate them.

The theory-of-planned-behavior approach ignores the cost of green behavior. It ignores the fact that consumers experience a conflict between altruistic values (for example, helping the environment) and egoistic values (for example, the pain of paying a premium). Taking the bus instead of driving benefits the environment by reducing carbon emissions. But buses can take more time, be less comfortable, and reduce freedom of mobility. Commuters often decide that acting on values alone is a bad deal, that the personal costs associated with the proenvironmental behavior outweigh the benefits. When altruistic values conflict with egoistic ones, people are tempted to base their decisions on what benefits them the most.[16] Egoistic values play a particularly important role when the individual costs of environmentally friendly behavior are high.[17] Concerns about gains quickly displace altruistic motives as costs go up.[18]

Accordingly, few are willing to pay a premium for green products, stating in our survey that price is a deterrent. This is consistent with previous research, which shows that most consumers are not willing to pay a price premium above 10 to 20 percent and that demand for organic products declines sharply with premiums above 20 percent.[19] Since price premiums for organic products are often above 20 percent—and reach 100 percent in some cases[20]—it is not surprising that demand remains low overall despite rapid growth in the industry. Customers are unwilling to trade quality for green attributes unless the private benefits are significant.[21]

Price acts as a psychological barrier too. High prices signal that a product is for rich people, not the majority. Premiums compound the perception that green products are somehow different—not normal, not for the mainstream. According to one study, 50 percent of Americans think green products and services target "rich elitist snobs" or "crunchy granola hippies" rather than people like them.[22] Thus, psychologically, the higher price of green products intensifies the gap between altruistic and egoistic values.

Educating consumers about the environmental benefits of green products will not bridge the gap between green aspiration and green behavior. Information campaigns are not enough. When the conflict between egoistic and altruistic considerations is strong, supporting altruistic values will not completely overcome the costs of acting proenvironmentally.[23]

This is not to say that we need to throw the baby out with the bathwater. The theory of planned behavior's motivation factor is integrated in our approach. But before we get to that, we must deal with the second false assumption: that the conflict between altruistic and egoistic values is irreconcilable. By definition, altruism helps someone else to the detriment of one's self. This tension is revealed in the fact that many consider green consumption to be problematic and an apparent oxymoron. Indeed, *green* implies conservation of environmental resources, whereas *consumption* generally involves their destruction.[24] Conservation is an altruistic act, incompatible with the egoistic act of destructive consumption. In other words, this assumption asserts that people are either altruistic or egoistic. They cannot be both.

This neglects reality. It is possible to value things that help yourself and others at the same time. Even actions as seemingly selfless as volunteering at a soup kitchen can benefit volunteers. They benefit emotionally from helping people, and their social status may improve because of their altruistic behavior. Philanthropists benefit from giving to nonprofit organizations that put their names in brochures or on the walls of their buildings.

This dynamic was portrayed to great comedic effect in the HBO series *Curb Your Enthusiasm*. In an episode titled "Anonymous Donor," creator and lead actor Larry David makes a donation to build a wing for the Natural Resources Defense Council. At a social event organized by the nonprofit organization, he notices that his name is displayed on the wing of the building, and he says he feels "pretty good" about it. The feeling doesn't last long, though. He soon finds out that the other wing in the building was donated by "anonymous." He admits to his wife that he now feels bad about getting his name on the wing while someone else donated anonymously. He fears it will make people think he did it for the credit. His wife scoffs that she knows who the anonymous donor is: Larry's friend and nemesis, Ted Danson. The employees of the nonprofit know Danson is the anonymous donor, and he ends up getting the lion's share of praise for his perceived modesty. Finally, a frustrated Larry concludes that the next time he gives a donation, he's going to do it anonymously and just tell everybody about it.

In fact, many behaviors include both altruism and egoism. Some describe altruism as the consumption of "warm glow"[25] or the purchase of "moral satisfaction."[26] Similarly, there are products that are not only better for the environment than conventional ones but that provide personal benefits to the consumer.

When communication efforts seek altruistic behavior by emphasizing environmental benefits of products, they often do so to the detriment of egoistic values. This all-too-common strategy limits the appeal of green products to a tiny, committed minority. Marketing scholars argue that "green marketing must satisfy two objectives: improved environmental quality and customer satisfaction. Misjudging either or overemphasizing the former at the expense of the latter can be termed 'green marketing myopia.'"[27] Such myopia has led to many failures. They also argue that consumers evaluate their green purchases based on two main components. The first component is the degree of compromise, or sacrifice, in the performance of the product. The second is the degree of confidence in the environmental benefit. Firms need to address both of these components to increase the attractiveness of green products.[28]

The most effective way to motivate green consumers is to communicate and elevate the personal benefits of green products. Consumers will pay a premium for sustainable products when they have additional benefits, such as being healthier or better in quality. Combining these benefits creates what we call the green bundle. This is a less explored piece of the puzzle in green markets, but it is the key to effective information strategies for sustainable goods.

The green bundle strategy has two main parts. First, firms must frame their environmental message in terms of private benefits. Second, they must provide credible information about the environmental benefits of their products. It bundles credible information about public benefits to the environment with information about private benefits to the consumer.

Motivations

Consumers weigh their motives against the costs of their actions. Green aspirations become actions when people see products that are bundled with private benefits. Environmental benefits become part of the overall package, integrated with private benefits and valued in comparison to other products they can buy or actions they can take.[29] Buyers' perceptions of value represent a trade-off between the quality and benefits they perceive in a product versus the sacrifice they perceive in paying the price.[30] Bundling frames environmental messages with private benefits to motivate behavior. Private benefits include better performance, status, health, money, and even emotional returns.

These benefits have been discussed in detail by the marketing literature, which describes how consumers work their way through a mental list of values when they evaluate an item for purchase.[31] In business markets, that value is "the worth in monetary terms of the technical, economic, service, and social benefits a customer company receives in exchange for the price it pays for a market offering."[32] For example, it has been suggested that consumers consider at the point of sale five consumption values: functional, social, emotional, epistemic, and conditional values.[33]

Functional value is a consumer's perception of a product in terms of price, quality, durability, dependability, and reliability—the value derived from its utilitarian, functional, or physical performance. Examples include the thirst-quenching from of a bottle of water or the cozy warmth of a wool sweater. Social value comes from association with one or more specific social groups. This includes wearing specific clothing brands to fit in. Emotional value is the feelings or affective states a product generates, whereas epistemic value includes feelings of novelty and curiosity or knowledge from a product. Good examples of this are travel and other leisure activities such as going to concerts or the movies.

Finally, conditional value is the temporary value received during a specific set of circumstances. A Christmas card is one example of a product that has conditional value, since the value is only there during the holiday season. Conditional value arises when situational factors, including ill-nesses or specific social situations, moderate the perceived value-outcome process. It can therefore be derived from temporary functional or social value.[34] Hence, scholars have described conditional value as a specific case of other types of value.[35]

Building on this approach, researchers developed a scale with specific questionnaire items along four dimensions—quality, price, emotional value, and social value, with quality and price being seen as subcomponents of functional value.[36] They found that these multiple dimensions of consumer value, with both utilitarian and hedonic components, explain consumer choice better than a single "value for money" item.[37] As the authors state, the scale "demonstrates that consumers assess products, not just in functional terms of expected performance, value for money and versatility; but also in terms of the enjoyment or pleasure derived from the product (emotional value) and the social consequences of what the product communicates to others (social value)."[38]

This consumer-value perspective forms the foundation of the green bundle approach. Each of these private benefits can be successfully bundled with environmental benefits. Past research in marketing has shown that successful, established green products showcase nongreen consumer value, and studies have described several desirable benefits commonly associated with green products: efficiency and cost effectiveness, health and safety, performance, symbolism and status, and convenience.[39] Building on this research, we expand the list of private benefits associated with green products. We also describe the various contexts under which these cobenefits have the most potential to stimulate consumer demand for green products and how firms can effectively communicate about these cobenefits.

With Cobenefits

The foundation of the green bundle is the idea that coupling private benefits with public or environmental benefits create complementarities—relationships "in which two or more different things improve or emphasize each other's qualities."[40] Enjoying a fine French dinner provides hedonic pleasure, maybe with a little guilt from self-indulgence. The pleasure of the meal can benefit from the warm glow generated by altruistic behavior. What if the meal is provided at a fundraiser for charity? In such a situation, enjoying a fine dinner could increase the attractiveness of a donation while minimizing guilt. The bundle of a fine dinner and a donation would thus create more value than each does separately. This suggests that affect generated from hedonic consumption may be especially complementary to the utility derived from contributing to a good cause. Gala dinners often also include appeals to improve public status by showing friends that you are a good citizen.

Similarly, product categories highly related to social identity are likely to benefit from bundling sustainability to social-status benefits. Products that invoke the social-identity function are those that elicit concerns in consumers about their relationships with others or the expression of their self-identity.[41] These products allow consumers to publicly express support for a social or environmental issue, activities that become more salient when the product is purchased with a social-identity intention.

Not all products evoke the same emotional states or status when consumed.[42] Feelings associated with buying practical items, such as school supplies, toilet paper, or bleach, are different than the feelings associated with more hedonic or frivolous items, such as Belgian chocolate, expensive perfume, or a luxury vacation.[43] Experts classify products as experiential, symbolic, or functional based on the primary needs they satisfy.[44] Experiential products satisfy the need for sensory pleasure; symbolic products fulfill needs for self-enhancement or group membership; and functional products solve consumption-related problems and resolve conflict.[45] Appeals that more closely match the specific needs satisfied by a product category will be more persuasive to consumers than appeals that address less relevant needs.[46] Each form of consumption value presented will likely increase the salience of environmental attributes depending on the main private benefit of the product category.[47]

And not all values work for all products. Emotional value can be highly salient for consumers purchasing items with experiential characteristics because of the complementarity between the emotionally driven purchase experience for experiential goods and the value source. Research shows that consumers are more likely to respond positively to messages about social issues when faced with the purchase of an experiential, or hedonic, product versus a practical one such as a textbook.[48] Experiments compared the effectiveness of promised donations to charity in promoting "practical necessities" (for example, a box of laundry detergent) to their effectiveness in promoting "frivolous luxuries" (for example, a hot fudge sundae). The results suggest that charity incentives are more effective in promoting frivolous products than practical ones.[49] With products that are primarily functional, rational thoughts and functional attributes dominate the decision-making process.[50] Complementarities are at their best when products' environmental attributes themselves enhance performance, as is the case, for example, with the increased torque of an electric engine.

For the purposes of the green bundle, we see five likely

cobenefits for green products: quality, health, money, status, and emotion (see figure 2.1). These benefits build on the categorizations of quality, price, emotional value, and social value.[51] We have added to this list health, another important cobenefit of environmental activities, which marketing scholars described as providing great appeal among health-conscious consumers.[52]

It is easy to see how purchasing green products can have emotional value. Emotional benefits include the "feel-good" factor when purchasing groceries with a fair-trade label or when donating to nonprofit organizations.

In many cases, there is a natural overlap between quality and greenness. Performance, functionality, usability, durability, comfort, and convenience are all attributes that can be bundled with sustainability. Products that use less energy or are more durable provide good examples. Although green products have traditionally been seen as having lower quality, that is not always the case.

Status can be a powerful tool to compel behavior. It is particularly effective with products that are highly visible and in a context in which other people care about the environment. Car ownership is an example of one of the most visible consumption choices we make, and cars come in different shades of green.

We included health benefits because environmental harm and human health are often closely linked. When consumers make the connection between environmental impacts and health, it becomes a powerful motivator to change consumption behavior. Awareness of the connection between environmental impacts and health can lead consumers to seek out green products to protect their health.[53] For example, consumers often purchase organic foods because such foods

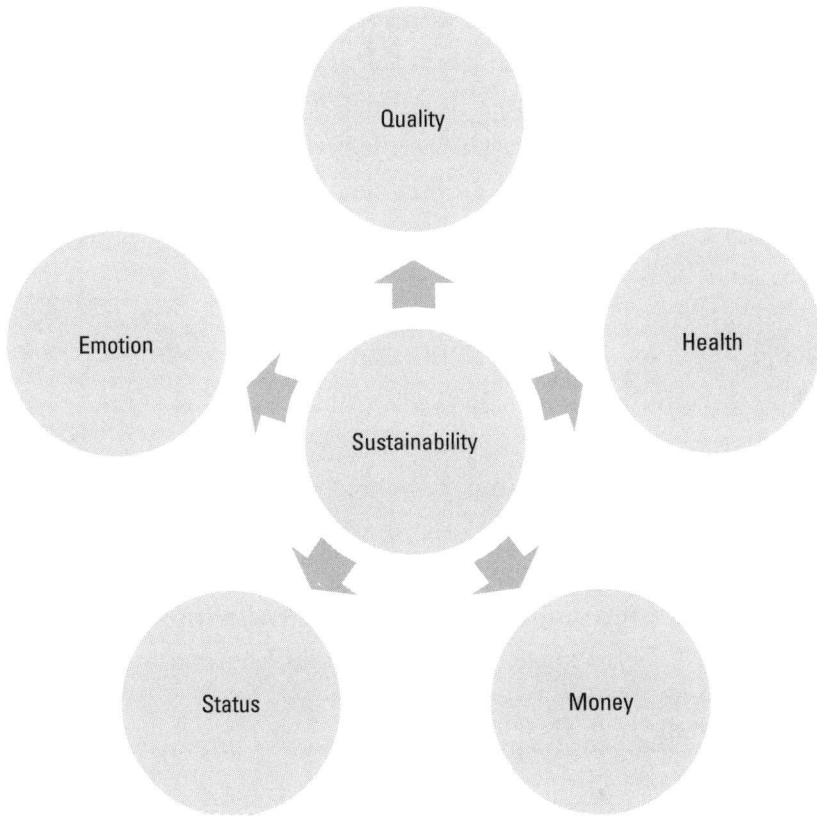

FIGURE 2.1.   The Cobenefits of Green Consumption

have not been treated with chemicals that have been shown to have negative health impacts.

On its own, sustainability remains a sufficient benefit for some consumers. It's just not enough for everyone, or even for most. The green bundle offers a way to reach this largely untapped majority of the consumer base.

The relevance of these benefits will vary according to context. Situational aspects moderate perceptions of functional, social, health, or emotional benefits. For example, people might become more aware about the connection between the environment and health when they face illness.

Sometimes the complementarities between sustainability and the product value will be obvious to consumers, but often they need to be described. This is where information becomes important.

Information

The second part of the green bundle strategy is helping consumers realize the environmental impact of their consumption by informing them about the negative environmental impact of their current consumption or about the environmental benefits associated with purchasing green products. In economic terminology, this is called reducing information asymmetry between the producer, who knows about the environmental impacts of his products, and the consumer, who doesn't. This is what most information campaigns have focused on thus far, but they have often done so inaccurately. This is often seen as the key step rather than as a precursor. In most cases, without the realization of a problem, consumers will not change their consumption patterns. But there is a difference between understanding a problem and knowing what to do about it.

Transparency is unavoidable. Computers, wireless communications, remote sensing, and other technological breakthroughs are reshaping every facet of modern life by vastly increasing our capacity to collect, disseminate, and utilize information.[54] The information age makes the invisible visible. Environmental problems are now easier to spot, and consumers' awareness of environmental issues is mounting. Let's take air pollution as an example. Poor air quality affects everyone, yet it often flies under the radar—especially when the pollutants can't be seen. Now, smartphone applications make the pollution visible. UCLA's AirForU app tells users whether the air they're breathing is healthy or not each day according to the Environmental Protection Agency's air-quality index. This information, presented in an easily accessible and digestible form, helps people decide whether they should take preventative measures or engage in breathing-intensive activities such as strenuous outdoor work or exercise.

Although consumer awareness of environmental issues is a necessary first step, it must be coupled with the ability of consumers to understand the environmental information to the extent that it influences purchase decisions. Recent research shows that only 20 percent of coffee consumers have a good understanding of the organic-coffee eco-label, with much less understanding of competing coffee eco-labels, including the Rainforest Alliance, Bird Friendly, Fair Trade, and UTZ eco-labels. This makes things challenging. Measuring consumption impacts is difficult and depends on what types of impacts are included, the relative weights attached to them, and how they are allocated. If only one environmental impact is measured, how do you know whether this is the main impact of the product? If, say, only the environmental impact of the production of the product is included, how do you know it is the most important impact throughout the life cycle of the product?

While the information needs to be grounded in sound science, simplicity of the information communicated is key. The literature shows that sustainable signals are not always processed in a rational way. For example, when people were asked to value the protection of different animals such as muskrats, squirrels, and other wild rodents together or to value the protection of only muskrats, people valued muskrats similarly to the entire rodent category.[55] This effect has been termed *em-*

bedding, and it "refers to the general finding that sometimes two or more environmental goods are valued less highly together than they are separately."[56] In other words, when environmental attributes are evaluated separately, individuals tend to rate their value higher than when the same two environmental attributes are presented jointly on the same product.[57] Consumers can also be overwhelmed by complex environmental metrics. It is important to use these metrics parsimoniously and to ensure that they are standardized, contextualized, or even translated into things consumers are more familiar with or better understand.

Once consumers understand the problem, they also need specific, actionable items. They need to see how their green purchase will make a dent in the problem. Studies show that perceived effectiveness is a significant predictor of pro-environmental consumption.[58] It is not sufficient to describe water shortages and request that consumers conserve. They need to understand the impact of specific appliances on their consumption. For example, they need to know how much water Energy Star appliances can save over conventional ones. The intent is to save water, but the specific desired action is the purchase of an eco-labeled appliance.

Finally, consumers need to trust the information they are given. The skyrocketing incidence of greenwashing can have profound negative effects on consumer confidence in green products, eroding the consumer market for green products and services.[59]

Consumer awareness, understanding, and trust in environmental information form the basis of the information pillar or the green bundle strategy. Thus, the green bundle brings together two components: information and motivation (see figure 2.2). Although we portray this as a linear process, there are many interactions that happen along the way between the

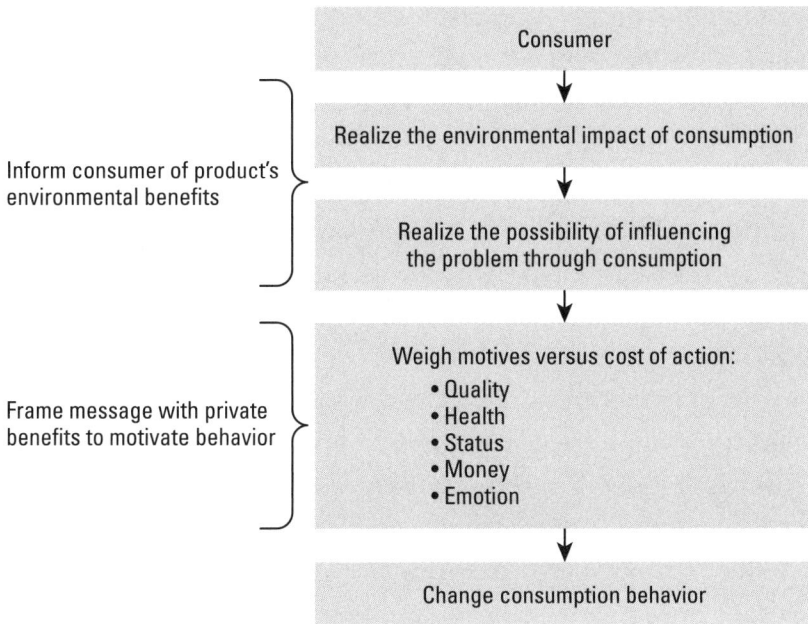

FIGURE 2.2.   Green Consumer Behavior-Change Framework

two main components of the bundle. Private benefits might even outweigh the costs at times. In such cases, the first steps of this approach—informing consumers about the environmental benefits of their consumption behavior—are not as essential. Private benefits will prevail.

A Holistic Approach

It is important to frame environmental messages in a way that is more appealing to consumers. Beyond the content of the message, the credibility of the messenger is important too.

As environmental issues become important within markets, green communication and the management of eco-performance transcend functional boundaries to become panorganizational management concerns.[60] Effective sustainable-information strategies go beyond applying good marketing principles. They also include knowledge from other disciplines and coordinate with other areas of a firm.

One challenge that often arises and leads to perceived greenwashing is lack of coordination among different units within an organization. This can cause marketers, for example, to overstate environmental benefits because they do not understand the complexity or impacts of a new product from R&D. It is not just the consumer who cares about a product's impacts. There are often a host of stakeholders who care, including employees, customers, suppliers, competitors, nongovernmental organizations, and communities. If one part of a company is attempting to gain competitive advantage on the basis of eco-performance but another part isn't living up to that image, competitors, nongovernmental organizations, the media, and regulators will queue up to attack. Firms cannot think about the bundle simply in terms of products. Internal incentive structures and ethical climates are also important determinants of firms' ethical and environmental behavior.[61]

As social and environmental pressures on businesses grow, those who communicate about green products need to have an appreciation of and provide input into all aspects of a business. How energy efficient is the production process? Where are raw materials sourced from? How well does the company treat its workforce and suppliers? These questions are not traditionally within the purview of marketers. But today, they are—because these factors are increasingly likely to influence the perceptions of important stakeholders, including customers.

Under the leadership of the CEO, a firm can improve information related to environmental-communication decisions, provide ethical leadership and training for employees, and properly incentivize employees to achieve sustainability objectives. This is another important part of the information pillar of the green bundle strategy.

Green bundle strategies are based on the idea that sustainability can be bundled with product qualities that are valued by consumers. For some products this bundle is natural, and communication strategies will emphasize the cobenefits of environmental improvements. For other products, the bundle needs to be put together. This is where sustainable-design practices can be beneficial. Design innovations can reduce negative social and environmental impacts of consumption.[62] To achieve this, designers need to gain a better understanding of what users do with products, how they interact with products, and what hidden factors are behind their daily decision-making process. In other words, although a better understanding of the environmental impacts of products is necessary to help consumers make better choices for the environment when shopping, a better understanding of consumer-desired functionality might help make sustainable design more effective. Therefore, design departments and marketing departments need to work hand in hand to design products that don't compromise between consumer value and sustainability.

In conclusion, green-communications efforts tend to fail not because of lack of consumer interest, as many have argued. They fail because the communications efforts are superficial, not grounded in the complexity of current cultural change, and end up sending messages that have the opposite effects of those intended. They are based on the incomplete idea that altruism is the main reason for purchasing green products. Communications have often relied on big-picture, apocalyptic narratives packaged with human guilt. This negative framing not only fails to resonate with most people but also risks painting the problem as too large and intractable for individual action to have any meaningful impact.[63] This outdated narrative fails to connect with today's consumers, and it seems more appropriate for fund-raising for the non-profit world.

Today, few consumers would like to be labeled as activists. Most of us want to do the right thing, but we don't want to trade product value for it. Our shopping includes both utilitarian and hedonic components. These motivations cannot be ignored. Without them, people will stop shopping. These outmoded strategies pose solutions to the problem of over-consumption, but people must still have their needs and desires satisfied. To be effective, green marketing must appeal to both the altruistic and egoistic values of consumers. We propose a different approach for information strategies, one that bundles environmental, or "public good," benefits with private ones to woo convenient environmentalists. The green bundle includes the following categories of values, or cobenefits, associated with sustainability purchases: quality, health, money, emotion and status. We will describe in the next chapters when to use each of these. We start with quality, or the functional benefit of a product.

Chapter 3

NO SUBSTITUTE FOR QUALITY

WHEN *CONSUMER REPORTS* released its 2016 owner-satisfaction index for automakers, one manufacturer stood above the rest: Tesla. Out of those surveyed, 91 percent said they would buy their vehicles again, seven percentage points higher than the second-highest-rated brand, Porsche.[1] And out of twenty-nine brands ranked by the venerable, long-standing consumer nonprofit organization, Tesla was the sole company that produced only zero-emissions vehicles.

The results reflect more than a "plugged in," environmentally conscious consumer base. Although the automaker has been criticized for reliability,[2] *Consumer Reports* also said in 2015 that its Model S P85D sedan "performed better in our tests than any other car ever has," in fact breaking their own ratings system by achieving an initial score of 103 out of 100.[3] Countering expectations of efficiency-focused electric vehicles, *Consumer Reports* described the Tesla as "brutally quick" and capable of making a two-hundred-plus mile trip on a single charge.

Teslas are one flashy example of our first way to reach today's convenient environmentalists—improving quality of products and services. Broadly defined, quality is the ability to consistently meet or exceed customer requirements or expectations while giving them satisfaction. More than simple speed or performance, it also includes elements such as durability and (less tangibly) aesthetics.[4]

Buyers of green products value the intrinsic quality of products separately from environmental or social benefits. According to research, people buy organic food because they think it tastes better than conventional food.[5] There may be truth to that. In a blind taste test, consumers perceived organic orange juice as tasting better than conventional orange juice.[6] Indeed, research shows that organic products might contain higher concentrations of sugars, resulting in a sweeter taste.[7] When consumers select organic food because it appeals to the palate, they are valuing the private benefits of products rather than the environmental benefits.

In many cases, there is a natural overlap between quality and "greenness." Performance, functionality, usability, durability, comfort, and convenience are all attributes that can be effectively bundled with sustainability.

Performance

Tesla is the prime example of a product that marries performance with a lower environmental impact, thus appealing to today's convenient environmentalists. As pointed out by Alfred A. Marcus in his book *Innovations in Sustainability*, "Tesla did not sell its electric cars as two-seat boxy vehicles for environmentalists as had GM in the 1990s, but as an object of desire that exceeds buyers' expectations for styling, handling, speed, safety, resale value, and maintenance."[8] When Tesla owners are asked why they bought their cars, they cite acceleration, cargo space, aesthetics, and safety records—but generally not the low carbon footprint. These discerning consumers are more likely to purchase a new generation of other green products, but only if they offer better performance.

First, let's take a figurative peek under the hood of the Tesla S, a luxury sedan introduced in 2012. As a fully electric car, the Model S produces zero tailpipe emissions. Despite such an obvious benefit, no marketing materials or reviews focused on this environmental advantage. But one attribute that was highly publicized is acceleration: the 2015 Model S blasts from 0 to 60 mph in as little as 3.1 seconds. Electric motors are naturally always at peak torque and don't require a transmission as do internal-combustion engines. This gives the Tesla an advantage in performance. And by positioning its battery beneath the cabin floor, the Model S possesses a low center of gravity and superior handling.

As a bonus, the Tesla Model S has more storage space than other cars of its size—electric motors are smaller than internal-combustion engines. Reviewers have praised the added storage of its front trunk (or "frunk," as it's been unfortunately dubbed). Because Teslas do not require a transmission, they lack a driveshaft hump, freeing up legroom and storage space for passengers.

As befitting a Silicon Valley start-up, technology is highly integrated in the Model S. The car boasts a seventeen-inch touch screen that controls most of its functions. The vehicles are further equipped with wireless internet on cellular networks, allowing software and firmware to be updated remotely, improving functionality. For example, real-time updates to the enhanced autopilot allow the car to match its speed to traffic conditions, automatically change lanes, and self-park. Last but not least, the Model S boasts an excellent safety record; the National Highway Traffic Safety Administration rated it five out of five stars for frontal-crash, side-crash, and rollover safety. As one reviewer put it, "The Model S is not just a great electric car. It's a great *car*, period."

Taking a deeper look at the motivations for buying vehicles such as the Tesla, a survey was conducted of 19,460 electric-car-rebate applicants about their purchasing decisions and experiences.[9] Tesla and BMW are the big players in this arena of high-end electric cars. Owners cited concern for the environment more often than the average respondent, but they are much less concerned about fuel savings. And they aren't identical. Tesla owners are more concerned with vehicle performance than are BMW owners.[10] But BMW and Tesla owners were two and three times more likely to be motivated by owning the latest in electric-vehicle technology, respectively. The results indicate that there are two types of consumers who purchase high-performance electric vehicles. The first is an environmentalist with a taste for high quality and high-performance durable goods. These consumers support the environment but want the highest quality and top performance. The second type values quality and performance but views environmental benefits secondarily. When analyzing the stated motivations on Tesla forums,[11] researchers found many quotes that echo this remark: "The Tesla S class is more efficient than a Prius, quicker than a Porsche 911, and has more cargo space than many SUVs." Few mentions were made about sustainability.

Contrast Tesla's success with the 2010 Nissan Leaf. Tesla's advertising focuses on performance, letting the obvious environmental benefits speak for themselves. The makers of the Leaf, though, put together one of the most clichéd advertising campaigns imaginable. One TV placement featured collapsing glaciers, sad piano music, and a wandering polar bear who cruises city streets and eventually hugs a man getting into his Nissan Leaf. There's nothing like looming extinction and fear of global warming to get buyers out to dealerships, apparently.

The campaign was lambasted by advertising and environment reporters and experts.[12] One called it "as subtle as a box of hammers to the face." Andrew Sullivan, writing for *The Atlantic* under the headline "Smug Alert," pulled no punches whatsoever: "Dying polar bear travels thousands of miles to thank man for buying an electric Nissan. What an absolutely outrageously manipulative insensitive hubristic piece of Green advertising bullshit. From a fucking car company! A car company who's (non-electric) cars are helping to destroy the bear's ice pack!"[13]

Perhaps Nissan can be forgiven for this misstep. After all, the 2010 Leaf was its first foray into the world of plug-in electric vehicles. And the company seems to have learned from its mistakes. The advertising campaign for the 2018 Leaf does almost a complete 180 from the sad polar bear, focusing on performance, comfort, and technology that will "amaze your senses." It still includes a mention of the car's environmental benefits, but that is clearly secondary to the performance aspects of the vehicle.[14] The new campaign seeks to excite, not depress.

Functionality

Another important aspect of quality is functionality—the action opportunities a product affords.[15] In other words, people value features that give users a set of capabilities. Energy-efficient LED lights function better than do traditional incandescent or fluorescent lights. According to the US Department of Energy, its advantages include compact size, increased lifetime (longer even than compact fluorescent bulbs), and greater dimming and control capability.[16]

LEED buildings are another high-profile example of environmentally conscious design with high functionality. LEED, or Leadership in Energy and Environmental Design, is a world-renowned green-building certification program. LEED-certified buildings improve air quality, reduce energy and water consumption, and save money.[17] Certifying 1.85 million square feet every day, LEED provides independent verification of a building or neighborhood's green features, allowing for design, construction, operation, and maintenance with improved functionality. Those nonenvironmental improvements haven't gone unnoticed. Surveys of the buildings' occupants find greater satisfaction with air quality and thermal comfort.[18]

This matters to occupants' health, an important factor we'll touch on in later chapters. Poor air quality in buildings influences rates of communicable respiratory illness, allergy and asthma symptoms, sick-building symptoms, and worker performance. A better indoor environment significantly reduces these health effects and directly improves worker performance.[19]

In addition to energy-bill savings, improved employee performance because of the functionality of LEED buildings is another reason why they are important. Certified buildings increase productivity, cut down on absenteeism and turnover, and reduce financial liability.[20] LEED office spaces are dominated by industries that benefit most from improved productivity, such as legal and financial services. Firms in these office space–intensive sectors are likely to profit most from the operational and productivity benefits of green buildings.[21]

Form indeed follows function, and so does consumer demand. As a result of these nonenvironmental benefits, the green-building business has grown rapidly, reaching $260 billion as of 2013.[22] The main reason given for this, as stated by 40 percent of those surveyed, is client demand—up from 34 percent in 2008.[23] Perceptions of green buildings are positive and improving. The LEED stamp of approval also allows owners to charge a premium, a reflection of how the public values this certification. In 2010, one study found that LEED buildings charged an average rent premium of 4 to 5 percent and sold at a 25 percent price premium.[24] The elevated performance of LEED buildings is in high demand, and builders are responding accordingly.

Beyond LEED, architects have developed modular homes that match sustainability with functionality. These houses are made up of building blocks, built piece by piece in a controlled factory environment before being transported to the construction site. Sustainable modular buildings reduce construction time, waste, and cost, and they get people into new homes faster. Modularity increases performance by making the products easy to update, fix, and customize, all while decreasing life-cycle costs.[25] They also allow customers to adjust their homes to their evolving needs over time.

KB Home, a residential builder, developed the KB Home Projekt, which builds houses that combine modular and sustainable designs.[26] The project aims to be net-zero energy by 2020 and to able to adapt and improve over time to meet the needs of a household in 2050.[27] From the consumer perspective, modularity allows homeowners to personalize or adapt their space to meet changing needs. These adaptations can be made in the moment or slowly over time. For instance, the KB Home Projekt house includes a moveable wall between the home office and living room, creating a flex space. "When this wall moves forward it contracts the living room and expands the office," explains Joe Wheeler of Virginia Tech's Center for Design Research. "When it moves backward it expands the living room and contracts the office. So depending on if you are working during the day you can have a larger work space or if you are entertaining at night you can have an expanded living room." Wheeler's team is exploring the idea that houses should be built more like phones or cars. He says, "Components of homes such as kitchens and bathrooms and office walls like [the moveable wall] are built in a factory, then these are brought out to the site and the house is built around them. . . . It allows for the deliverance of technology which is what we are going to need in the near future."[28] Modular homes are easier and more efficient to update with emerging technology and needs, and they provide a dynamic component to living spaces.

The KB Home Projekt was exhibited at the 2016 Greenbuild International Show and Expo in Los Angeles. Over a thousand visitors flocked to the showcase, which included a movable wall as well as hydrogen batteries and facial-recognition software in mirrors. Dan Bridleman, senior vice president of sustainability, technology, and strategic sourcing at KB Home believes that the design will eventually allow "sustainability to be integrated into everyday thinking . . . and [can be brought] to everybody."[29]

Usability

Usability is another component of quality and is closely related to functionality. It has been defined as the ability to utilize the functionality of a product in practice.[30] Usability is particularly important in software development, and more recently has become so in consumer electronic products, for product acceptance and success. Usability is related to sustainability because a mismatch between intended functional use and actual use by consumers could lead to the squandering of resources. Let's take a personal example that illustrates the concept and its role in the green bundle.

Last summer, I rented an apartment in Paris during a heat wave. Paris is not well set up for such excruciating heat. Our fridge was barely cooling drinks. One morning, I opened the fridge and found everything melted. There was no difference between the room temperature and the temperature in the fridge. I moved the fridge temperature dial, but there was no change in the temperature, and I didn't hear the compressor start. After an hour or so, I called the owner and told him that the fridge was broken. He said he would replace it. Then, my husband came back from his early run and told me that the evening before, he'd moved the temperature dial because he thought the fridge wasn't cool enough. In fact, though, he had changed the dial in the opposite direction of the way he should have to cool the refrigerator. Basically, he had turned the dial to the maximum warm temperature rather than the maximum cold temperature. It takes up to twenty-four hours for a fridge to go back to its initial temperature. Even after I dialed it back, I did not see a change in temperature in the fridge. Whether it needed to be or not, the refrigerator was replaced.

This illustrates that there can be unintended consequences of product design. People often misunderstand the fridge temperature dial. Most refrigerator temperature settings are controlled with a dial or slider. They are sometimes labeled 1 through 5 or 1 through 9.[31] Because most people are not sure how to set it, they settle on somewhere in the middle, which might not be the optimal temperature.

Usually, the higher the number on the temperature-control dial, the colder the temperature will get inside the refrigerator. In other words, in most fridges that have a manual thermostat, the scale on the thermostat is inverse, so that 1 keeps a fridge hotter and 5 keeps it colder. This also correlates with energy usage. The colder a fridge is, the more energy it uses. The reason dials are designed that way is because they are not thermostats. They are power dials, similar to volume knobs on audio equipment.

The "power of coldness" concept confuses most people. The user's mental model when adjusting temperature is that of a thermostat.[32] We turn it higher to make our home warmer and lower to make it cooler. To adjust volume, the user's mental model is a volume dial on the radio. We turn it higher to make it louder and lower to make it quieter. We actually say, "Turn down the volume."

With refrigerators, the dials do not match a person's mental model.[33] Almost everyone in the developed world has a fridge, but they infrequently adjust its temperature. Until recently, most models did not offer feedback to tell users when they were making things warmer or colder, so most of us never formed a consistent mental model of how a fridge dial works as we have with other devices we use daily. On the internet, there are many forums in which people post topics such as, "Fridges—temperature settings help please!"

A digital temperature reader would help deal with the problem. Manufacturer LG now provides temperature controls on a front-door display panel of their Energy Star refrigerators. The fridge comes set at the recommended temperature setting of 37 degrees Fahrenheit (about 3 degrees Celsius). This improves usability of the fridge functions while promoting energy efficiency—it is likely that many people will not change the default setting.

But going back to the concept of usability, we can see that in the case of refrigerators, the temperature dial has low usability, hampering consumers' ability to utilize the functionality of the fridge. There might be a mismatch between manufacturer intent and actual use. Research shows that fridge users do not use all of the appliances' features as they were planned.

Opening our refrigerators is such an automatic task that we autopilot our actions. That is fine for us but not so great for designers who need feedback to create an ideal refrigerator for consumers. Observation of how fridges are used reveals opportunities to make improvements. One study looked at the interactions of eight families with their fridges during a week.[34] The results showed that the doors and shelves were poorly designed, which increased the time fridge doors were open to reorganize food after shopping. The study describes how time was wasted when doors were open, as people searched for their desired items and shuffled food around to make things fit when restocking between shelves and in doors and drawers. The participants designed and rearranged their fridges to meet individual needs so tasks could be accomplished with less effort. They rearranged narrow shelves for storage according to the size of the food packaging, often storing things that were not taken out on the top shelf.

Designing to improve usability varies by market. In developing countries, for example, poor infrastructure makes for shaky power grids. Refrigerators in these markets need to conserve energy and be more efficient. A team of researchers at UC Berkeley designed an environmentally friendly fridge for the Mexican market.[35] It needed to be not only environmentally friendly but also affordable for the company and the user. They conducted life-cycle assessments of the environmental impacts of their refrigerators and realized that reducing energy used during the operation of the fridge—rather than in the manufacturing of the fridge—was the most effective way to improve environmental performance. The final design includes a quick-access tray that allows people to get the food they use most often without opening the full door. It also includes an insulated window that allows users to see inside the fridge, limiting the time they need to locate or rearrange food and drinks. Adjustable shelves and a large vegetable tray make it easier to organize and access the food. These design elements combined to keep fridges closed longer, saving energy by preventing cold air from escaping.[36] The team also used innovative phase-change material that acts as a thermal battery. By running the compressor only to "charge" the battery at night, when electricity rates are low and ambient temperatures can be cooler, the fridge is able to remain cold all day, saving money spent for utilities. The team estimates that the design could reduce energy use by 40 percent.

User-centered design improves product usability and sustainability by making the people who use products a focal point during the entire design process.[37] As described in a study by Renee Wever and colleagues, "Instead of focusing on technological possibilities and quality measurements in terms of components, user-centered design takes solutions that fit the user as a starting point and measures product quality from a user point of view, taking into account needs, wishes, characteristics and abilities of the projected user group."[38] The aim of adopting this design approach is improving the quality of interactions between users and products.[39]

While sustainable design has historically focused primarily on reducing material use or improving recyclability, a user-centric approach of sustainable design concentrates on reducing the product's environmental impact during its use phase. Hence, sustainable-design strategies can bundle sustainability with usability.

Durability

Claims that consumer durables don't last as long as they did in the past have been made since the end of World War II. Manufacturers have been accused of creating products with the deliberate intention that their life spans will be less than the known technical potential, designing them in such a way as to make disassembly and repair work difficult and not stocking spare parts for long enough periods. Under what is termed "planned obsolescence," some manufacturers produce goods that rapidly become obsolete and require replacing; this is achieved by frequent changes in design, termination of the supply of spare parts, and the use of nondurable materials.

Product life span is a key component in assessing environmental impact. Concerns about waste have led to product durability's emergence on business and environment agendas. At the same time, durable goods must provide higher utility to consumers than do goods that quickly wear out. Tim Cooper, author of *Beyond Recycling*, defines durability as "the ability of a product to perform its required function over a lengthy period under normal conditions of use without excessive expenditure on maintenance or repair."[40] Durability is closely linked to reliability, the likelihood that a product will not break within a specific time period. This is a key element for users who need the product to work without fail.

Durability is an important characteristic of construction products in general and of green building products in particular, according to the findings of a survey of US architects.[41] The environmental and economic benefits of durability should be obvious. According to Peter Yost, a building science expert with 3D Building Solutions, "a durable building—one that lasts a long time—provides a long period of time to amortize the environmental and economic costs that were incurred in building it."[42] The same argument applies to products and materials that go into those buildings. Durable products and materials will not need to be replaced or repaired as frequently, so the raw materials, energy, and environmental impacts invested in them can be spread out over a longer time.

Longer-lasting materials and products increase the resourcefulness and sustainability of product groups with rapid turnover, such as fashion, in which cycles are defined by seasonal changes. These cycles are now being shortened further in what is called fast fashion, designs that move quickly from catwalk to consumer. To maintain the pace, the fashion industry has optimized its supply chain to design and manufacture clothes quickly and inexpensively, allowing consumers to purchase current styles at a lower price, often to the detriment of quality.

Countering this trend, environmental paragon Patagonia found success by providing customers with durable, high-quality clothing that minimizes its environmental footprint. [43] Patagonia's mission is to "build the best product, cause no unnecessary harm, use business to inspire and implement solutions to the environmental crisis."[44] In Patagonia's eyes, durability and environmental sustainability go hand in hand. The fewer items that need to be replaced, the less the burden will be on the planet. As the company's vice president of public engagement Rick Ridgeway stated, "At Patagonia, we are committed to making products with as high quality and as much durability as possible. The durability of a product turns out to be one of the most important elements of a product's environmental footprint. So if a product can last for years—and, in the case of a jacket, maybe a decade or more—then the overall footprint of that product on the planet goes way down. It exponentially starts to decrease as its usability increases."[45]

Beyond their jackets' physical longevity, Patagonia invests in emotional durability with its customers. In order for their jackets to be truly durable in the eyes of consumers, Patagonia cultivates a lasting connection between product and consumer. As researcher and design activist Kate Fletcher put it, "By cultivating an emotional and experiential connection between person and object, we can disrupt our dependency on consumption of new goods to construct meaning and our sense of self." [46] By staving off obsolescence with high-quality clothes that carry an environmental message, Patagonia fosters this emotional connection and sells clothing that is both physically and emotionally durable. Evidence shows that consumers value their Patagonia fleeces. For example, Patagonia products have been said to be "inescapable" in Silicon Valley and "the most quintessentially-VC [venture capital] item in an investor's wardrobe."[47] "It has a kind of romance to it," menswear designer Patrik Ervell said. "I always think of San Francisco, where I'm from. The captains of industry [there] aren't wearing suits. They're wearing fleeces half the time." Branding impresario Andy Spade, who has been wearing Patagonia since the 1970s, said, "They have authenticity. There's a guarantee to everything they make."[48]

Demand for durability has been trending in recent years. According to Juliet Schor, professor of economics and sociology at Boston College, people are starting to reject mass production and fast fashion. And producers of quality products that are made to last are benefiting as a result.[49] Patagonia has audaciously gone so far as to encourage customers to not buy new products, taking out a full-page ad in the *New York Times* that stated in bold text, "Don't Buy This Jacket."

Although setting a marketing goal to limit growth may seem surprising, it has led to increased revenue by winning over customers from other brands.[50]

Patagonia encourages consumers to buy less because their products are high quality. Simply put, they last longer. In addition, the company offers repairs to damaged clothing and even allows buyers to trade in their older Patagonia clothing. The company's website features more than forty repair guides on how to fix damaged products, further displaying their commitment to making products last as long as possible.[51]

Due to their commitment to the environment and product durability, Patagonia is on track to have their most profitable year to date, with sales projected to reach $750 million. Profits have tripled since 2008, and the compound annual growth rate has been 14 percent.[52]

The French translation of the word *sustainability* is "durabilité." Indeed, there is a natural connection between durability and sustainability. Things that last longer will not need to be replaced. This is the case for buildings and clothes but also for many other products. Durability is actually one of the criteria that must be met to obtain the European eco-label for products such as electronic equipment, furniture, household appliances, bed mattresses, and clothing.[53]

Comfort

Green products can also provide a more satisfying or enjoyable experience. For example, better air quality in green buildings, as mentioned earlier, enhances the comfort of those working or living there. People are less prone to allergies or asthma that can make them uncomfortable.

One product that is deeply associated with comfort is the mattress. A good bed can mean the difference between sound sleep and a night of tossing and turning. Unfortunately, mattresses are also a major source of pollution, filled with chemicals and plastics. But the journey of Jack Dell'Accio and his greening of Essentia's mattresses offers an alternative narrative.

The Dell'Accio family was already in the mattress business when a family member was diagnosed with cancer. Physicians told Jack that toxins are found in everyday items such as TVs, microwaves, couches, and dashboards. He instantly realized that mattresses were manufactured with poor-quality components, filled with chemically derived foams treated with harsh chemicals, and layered together with glue. In 2006, he decided to explore alternative, nontoxic mattresses and designed a model made of organic foam.

People spend a significant amount of time in bed and on couches that are often rife with chemicals. According to the US Department of Labor, the average American spends a little under 9 hours a day sleeping. Add to that the additional 2.78 hours a day we spend watching television on average, and we spend nearly half our lives in bed or on the couch.[54] Due to flammability standards, most of these furniture items have been doused in toxic flame-retardant chemicals that seep out and wind up in dust, which we then breathe. Potential health effects include increased risk of cancer and altered hormone levels. Prenatal exposure has been found to decrease IQ and cause cryptorchidism—undescended or maldescended testes.[55]

So why do furniture manufacturers continue to use flame retardants? To prevent house fires (at least ostensibly), regulators require mattresses and other flammable home furnishings to be treated with chemical flame retardants as a safety procedure. Yet California, a state that leads the way for the United States because of the size of its economy, amended its regulations in 2013. The code still requires mattresses to pass flammability tests. But due to the work of researchers and to activism by firefighters who have been affected by the toxic impacts of the chemicals, the state's population was made aware of the issue. Changes were made to allow the use of natural flame retardants such as wool and latex.

The statewide change began in 2008 when a UC Berkeley scientist, Arlene Blum, founded the Green Science Policy Institute—an organization devoted to fighting flame-retardant requirements worldwide. The institute's scientific publications and outreach campaigns contributed greatly to the public debate about the health impact of flame retardants. Blum was featured in the 2013 HBO documentary *Toxic Hot Seat* along with Tony Stefani, a former firefighter who was diagnosed with cancer, and Mark Leno, a California state senator who introduced numerous policies for increased chemical safety. Firefighters are particularly vulnerable to furniture chemicals, which are released during fires and result in extremely high cancer rates within the profession. The documentary raised awareness of the problem with flame-retardant requirements. Soon after its release, the state's standard was updated. Although it still contains a modified smolder test, it no longer contains an open-flame test. This new standard allows manufacturers to meet the requirements without using chemical flame retardants. The law also requires a tag on furniture verifying products that do not contain flame retardants. The amended standard created an opportunity for businesses to provide a solution to consumers concerned about the health problems of chemical flame retardants.

A few companies took advantage of this surge in awareness to sell organic mattresses without flame retardants, creating thriving businesses in the process. Mattress companies Essentia, Naturepedic, and Organic Mattresses Inc. (OMI) successfully marketed the health benefits and sustainability of their products. Their founders drew inspiration from a range of sources: a relative's cancer diagnosis, a search for a safe mattress for a grandchild, and personal chemical sensitivity. In 2008, at a time when industry sales were falling by double digits, OMI doubled in physical size and reported continued steady growth. Naturepedic went from selling $1 million worth of mattresses in 2005 to $10 million in 2013. Despite luxury prices, sales of organic mattresses continue to rise. These companies offer products that are healthy and chemical-free, and they are flourishing as a result.

Mattress manufacturer Essentia launched its business in 2006. It produces memory-foam mattresses that are made from the sap of the rubber tree. Their motto? "Organic mattresses, but better! You no longer need to compromise on comfort when committed to a healthy lifestyle." According to owner Dell'Accio, it wasn't easy to convince storeroom retailers about his value proposition. Salespeople didn't want to promote the health benefits of his mattresses because it meant pointing out that their other mattresses were toxic. Essentia decided to vertically integrate and sell directly to customers. They sold products online and opened their own stores. The market base for Essentia has evolved over the years. What started with a few grassroots customers who had allergies or health problems evolved to include people generally seeking better sleep solutions. In 2012, the professional sports industry took notice and sought these high-performance mattresses that also helped with recovery from injuries.

Essentia's website features testimonials by professional athletes who use its mattresses as part of their health regimen. The company has never advertised on TV, in newspapers, or on the radio, but it has been featured in *Forbes* and the *Huffington Post* as well as on television shows such as *The Dr. Oz*

Show and Anderson Cooper's *Anderson Live*. Essentia's sales have grown steadily at about 40 to 50 percent annually. It expects them to triple next year. The advantage of going green, in their case, has been unpaid-for publicity and accelerating profits.

Convenience

Convenience is a staple of modern society. Technological advances have powered new levels of convenience at home, in the office, and nearly everywhere else. By connecting on mobile devices and the so-called Internet of Things—a network of smart physical devices, vehicles, buildings, and other items—everyday tasks are easier to complete and information is available in real time. Nowadays, people cannot imagine life without technology. It makes life convenient and simpler. The rise of information and communications technologies have also enabled a sharing economy in which peers obtain, give, or exchange goods and services through online coordination.[56] The environmental promise of sharing platforms is that consumers become much less reliant and dependent on individual, private ownership.[57] As a substitute, they can have relatively inexpensive and convenient access to goods owned by other consumers that would otherwise stand idle. So, ownership of resources is replaced by access to these resources, and consumers not only save money but use less resources. Therefore, the sharing economy can be considered as contributing, at least potentially, to a sustainability transition. Several scholars have described the sharing economy as a potential new pathway to sustainability[58] that could disrupt the unsustainable practices of hyperconsumption that drive capitalist economies.[59] At the same time, critics denounce the sharing economy for being about economic self-interest rather than sharing and for being predatory and exploitative.

Giants of this emergent economy include Uber, which provides shared transportation services,[60] and Airbnb,[61] which provides shared hospitality. In addition to providing services to millions worldwide and reaping large profits, both companies say they help the environment by reducing overall resource consumption. Former Uber CEO Travis Kalanick described a city with Uber as "a cleaner city, where fewer cars on the road will mean less carbon pollution—especially since more and more Uber vehicles are low-emission hybrid vehicles."[62] Airbnb cofounder Joe Gebbia said, "We have always believed that the Airbnb community supports environmental sustainability around the world, and it's truly amazing to see that the impact is even bigger than we could have imagined. In North America alone, Airbnb guests use 63 percent less energy than hotel guests—that's enough energy to power nineteen thousand homes for one year. With an impact that big, it's clear that the Airbnb community is making a huge difference."[63]

Both companies have grown at an incredible pace. Uber's total rideshare bookings rose from $688 million in 2013 to a projected $26.12 billion for 2016,[64] while Airbnb's summer bookings skyrocketed from forty-seven thousand people in 2010 to seventeen million in the summer of 2015.[65] Much of this popularity can be attributed to the services' convenience. Uber customers typically wait no more than three minutes to be picked up at any time of the day. For many urban dwellers, the service has altogether eliminated the need to own a car.[66] Meanwhile, Airbnb is often cheaper than hotels and provides a personalized, unique travel experience. The company makes it easy to rent an entire home for a just a few days, with options that previously didn't exist or would have been difficult to find. The online search interface allows users to filter by price and amenities and by reviews to hear what fellow travelers have to say about a particular space. "Airbnb has fantastic listings, fair prices and their staff are very eager to help and easy to reach by phone or email," Airbnb user Julie Richards said. "We have booked three different places through Airbnb, and so far I've been happy with their service and ease of [using the] website."[67] Customers of Airbnb and Uber view the services as inexpensive and simple to use.

Overall, more studies must be done to truly assess the environmental impacts of the shared economy. Although sharing resources is environmentally beneficial, the increase in travel facilitated by Airbnb and Uber is not.[68] One study found that car sharers emit between 240 and 390 fewer kilograms of CO_2 per person per year. This corresponds to between 13 percent and 18 percent of the CO_2 emissions related to car ownership and car use.[69] Another study that examined ridesharing services found a measurable decrease in carbon emissions, but only because of significant decreases by car-holding households. A majority of households without a car actually increased their emissions slightly.[70]

A survey of shared-economy participants found perceived sustainability to be a major factor in positive attitudes toward services like Uber and Airbnb, but "economic benefits are a stronger motivator for intentions to participate."[71] This might explain why operators in the sharing economy don't use many environmental framings around their activities but rely abundantly on economic framings to emphasize price and convenience.[72]

The convenience and economic savings provided by Uber and Airbnb as opposed to traditional taxicabs or hotels have made both companies popular. Environmental benefits are not driving this trend.

Trojan Horse?

The effect of quality on consumer willingness to pay is a double-edged sword. Early iterations of eco-labeled products were associated with lower quality. Many consumers still associate these labels that way and thus may be reluctant to purchase products.[73] For example, although wine experts often provide higher ratings to eco-labeled wines,[74] evidence shows that consumers do not associate eco-labeled wine with increased quality, and so the label does not garner a price premium.[75] In fact, organic labeled wine is associated with a 7 percent *reduction* in price, confirming that consumers see a negative connotation with "green wine."[76] This may be due to a poor understanding of the organic label and its effect on the winemaking process, but it raises questions about the general perception of the association between green products and quality and about whether advertising sustainability impacts this perception.

A recent study looked at green-product enhancements and how the communication of those environmental benefits affected consumers' purchasing decisions.[77] It describes the following scenario: A firm develops a new product that is better for the environment. One option is to communicate that the green benefit was intended—the firm may highlight that it is concerned about sustainability, and as a result, it developed a product that is better for the environment. Alternatively, the firm may communicate that the green benefit was actually an unintended side effect; it may advertise that it was trying to develop a new product that satisfied some other goal and that the environmental benefit was merely a by-product of those efforts. Which communication will be more effective?

There are a number of real-world examples of how such communication strategies operate. For example, Method, a certified benefit corporation that manufactures household cleaning and personal-care products, advertises that "we keep the planet in mind with every bottle we design." At the other end of the spectrum, when Anheuser-Busch released new aluminum bottles for their top-selling beers in 2005, the campaign highlighted the distinctive design. It downplayed the significant environmental benefits of switching to aluminum. And, as previously discussed, the giants of the shared economy didn't put the environment at the forefront of their communication strategies, and neither did Tesla. Yet they all found success. There is no one-size-fits-all strategy to marketing sustainable products, but modesty has proven effective in many cases.

All else being equal, one imagines that intentionally improving a product would be preferred to doing so without purpose. A 2014 study on the matter showed the opposite effect, however. When a company manufactures a product that is better for the environment, consumers are less likely to purchase it when the green benefit is perceived as intentional than when the same benefit is perceived as an unintended side effect. This counterintuitive effect may actually lead to a decrease in consumer interest. In other words, Airbnb and Uber are likely better for the environment than conventional alternatives, but this effect is presented as an afterthought rather than as an intended outcome. Or as Eric Ryan, Method's cofounder, put it, "We don't run from the green, we just don't make that the lead story."[78] Instead, Method sells an experience and the technology that enabled the company to turn the laundry-detergent industry on its head with a product that's eight times as concentrated as its conventional counterpart. In other words, some firms could use a Trojan Horse strategy that will let sustainability enter a securely protected brand. This might ensure that consumers will not perceive a compromise in quality associated with sustainability.

In conclusion, quality and sustainability often go hand in hand. Performance, functionality, usability, durability, comfort, and convenience can all be bundled with sustainability. This bundle not only is possible but may even be a natural outcome of product design. There does not need to be a tradeoff of quality for sustainability. And yet, perhaps counterintuitively, emphasizing environmental benefits can backfire, or at least fail to be effective. Using the Trojan Horse approach may be the wisest course of action in many cases. Who is your customer base? Are they true-blue greens or the majority of consumers who value things beyond environmental concerns? Understand them and what they seek. Product and service performance grants access to convenient environmentalists. But there's more to this equation. People do not exist in a vacuum. They value the opinions of their tribe—the people they interact with on a daily basis. We'll turn to this powerful force next.

Chapter 4

A STATUS UPDATE

THE TOYOTA PRIUS made its debut in 2000, but the real coming-out party was not until 2003. By that time, environmentally conscious Hollywood A-listers such as Leonardo DiCaprio, Meryl Streep, and Cameron Diaz had already taken a shine to the car, and, seizing on the apparent interest, a public-relations firm requested five vehicles for the Academy Awards.[1] Toyota allegedly paid nothing for the placement, but a local dealership loaned the cars out for free. What the company got in return was priceless: images of stars like Harrison Ford and Susan Sarandon—preened and coiffed for the red carpet—stepping out of their vehicles and into the living rooms of 30 million worldwide viewers.[2]

The Prius was as striking as the celebrities that night. As *The Hollywood Reporter*'s Daniel Miller put it, "Amid a sea of hulking black Lincoln Town Cars, the compact gas-electric hybrids stood out to viewers at home and attendees walking the red carpet."[3] The power of celebrity prevailed on potential consumers, and sales grew rapidly in the following years. In many major cities, it is now unthinkable to pass a morning commute without spotting at least a few Priuses. In cities such as Los Angeles, they are nearly ubiquitous. In 2013, it was the top-selling car in the state of California.[4]

Most people care what others think of them, despite statements to the contrary. And they care about their status—their relative standing or rank in a group.[5] Status is awarded by others based on prestige and deference, and it typically, although not always, correlates with wealth or other socio-economic indicators.[6] Simply put, we tend to evaluate and contextualize each other socially based on the products we consume. In this chapter, we will describe the status element of the bundle, or how to bundle environmental performance with green products in a way that makes people want to show off their greenness.

Status is why celebrities hopping out of Priuses was a big deal. In this case, it correlated with sustainability, but status can be a powerful market force on its own. It leads people to indulge in conspicuous consumption—the purchase of unnecessary expensive items to display wealth and income. Opulent mansions, cars, and jewelry are traditional examples. Ostentatious tech gadgets, gold teeth, and diamond-encrusted iPhone cases are modern variations on the theme. Economist Thorstein Veblen first introduced the term *conspicuous consumption* in 1899 to describe the purchasing behavior of extravagant consumers. They spent money simply to demonstrate that they could, and they used that behavior to signal their influence over other classes, whose members sought to emulate them. The result of such consumption, Veblen argued, is a society characterized by wasted time and money.

Conspicuous consumption provides one explanation for overconsumption. We consume luxury goods we do not really need to signal wealth and acquire status. In today's society, such behavior contributes to environmental degradation by incentivizing unnecessary purchases that waste diminishing resources. With its cities mired in severe air pollution, China tried to counteract the problem in 2016. Luxury cars, which generally use more energy and produce greater emissions than other vehicles, were becoming increasingly popular among Chinese consumers. To curb the largesse, the Chinese government slapped a 10 percent tax on the most expensive models from Ferrari, Bentley, and Aston Martin. People buying cars that cost more than 1.3 million yuan ($255,840) are now hit with this tax.[7] But it is unclear whether the strategy will be effective. In fact, it might have the opposite effect— as the cars become more expensive, their purchase will more clearly express buyers' wealth, possibly leading to further conspicuous consumption.

Status is not all about selfishness, though. We also like to show off the good things we do. We take prosocial actions to signal virtue and boost our reputation. As concern about environmental damage and global climate change mounts, status is increasingly conferred on demonstrations of austerity rather than those of ostentation. This is particularly true of austerity that minimizes environmental impact. Consumers are increasingly willing to take on additional costs to show off this austerity in a phenomenon that has been termed *conspicuous conservation*.[8] Conspicuous consumption signals how much green is in your wallet; conspicuous conservation signals how green you are as a consumer.

There are psychological benefits to socially visible consumption of environmentally friendly products. Buying green and engaging in conservation behavior says something about a person. It reveals personal traits and preferences that may be hard to notice otherwise. These actions signal that a person is prosocial rather than pro-self. Psychologists find that a prosocial reputation is valuable, leading to benefits such as trust,[9] friends, allies, romantic partners,[10] and the achievement of leadership positions.[11]

To engage people with proenvironmental, reputation-driven consumerism, a few elements must be present. First, the signal must be costly: the more you give up, the more prosocial you are perceived to be. Second, the signal must be visible. People need to be able to clearly recognize the product or behavior as green. Third, it must be a choice rather than a necessity. Choosing to ride a bus is less convenient than driving, but doing so to reduce one's environmental impact could be viewed as prosocial behavior—bearing the loss of convenience for the greater good. Taking a bus out of an inability to afford a car, however, is not costly in relative terms. What is functionally prosocial behavior might actually be associated with low status in that case. Finally, the signal needs to be communicated to people who value green behavior. Conspicuous conservation has higher value in proenvironment regions. We break down these different elements in this chapter and explain how to use social status in green bundle strategies.

Panurge's Sheep for Good

People pay attention to and care a great deal about what others do. François Rabelais, the famous Renaissance French writer, humanist, and physician, described the strength of social norms in his story about Panurge's sheep. It goes as follows: Panurge buys a sheep from a vendor but is overcharged. In revenge, he tosses it into the sea. The rest of the herd instinctively follows it over the side of the boat, despite the shepherd's best efforts to rescue them. The phrase *mouton de Panurge* is now commonly used in France to describe an individual who will blindly follow others regardless of the consequences. As the story goes,

> Suddenly, I do not know how, it happened, I did not have time to think, Panurge, without another word, threw his sheep, crying and bleating, into the sea. All the other sheep, crying and bleating in the same intonation, started to throw themselves in the sea after it, all in a line. The herd was such that once one jumped, so jumped its companions. It was not possible to stop them, as you know, with sheep, it's natural to always follow the first one, wherever it may go.[12]

Peer pressure is a compelling force on human behavior. It differs from general social pressure because it has the ability to make individuals not just conform but change behavior. Parents are well aware of the threat it poses to teenagers, who might copy friends' bad behavior out of a desire to be accepted or the fear of being ostracized. Although much public focus is on the negative aspects of peer pressure, it can also be used to effect positive behavior, and it can be leveraged to entice people to live and buy more sustainably.

Basic moral appeals are minimally effective in convincing people to buy green; telling them others are already doing it works much better.[13] A 2008 case study looked at messaging intended to get hotel guests to reuse their towels. Signs noting that other guests at the hotel reused them were 25 percent more effective than traditional messaging.[14] A similar experiment looked at two recycling messages. The first was a basic moral exhortation to recycle. The second featured a statement saying that their neighbors were already recycling. The latter, crafted to activate social norms, increased curbside recycling rates by 19 percent. People felt guilty about not recycling when they believed that their neighbors were already doing so. Peer pressure works by changing what we perceive as norms,[15] changing what behaviors are considered immoral or antisocial, and increasing the moral cost (or benefit) of a given action.[16]

As Per Espen Stoknes stated in his book on the psychology of climate-change action, "If we stop communicating our worst behaviors (how much energy we consume, how big a house we built, how many miles we fly) and instead model our best behaviors—inspired by and in competition with friends, celebrities, or anyone else we think well of—change can happen, and happen faster. We can start social cascade effects."[17]

Star Power

As previously noted, celebrities have the power to influence how people perceive green behavior. For example, after the Environmental Media Association—a nonprofit that works with the entertainment industry to encourage green production and raise environmental awareness—organized the aforementioned red-carpet Priuses in 2003, sales took off.[18] Prior to that moment, most people had not seen the vehicles.[19] "Watching celebrities climb out of small green cars is a visible symbol that you can be environmentally friendly and cool at the same time," said Matt Petersen, president of Global Green.[20] The Prius gained further momentum when it was featured prominently in Larry David's hit HBO comedy *Curb Your Enthusiasm.*

The boost from the Oscars and other publicity events (with an assist from steadily rising gas prices) stoked massive interest in the second-generation Prius, which was launched in the fall of 2003. The new model quickly became a fashion statement.[21] Toyota doubled sales in 2004 and doubled them again the next year. People were waiting months for a chance to buy one.[22]

Since then, the power of celebrities has also been harnessed to speed the adoption of other green products. Artificial grass, used to save water in arid parts of the world, has benefited from the endorsement of celebrities such as Jessica Alba, Kristen Bell, and David Basche, who have installed it at their homes.[23] PR Newswire called fake grass the new "celebrity trend."[24] Apparently, the motivation isn't pure altruism; celebrities switch not just to save water but for the convenience of not having to maintain a real lawn. Artificial grass stays green year-round without constant maintenance.

Artificial-grass companies have actively taken advantage of this trend. The website of Artificial Grass Direct (AGD) tells consumers that "you may not be able to afford a house as large as these celebrities, or live the same lifestyle, but with AGD you are able to have the same lush, green grass!"[25]

When Altruism Meets Narcissism

What happens when conspicuous conservation meets conspicuous consumption? Can the two be mixed? Yael Aflalo, owner and founder of the clothing brand Reformation, thinks so. "I want altruism and narcissism to be combined," she said.[26] Coincidentally, the word *narcissism* derives from the Greek myth about Narcissus, a handsome young Greek who fell in love with his own reflection in a pool of water, finally transforming into the flower that bears his name. Thus, the term *narcissism* has an inherent nature connotation. Why not use that for a good purpose such as the environment?

Dressing in an eco-friendly manner used to be associated with loose hippie or outdoorsy clothing. Green clothing was perceived as practical but not chic. It could be used to climb mountains but not for a night at the opera. Patagonia fleece jackets are a typical example—functional but certainly no fashion statement. The paradigm and materials have changed, though, and this is no longer the case. Green is chic, and it has been embraced by luxury brands. Nonprofit Runway to Green tapped twenty-five luxury designers to develop a limited-edition green collection. Each crafted an exclusive item to be sold in selected retail stores around the globe and online. Brands included such luminaries as Prada, Marc Jacobs, Gucci, Balenciaga, Burberry, Yves Saint Laurent, Alexander McQueen, and Manolo Blahnik.[27] High-end department stores and boutiques now regularly feature green fashion, and many top designers have embraced synthetic and recycled materials. And although green apparel and accessories still only account for a little over 2 percent of the $200 billion fashion business in the United States, that's around $5 billion.[28]

You may have already heard about Stella McCartney's commitment to green fashion.[29] She launched the first luxury fashion company to brand itself as antileather and antifur and the first to focus on both stylishness and sustainability. Before the company's launch, environmentally sustainable and ethical clothing was disdained by fashion insiders. As the market grew, new labels seized the opportunities provided by eco-fashion.

Reformation is the prime example. Yael Aflalo founded Reformation after a life-changing trip to China, where she witnessed high levels of pollution and wretched working conditions in a region that is known for fashion manufacturing.[30] She decided to make her clothing line more sustainably and less wastefully.[31] Reformation's clothes are crafted from sustainable materials: carefully selected fabric and repurposed vintage or previously produced deadstock.[32] In addition, the factory claims to use "the most efficient, eco-friendly and pro-social technologies and practices available" and "invest[s] in green building infrastructure to minimize our waste, water, and energy footprints."[33]

Aflalo did not promote the company's greenness at first. On advice from its former public-relations agency, the company did not promote its use of recycled and overstock materials for a few years after the 2009 launch. The agency advised Aflalo that such messaging would not resonate with fashion consumers.[34] They took a more organic approach.[35] "It just kind of happened. I think we made really great clothes that girls wanted to wear. That's always been our guiding light: Just focus on making really awesome shit, and people will come and want to buy it."[36] Although there are other sustainable brands, Aflalo contends that "they're not fashionable. That's really the issue."[37]

As Reformation grew in popularity, it caught the attention of stars such as Taylor Swift, the Haim sisters,[38] Rosie Huntington-Whiteley, Rihanna,[39] and Emily Ratajkowski, who all wore Reformation to a range of events.[40] The Red Carpet Green Dress campaign, led by advocate (and former actress) Suzy Amis Cameron, teamed up with Reformation to raise awareness about sustainable clothing and produce versions of red-carpet gowns that are available to the public. They created Red Carpet Green Dress, an annual design competition, "to create a Red Carpet worthy dress, and now tuxedo, environmentally and socially responsible fabrics." Red Carpet Green Dress has been supported by celebrities such as actress Sophie Turner, who stars in HBO's hit *Game of Thrones*.[41]

Reformation has a program called RefRecycling to promote donating clothes. It eases the process and offers incentives such as credit to spend on their website.[42] "Making sure that the clothes they buy are made sustainably is obviously a priority," Aflalo said. "But it is also important to help them with garment care and what to do with their old clothes when they're over them, and to make that as easy as it possibly can be."[43]

Reformation's revenues have grown steadily, doubling for four years straight and topping $25 million in 2014.[44]

Competing with Friends

Most of us depend on our friends, emotionally and otherwise. We also compare ourselves with them to determine where we stand socially and how to adjust. Although people tend to be more altruistic when they're being watched, such behavior is not necessarily competitive. Individuals often strive for a positive reputation without trying to be superior to others.[45] Competitive altruism comes into play when people actively try to be more altruistic than one another. Within individuals' closest-knit circles, they regularly compare themselves to one another.

Leveraging this phenomenon, online magazine *Slate* created Slate 60, a public list of philanthropists. According to journalist David Plotz, the list "attempts to fuse two essential but conflicting aspects of the American character: generosity and competitiveness." The idea came after editor Michael Kinsley was struck by Ted Turner's remarks in an interview with Maureen Dowd. The CNN founder bemoaned the Forbes 400 list of richest Americans, saying it discouraged the wealthy from giving for fear of slipping down the rankings. Turner suggested that a list of charitable contributions could inspire the rich to compete in a more publicly beneficial way.[46]

Similarly, Warren Buffett and Bill Gates created the Giving Pledge in 2011 to enlist fellow billionaires to donate at least 50 percent of their wealth to charitable causes. The vast majority who signed up said they were already giving plenty but went along with the highly publicized pledge anyway, some because they thought it would encourage other billionaires to do the same, and others, as Oracle founder Larry Ellison remarked, simply because Buffett and Gates asked. "Many years ago," Ellison wrote in his pledge letter, "I put virtually all of my assets into a trust with the intent of giving away at least 95 percent of my wealth to charitable causes. . . . Until now I have done this giving quietly—because I have long believed that charitable giving is a personal and private matter. So why am I going public now? Warren Buffet personally asked me to write this letter because he said I would be 'setting an example' and 'influencing others' to give. I hope he's right." There are now about 138 billionaires listed on the Gates/Buffett website givingpledge.org. "Brilliant!" wrote real-estate titan Sylvan Adams. "Directing the same competitive instincts that these driven people employed to achieve the pinnacle of financial and social success, the Giving Pledge is encouraging us to outdo one another in giving our wealth away."[47]

Who Are the Neighbors?

The success of the Prius is attributable in part to Toyota's brand equity and its aggressive and innovative marketing. But these factors alone do not explain why the Prius fares better than comparable cars within green communities. That's where another important feature comes in: the Prius's distinctive design. Indeed, Toyota executives reportedly instructed engineers to develop a unique design regardless of quality. Because of this distinctive look, driving a Prius sends a signal of conspicuous conservation. The BMW i-series appears to have followed suit, employing a distinctive look and light-blue trim.[48] Two different studies found that the Prius's "green halo" led people to value it more—and the greener the neighborhood, the higher the value.[49] They compared the Prius to other hybrids to explore the difference. As one study's author, Steven Sexton, noted, "The Honda Civic hybrid looks like a regular Honda Civic. The Ford Escape hybrid looks like a Ford Escape. And so, our hypothesis is that if the Prius looked like a Toyota Camry or a Toyota Corolla that it wouldn't be as popular as it is."[50]

The first study estimated an average willingness to pay for the green signal provided by the distinctively designed Toyota Prius in the range of $430–4,200 depending on the owner's location. The second study found that the Prius commands an environmental signaling value of $587, or 4.5 percent of its value.[51] This means that, after controlling for mechanical differences across vehicles and accounting for the fuel-efficiency benefits of the Prius (and hybrids in general) and for general behavioral motivation for purchasing hybrids (for example, altruism), the Toyota Prius has on average a social-status-signaling value of $587.

Willingness to pay varied by community. Communities with a larger share of potential green consumers, as measured by political preferences, place a higher value on Priuses because of the environmental signal they send. The effect correlates with previous research showing that communities in California with more registered Green or Democratic Party members are home to more Priuses. People anticipate that their greenness will be noticed and acknowledged when they drive a Prius down the block. At the other end of the spectrum, communities with more Republicans tended to have more gas-guzzling Hummers.[52]

The neighbor effect is not limited to cars. When residents of a major California county were given two green electricity choices—visible solar panels or participation in a green-energy program—the solar panels were preferred despite the fact that they were five times more expensive than the alternative.[53] Again, it was the value of the green signal, and, again, people were willing to pay a premium for their green behavior to be seen. People who purchased solar panels also kept a contractor-posted sign that read "Solar panels installed here" long after installation, thus ensuring that their neighbors did not miss the green behavior that was already displayed on their roofs.[54]

The neighbor effect is not limited to environmentalists. Consumers in green-leaning neighborhoods were significantly more likely to purchase solar panels regardless of their own ideology. Meanwhile, ideology had zero effect on the invisible but cheaper green-energy program. Moving an average resident from the brownest neighborhood to the greenest one would make her five times as likely to buy the solar panels.[55] This is the power of reputation to motivate environmentally friendly behavior. The virtue-signaling value of solar panels has been estimated at 3.5 percent of the market price of a home in California,[56] and the premium is larger in communities with more college graduates and registered Priuses.

Social status is a relevant demand component for any environmental product that is obviously visible to others. Car-ownership decisions are among the most visible consumption choices that households make,[57] so it is unsurprising that the Prius is probably the most famous example of conspicuous conservation. Writing for the *New York Times*, journalist Micheline Maynard noted that "the Prius has become, in a sense, the four-wheel equivalent of those popular rubber 'issue bracelets' in yellow and other colors—it shows the world that its owner cares."[58]

Making the Inconspicuous Conspicuous

We have seen the power of status to market behavior and consumption that is highly visible, but what about unseen products and services? Electricity use is an interesting topic with which to assess status-based strategies because it is generally invisible to consumers and those around them. In the United States, most residential and commercial electricity users receive no information about their usage aside from monthly bills, which generally do not disaggregate into time periods or sources. Public-information campaigns are one way to manipulate the power of status, making the invisible visible and motivating consumers to reap reputational benefits.[59] But how effective are they?

We tested the effects of information about electricity usage on conservation behavior with university students through a field experiment.[60] We offered real-time information to students in residence halls about their electricity usage at the appliance level over the course of a year. They received information on a dashboard that detailed in real time their use of lights, heating, cooling, and anything plugged into a wall, such as computers, minifridges, and hair dryers. Both current and historical electricity-usage information was provided, and they received a comparison to their neighbors' usage. We then compared that to a control group that did not have access to such information.

Changes in behavior occur when a person is aware of an issue, thinks his or her actions can influence it, and feels capable of engaging in such action. Under such preconditions, detailed feedback on how to perform conservation activities and on the outcomes of these activities can facilitate conservation behavior.[61] Information about such social norms as *aggregate* energy usage by others can also increase the moral benefit from engaging in conservation.

Residence halls were the ideal location for our study. The rooms are standardized so there are no differences in efficiency or size of the housing stock to account for. And students don't pay electric bills, so there were no price effects to confound our behavioral interventions. This is particularly important when analyzing reputation motivations—rewards such as money savings dilute the green signal. Finally, the students had enough control over their environment (lights, thermostats, plug load, windows) to meaningfully engage in conservation.

The response to this information campaign? None. Detailed data about electricity use had no significant effect. And it was not simply because participants did not look at their dashboards. Using Google Analytics, we tracked who looked and when. More than 90 percent viewed the dashboard (and nonviewers may still have seen email reports that were circulated). The participants got the information; they just did not really care.

For the next iteration, we decided to make the information public. We hypothesized that visible conservation behavior might influence how individuals perceived one another. Weekly reports on each room's electricity usage were posted next to the elevator where everyone could see them. The posters displayed red dots for those consuming above average amounts of electricity and green dots for those whose consumption was below average. The results? A 20 percent reduction in usage. Individuals seeking a reputation for conservation now had adequate motivation to conserve—they did not want to be perceived as high users.

After two months of the public-information treatment, even those who had previously consumed more energy had formed better habits. These habits persisted until the experiment ended three months later. We also observed actions taken by participants to reduce their energy use. Whereas participants in the first study learned how much of their energy use came from heating and cooling via the dashboard,

only participants in the public-information treatment reduced use of those systems.

Focus groups and exit surveys at the end of the experiment supported our analysis. Students said they were aston-
ished how much energy was taken up by heating and cooling. "I feel that having access to my power usage made me
more aware and considerate of the amount of power I used,"
one noted. And yet, for students who weren't intrinsically motivated, private information just was not enough. One said,
"The amount of energy that I consume compared to other
rooms was not a great enough incentive to cut back."

That stands in stark contrast to reactions to the public-
information treatment poster, which were far less equivocal:

- "Once the poster got up, it became serious"
- "I liked the poster, it made us want to get green dots."
- "We want to make it green because red looks bad."
- "I thought the posters were pretty crucial to the whole
  process. It gets everyone else involved."
- "We did not want to attract attention because we were red."
- "I turned off all the lights and wore a lot of sweaters so I
  could get a green dot."
- "When I got a green dot, I received high five."

These results are consistent with previous research on conspicuous conservation, which describes how individuals take
benefit from prosocial behavior as a signaling mechanism.[62]

Unfortunately, our experiment did not allow us to investigate the finer points of reputation as a mechanism, such as
whether people were seeking recognition and status or avoiding shame or symbolic punishment.[63] Some of the comments
in the list seem to indicate the latter, although shaming is at

odds with the incredible number of positive comments about the public-information treatment. Not only did we not receive a single negative comment or complaint about the posters, but some students even reported missing them after the experiment.

Shaming

Although shaming was not used explicitly in our experiment, the mechanism has been used effectively in other conservation contexts. During California's most recent severe, statewide drought, the top water consumers in Beverly Hills were made public. Thereafter, the city saw a significant reduction in water use.

Beverly Hills consumes water at a much higher rate than other areas. It is estimated that residents wasted 175 million gallons of water between June 2015 and October 2015 alone.[64] Most people seemed unmotivated to save.[65] They were concerned about "reducing property value, or did not want to give up the lush landscape that is part of the heritage of old, wealthier neighborhoods in the area."[66] City educational campaigns, usage restrictions, and written notices for people suspected of wasting water had no effect—the community missed a mandated state-savings target and was fined by regulators, who stated publicly that its water wasters "should be ashamed."[67] After the episode, the city issued warning letters to eighty-six single-family residential water customers—the highest users among those failing to meet the city's 30 percent reduction mandate.[68]

The *Los Angeles Times* obtained these letters and corresponding water bills in response to a California Public Records Act request. The newspaper decided to publish the names of some of the most excessive users. The list included actress

Amy Poehler, whose home allegedly used about 170,000 gallons from May 14 to July 14, 2015—roughly 12,000 gallons per day.[69] The average Los Angeles resident, meanwhile, uses only 196 gallons daily. Other big names included real-estate developer Geoff Palmer, film producer and director Brett Ratner of *X-Men* fame, and music mogul David Geffen. Geffen and Ratner were identified among Beverly Hills residents as some of the most wasteful water customers. One unidentified person used an astonishing 11.8 million gallons of water per year and was nicknamed the "The Wet Prince of Bel Air."[70] Celebrities made easy drought-shaming targets. The lush landscapes they maintained during the drought symbolized their wealth and excess. Some sent responses to the *Times*. The spokeswoman for Brett Ratner told the *Times* that he was unaware of excessive water use. When an investigation uncovered leaks, he decided to replace his entire water line.

The shaming campaign was highly effective. After the costly public scolding, residents in the Beverly Hills area finally began conserving.[71] The city cut water usage by 26 percent in January of 2016—its highest percentage in eight months of reporting.[72]

Technology has made drought shaming easier than ever.[73] Several mobile applications were developed to empower snitching on water wasters. They are being developed by local governments,[74] but private entrepreneurs have gotten in on the action too. DroughtShameApp was created by Dan Estes, a Santa Monica, California, real-estate agent. It allows people to post geotagged footage of water misuse.

The Schwarzenegger Approach

Using status to sell green products works better when the signal is visible and in contexts in which people are more likely to admit that they care about the environment. This is why the Prius sold better in communities with a larger share of liberals. Likewise, shaming works better when people don't want to be perceived as excessively wasteful. If you are one of the unconcerned "brown" environmental consumers, you might be immune to such strategies. Underlining the ecological benefits of a product could actually turn away such people, who don't want to be identified as environmentalists. This group includes political conservatives and is more male than female. Is there a way to reach those who shy away from green?

One study found that men were less likely to buy green products when they felt their masculinity was threatened.[75] But that may mean that eco-friendly behavior can be encouraged by affirming masculinity.

There is a gender gap in sustainable consumption.[76] Studies have found that men recycle less,[77] litter more,[78] and exhibit a larger carbon footprint than do women.[79] Men also scored lower than women on the ecological- and altruistic-intention scales.[80] Previous research attributed this gap to personality differences between genders, stating that women tend to be more caring and empathetic and more concerned with health and well-being.

Newer research proposes that this might also stem from a prevalent association between green behavior and femininity and a corresponding stereotype (held by both men and women) that green consumers are more feminine.[81] Proenvironmental messages tend to use font styles and colors that are more feminine than they are masculine. The researchers asked people to imagine someone with a reusable grocery bag or a plastic bag, and respondents were more likely to imagine a woman with a reusable bag.

Greenness and femininity may be cognitively linked, but

they do not need to be. Masculine branding can be used to promote green products and behaviors to men. Such branding may include references to traditionally masculine things such as grilling and barbecuing, rough and woodsy scents, or facial hair. With masculine branding, marketers are able to focus in on what most of the male demographic is drawn to or interested in. It has been used successfully before, for example to get men to purchase "diet" products that had been perceived to be for women.[82] Marketers changed their phrasing from "diet" to "zero-calorie" drinks. Pepsi Max claimed that it was the "first diet cola for men," while Dr. Pepper 10 warned about its product that "it's not for women." The same can be applied to green behavior. A recent study that was conducted in Chinese BMW dealerships focused on one of the automaker's eco-friendly cars.[83] In surveying shoppers, the researchers simply changed the name of the car from the traditional, environmentally friendly name to "Protection," a more masculine term in China. With all other descriptions of the car the same, the name change increased men's interest. Another famous example of a strategy aimed at men comes from the Texas State Department of Highways and Public Transportation. Since mostly young men were trashing Texas highways, they decided to send a masculine message to deter men from littering. They identified the values of the group, which included strength, honor, and loyalty, and came up with a slogan that emphasized those values: "Don't Mess with Texas." It worked. Between 1986 and 1990, highway litter dropped 72 percent.[84]

Political conservatives are another group less disposed to association with green products. In one study, they were less likely to purchase an energy-efficient lightbulb when it was advertised as being good for the environment.[85] When cost information alone was presented to the research participants, however, political ideology made no difference in whether they bought the light bulb. As the authors stated, "Environmental concerns are part of a politically liberal ideology in the United States and have been correspondingly devalued by political conservatives."[86] In the same vein, another study showed that providing electricity-usage feedback to households was two to four times more effective with political liberals than with conservatives.[87] In this study, conservatives were more likely than liberals to opt out of receiving the home electricity report and to express dislike for the report. This raises the question of whether environmental benefits should even be mentioned in some campaigns to promote energy efficiency. And more generally, it raises questions on how to engage political conservatives in conservation behavior effectively.

Bundle strategies related to status and social identity need to be mindful of how environmental issues are perceived by consumers. It is important to emphasize the aspects of green products that are in line with consumers' identity. Former California "governator" and action-movie star Arnold Schwarzenegger is arguing just that.

Schwarzenegger is far from your typical environmental activist. A Republican and former Mr. Universe bodybuilder, he initiated significant climate-change policies as governor. He said traditional environmental messages that stress conservation and downsizing are downers: "You should not make people feel guilty about driving big, fast, powerful cars. Instead, we should let them know they can be part of the solution by changing the technology in that car."[88] Schwarzenegger said this while explaining why he owns high-polluting Hummers. He said his Humvees are no longer the gas-guzzling type: "They are hydrogen engines and bio-fuel engines and one is being changed into an electrical engine."[89] Campaigns that focus on keeping and improving the items they love may be one way to get reluctant men and conservatives to be more green. Whereas Priuses appeal to liberals, Teslas or hydrogen-powered Hummers will appeal to more conservative consumers.

Status is a powerful tool to compel behavior in the marketplace. It should be strongly considered when promoting sustainable goods and services. People care a lot about how they are perceived within social groups. We want to be or look like those we admire, especially when they possess high status like movie stars and fashion models. We want our neighbors to think well of us, and we certainly do not want to be called out for antisocial behavior. We will even go so far as to compete with one another to peacock how green we are.

There are limits to conspicuous conservation as a marketing tool. By definition, the behavior must be observable. Using status as a marketing strategy is particularly effective when green consumption is highly visible, such as with cars, clothes, or houses. It gets more challenging when consumption is invisible to social networks, as in the case of electricity use. But, even then, there are ways to use public information to leverage this market force. Status is a powerful way to appeal to convenient environmentalists. It can even be used to appeal to those who have traditionally been reluctant environmentalists. In any case, it needs to match consumers' social identity. Next, we will turn to what may be the most powerful force of all—something consumers truly can't live without.

Chapter 5

A HEALTHY PERSPECTIVE

STAKES ARE NEVER HIGHER than in matters of life and death. Imagine that our archetypical convenient environmentalist is starting a family. She's pregnant and shopping for cribs. Tuned in to all things baby related, she learns that health in early life has long-term consequences on future health, education, and earnings.[1] After a quick round of smartphone research, she discovers that common materials in cribs, bassinets, cradles, and porta-crib mattresses may be harmful or even life-threatening to her baby—the majority of mattress manufacturers use toxic, unsafe materials.[2] After returning half of her baby-shower gifts, she goes to a specialty store and purchases a safe, healthy, organic mattress for her future child. Without hesitation, she chose a product that bundled environmental performance with health.

Health and the Environment: The Evidence

People interface with the environment at every moment of their lives, and it's a two-way street. We affect the environment, and it affects us. More specifically, it affects our quality of life and our health. People increasingly face exposure to harsh chemicals used by various business sectors. Exposure occurs through the air we breathe, the water we drink and bathe in, the food we eat, and the soil we touch. This exposure can lead to serious health issues, from learning disabilities to asthma and cancer. In 2014, the number of adults in the United States who had been diagnosed with cancer at some point in their lives was 20.3 million, about 8.5 percent of the total adult population.[3] That number represents an 18 percent increase since 2006.[4] The American Cancer Society estimates that 75 percent of cancers are the result of environmental factors, including exposure to pesticides and hazardous air pollutants.[5]

Such exposure is especially problematic for children, who are more sensitive to chemicals. It can result in asthma and hyperactivity as well as cancer—rates for children jumped more than 16 percent between 1999 and 2013.[6] In 2014, 6.3 million children under age 18 suffered from asthma, an increase of more than 188 percent since 1980. [7] About one in twelve school-aged children suffers from asthma, and the rate is rising more rapidly among preschool-aged children. According to the Centers for Disease Control and Prevention, autism diagnoses jumped almost 123 percent from 2000 to 2014.[8]

Environmental harm and human health are often closely linked. The World Health Organization defines the environment in the context of health as "all the physical, chemical, and biological factors external to a person, and all the related behaviors." Not everyone makes the connection between environmental impacts and health, but when they do, it becomes a powerful motivator to change consumption behavior.

People search for solutions when they become aware of health problems associated with their environment. Increased awareness leads them to seek out green products to protect their health.[9] They presume that organic foods offer greater health benefits.[10] They buy milk that is certified organic by the USDA, because it comes from cows that are not exposed to the carcinogenic hormones, antibiotics, and pesticides used in conventional dairy practices.[11] Along with the environment, health concerns have become a primary reason for buying organic food products.[12] With $43.3 billion in total sales for 2015, the industry has shown continuous and steady gains since the economic downturn of 2009, with a growth rate well beyond that of the overall food market.[13] Between 2011 and 2015, the industry grew 10.8 percent.[14]

Realization of the connection between environmental damage and health tends to be most profound at critical junctures in life: when starting a family, having children, or getting sick and wanting to understand why. Awareness can also be triggered externally through information campaigns and current events.

Information Campaigns

Organizations and governments frequently use information campaigns to raise awareness of important environmental issues that affect the public's health. Similar strategies can also work for private businesses. Well-executed campaigns can be highly effective in motivating consumers to protect themselves through the marketplace. In China, where air pollution frequently reaches perilous levels, the government issues announcements directly to mobile phones about the severity of air quality. Following these announcements, sales of masks and filters spike on Alibaba, the Chinese equivalent of Amazon.[15] A 100-point increase in the Air Quality Index—which ranges from 0 to 500, with larger numbers indicating poorer air quality—increases consumption of all masks by 54.5 percent and of anti-PM2.5 masks, the most effective and expensive type, by 70.6 percent.[16]

The same effect shows up in energy consumption. Information about the mechanisms that link environment, health, and green behavior alter the way people use electricity. When promoting conservation in the home, environmental messages that communicate the negative public-health outcomes connected with electricity production outperform those that focus on saving money.

Maladies that result from the negative environmental impacts of energy production include premature death and morbidities such as cancer, chronic bronchitis, asthma, and other respiratory diseases. Traditional conservation policies did not focus on these issues, despite decades of research showing electricity generation to be a top pollution source and a cause of the health problems. Since the 1990s, studies and rigorously parsed epidemiological data have provided strong causal evidence of the negative health effects associated with ambient air pollution.[17] These global public-health harms come primarily from coal and natural gas, which make up a majority of the current energy system. The costs associated with these illnesses are enormous, estimated at around $150 billion annually.[18] Electricity pricing does not normally reflect these costs.

The link between individual electricity use and its impacts on human health remains elusive for most consumers. Household electricity use is typically "invisible"—consumers have limited information about the external effects of their consumption. Behavioral theory suggests that disclosing the external environment and health impacts to consumers is an effective way to shift conservation preferences and reduce the perceived costs and moral benefits of individual consumption.[19] There are many ways to do this, and there are important differences in how effective various environmental cues are within the broader social context.[20] Messages that work in San Francisco probably will not have the same impact in Oklahoma City. Generally, however, when it comes to energy consumption, strategies that correct information asymmetries between consumption and pollution work to encourage conservation by reframing issues and creating new mental accounts of the costs and benefits of conservation.

Understanding consumer psychology helps explain how people connect the dots between health concerns and conservation behavior. Although some are motivated by the desire to help others or at least reduce harm to them, emphasizing to consumers the private health benefits of reduced consumption, including creating fewer harmful emissions, is a more inclusive route. It reaches prosocial folks as well as those who are more concerned about their own health and the health of their families. This strategy appeals directly to households that stand to benefit from cleaner air and fewer health problems. That is almost everyone, or at least a large portion of the population. It particularly includes urban communities, the elderly, and families with children.

Concentrating on urban communities and families with children, we conducted a field experiment to test the effectiveness of environment and health-related social messaging.[21] Focusing on household-energy-conservation behavior, we looked at household-energy usage of Los Angeles Department of Water and Power customers who pay their electricity bills. Our results represent the outcomes of real-life consumption decisions in natural settings. The experimental field site, University Village, is a large family-housing community with 1,103 units. On a per capita electricity basis, University Village residents are typical of California multifamily renter populations and only slightly below the national average in usage (due to the mild climate of the region).

The 118 participating households consisted of single, married, and domestically partnered graduate students with and without children. This population represents the next generation of homeowners—people who are used to working with mobile devices and who are increasingly reliant on electronic communications in their consumption habits. Our results indicate how future consumers will respond to high-frequency information, especially as utilities begin taking advantage of smart metering, which offers more detailed data that can be communicated to customers.

Building an intelligent, wireless-sensor network, we gave these consumers real-time access to detailed, appliance-level information about their electricity consumption.[22] Randomly selected households were assigned one of two messages. The first emphasized potential cost savings. The second focused on environment and health-related information. Both were delivered via a specialized, consumer-friendly website and accessible weekly emails. Households in the monetary-messaging group were provided not only with their electricity consumption in kilowatt hours but also with information about much money they would spend in a year compared to their most efficient neighbor. The other group received the same data but with tailored information about the environmental-health consequences of their consumption. They were told how many additional pounds of pollutants were emitted as a result, again as compared to their most efficient neighbor. They were also told that the pollutants are known to contribute to negative health effects including childhood asthma and cancer. Here is an example of a message sent to the first group: "Last week, you used 66% more/less electricity than your efficient neighbors. In one year, this will cost you (you are saving) $34 dollars extra."[23] And an example of a message to the second group is as follows: "Last week, you used 66% more/less electricity than your efficient neighbors. You are adding/avoiding 610 pounds of air pollutants which contribute to health impacts such as childhood asthma and cancer."

In order to provide a reference point for the households' consumption, we compared our participants to the neighbors in the complex that were in the top 10 percent for energy efficiency.[24] After a six-month baseline-monitoring period, the experiment was conducted for approximately one hundred days, matching the length of a typical information campaign.

Messages framed around environmental and human-health effects of electricity use induced more persistent energy savings than did the more conventional money-savings messaging. Participants who received messages stressing air pollution and health impacts reduced consumption by 8.2 percent. Households with children were more than twice as responsive, reducing consumption by 18 percent.

For a sense for what these savings mean to the typical two-bedroom family apartment, 8 percent is the equivalent of plugging in a laptop computer for eighty-seven hours per week or a flat-screen TV for thirty-six hours per week or of turning off a standard 60-watt light bulb for seventy-two hours per week.[25] These effects may be diluted across larger study groups, but the principle of using health damages and moralized consumer choice remains a promising strategy to promote residential energy consumption. By contrast, participants who received messages about monetary savings did not produce significant conservation by the end of the experimental period. But we will discuss this in more detail in our next chapter.

As mentioned in previous chapters, there is a gap between

what people say they will do and what they actually do. This gap was reflected in our experiment. Before the study, we conducted a survey asking independent, random samples of participants to select the messages most likely to alter their behavior and motivate conservation. Many said they were willing to change their behavior, and financial savings were at the top of their list of concerns. But when faced with decision making in a market setting, only the nonmonetary environment and health messaging produced lasting conservation.

This shows that health messages can be effective motivators of energy conservation. There may be limitations, though. We did not study the persistence of behavioral changes after the experiment ended. Results from an exit survey indicate, however, that some of the changes could persist. A majority said they saved energy simply by unplugging electronics, changing settings on computers, or programming different temperatures on thermostats. This suggests that the conservation could go on without further interventions.

Public Health Incidents

Although our experiment focused on scientifically researched, long-term risks, individual public-health incidents—especially high-profile ones that garner national or global media attention—also have powerful effects on consumer behavior. Widespread concerns about lead contamination were stoked by the Flint water crisis and by stories of contamination from major cities such as Newark, New Jersey, and Washington, DC. Within a very short period, large public audiences became acutely aware of issues such as decaying pipes and tap-water contamination.

Up to twelve thousand children in Flint, Michigan, were exposed to high levels of lead from the city's drinking water. Scientists, pediatricians, and public-health officials from the United States and around the globe agree that even the smallest amounts of lead can cause irreversible damage in children, including diminished IQ and behavioral problems.[26] The story quickly became national news, and not just because of the contamination. Environmental-justice issues played a major role, because Flint is a majority-black city in which 40 percent live in poverty.[27] Government misdeeds upped the drama further, as state and local officials repeatedly denied the problem while residents continued to be poisoned. Eventually, six officials were charged criminally and two companies were sued for their roles in the crisis. President Barack Obama took action, declaring a state of emergency and authorizing the Federal Emergency Management Agency (FEMA) to provide equipment and services to ensure access to safe water.

Flint was not an isolated case, despite its high profile. The Centers for Disease Control and Prevention estimates that more than five hundred thousand American children have had lead exposures that pose a risk to their health. The Natural Resources Defense Council estimated in 2015 that roughly 18 million Americans could be drinking lead-contaminated water.[28] Environmental activist Erin Brockovich ratcheted up awareness of the issue by creating a map of the United States that showed locations in which thousands of people had reported contamination.[29]

After Flint, people became wary of tap water. Many opted to drink bottled water instead. That was one reason why, in 2016, bottled water eclipsed soda in popularity for the first time.[30] In 2015, the total volume of bottled water consumed in the United States was 11.7 billion gallons, a 7.6 percent increase from the year before. That translates into 36.3 gallons per person.[31] Many switched from carbonated beverages for health reasons. Water is a calorie-free alternative, but after Flint, these increasingly health-conscious folks became more afraid of what was coming out of their tap.[32] This happened notwithstanding the high price of bottled water, which is two thousand times more expensive than tap water. This shows that customers are willing to pay a huge premium for their health to avoid the real or perceived risk of contaminated tap water.[33] The same trend is happening outside of the United States too. In China, pollution fears drive consumers to expensive, branded waters. Foreign-owned brands sell at premium prices of sixteen to eighteen times the price of local brands, but growing tap-water concerns—and a lack of trust in domestic brands—have made consumers willing to pay the price.

The Flint water crisis helped water-filter companies show the broader public the benefits of their water-filtration systems. For example, officials distributed twenty thousand Brita faucet-filtration systems to city residents.[34] At first, there was confusion about how effective the various models of pitchers and faucet-mount filters were. Company spokesman David Kargas intervened, confirming that "all Brita faucet mount filters, including the 20,000 faucet mount filters distributed this week by state and local organizations, are certified by NSF International to remove 99.3 percent of lead from tap water that has a lead concentration of 150 parts per billion— far higher than what has been reported in Flint."[35]

Brita lists health and safety among the top reasons for buying their filters and pitchers, while noting the general importance of drinking water rather than other beverages.[36] To that end, the company forged a partnership with Alliance for a Healthier Generation, an organization that works to reduce childhood obesity and encourage healthy habits. Together, they want to "show people there is an opportunity for the entire family to choose water and take this critical step in the fight against childhood obesity," said Ed Huber, general manager for Brita.[37] The company simultaneously touts the environmental benefits of choosing filtered water over bottled water, saying, "By drinking filtered water, you are reducing the amount of plastic bottles that end up in our landfills and oceans. 1 Brita® water filter used = 300 plastic bottles saved."[38]

Health maintains a consistent presence in Brita's marketing strategy. A 2014 advertisement stacked 221,314 sugar cubes, the amount someone who drinks just one can of soda each day ingests in a lifetime, into an intricate city replica. And more recently, Brita partnered with NBA star Stephen Curry to promote drinking water in general and the brand specifically. "You are what you drink," the two-time most valuable player says at the end of the commercial, as he sips from a Brita cup.[39] Brita's focus on health and environment paid off. In 2015, the filter company's market share was about 60 percent, with annual sales of $228 million.[40]

Well-positioned companies like Brita are able to capitalize on publicity from public-health incidents, but most firms have to initiate health-based appeals themselves. The aforementioned critical moments in consumers' lives are the times they are most receptive to making this connection between health and the environment.

Starting a Family

When people have children, their lives change completely. It's not just Facebook feeds filling up with baby pictures. They also realize that they are responsible for protecting the lives of these tiny, fragile beings. As Christopher Gavigan, author of *Healthy Child Healthy World: Creating a Cleaner, Greener,*

Safer Home, put it, "With parenthood comes a most spectacular wake-up call. This beautiful, mysterious, squirmy creature emerges—and so does our primal need to protect that miracle: to keep him healthy."[41] That primal call came in 2008 for actress Jessica Alba, when she became pregnant with her first daughter. After using baby detergent to prewash clothes she received at a baby shower, Alba was horrified to see big red welts emerge on her arms. If baby-detergent chemicals caused her to react that way, what would happen to her infant daughter? Seeking answers, Alba turned to Gavigan, who was head of the nonprofit organization Healthy Child Healthy World.

Their conversations led Alba and Gavigan to develop a healthy baby-product line that parents could feel good about. They launched The Honest Company in 2012 using seed investments of about $6 million.[42] They started off with seventeen products, including diapers, wipes, and lotion. The goal was not just to disrupt a singular market but to create a brand people would trust and return to.

The Honest Company's laundry detergent is pH neutral and boasts numerous certifications and awards. It guarantees safety for even the most sensitive skin. The irritant sodium lauryl sulfate (SLS) is absent from their products, as are glycol, enzymes, and other potentially harmful chemicals that are found in detergents. The company's sunscreen doesn't use any, either. Honest products commonly advertise themselves as being "chemical-free." The only active ingredient in its SPF 50+ sunscreen is non-nano zinc oxide. The hypoallergenic product is made without oxybenzone or octinoxate, two endocrine disruptors that are frequently used in sunscreen. As with its detergent and other products, the sunscreen touts a variety of green and safety certifications.

According to The Honest Company's website, they are on a "mission to build healthier, safer families" and "make products that are non-toxic and healthy as possible."[43] Since its founding, the brand has expanded to include items ranging from tampons to backpacks in addition to their trademark diapers, which still make up a majority of the company's sales. About 75 percent of their revenue comes from online shopping, but the products are also featured on the shelves of major retailers, including Whole Foods, Costco, and Target.

The diaper industry remains dominated by Procter & Gamble and Kimberly-Clark, creators of Pampers and Huggies, respectively. Together, they account for 80 percent of the US market. Still, by carving out a healthy, green niche, Honest has experienced remarkable growth.[44] In the first year, they sold $10 million worth of products. By 2015, The Honest Company was selling 135 products and generating $150 million in annual revenue. Current valuations of the company range from $500 million to $1.05 billion.[45] The Honest Company's success is one example of the market opportunities for healthy and environmental products.

Ironically, The Honest Company's honesty recently came into question. In 2015, it was sued over false labeling after customers claimed the sunscreen was ineffective. More recently, the Organic Consumers Association filed suit against the company, claiming that the "organic" label placed on Honest baby formula was deceptive. Even worse, a 2016 *Wall Street Journal* exposé found SLS in their laundry detergent.[46] The detergent clearly bills itself as being SLS-free. Meanwhile, customers have complained that canceling diaper subscriptions is unnecessarily difficult and that the subscription contains frequent and misleading charges.[47] It remains to be seen how these allegations will affect the company's future performance and customer relationships.

In other words, although The Honest Company found success using health to drive green consumption, it might have overlooked the greenwashing pitfalls we describe in chapter 8 of this book. For a company named Honest, these are troubling times indeed.

Facing Health Problems

The connection between the environment and health also emerges at times much less joyous than a baby's birth—when people become sick with a disease known to have environmental causes or when a friend or family member becomes sick. That's what prompted Bill Hayward, CEO of Hayward Lumber Company, to investigate healthy building materials. After moving into a new home in Pebble Beach, California, with his family, Hayward began to feel tired and depressed. His wife suffered frequent headaches and congestion. But what finally forced them to investigate the cause of the family's ailments was the health of his infant daughter. She had stopped growing for months, dropping from the ninetieth percentile for her age to the ninth.

The Haywards did some research and learned that their home was to blame for their health troubles. Damp and stale air from poor ventilation is a major issue in homes throughout the United States. The Haywards' house was no different. Although they are viewed as safe havens, homes negatively impact health across the country, a problem exacerbated by a society that spends about 90 percent of its time indoors.[48] Damp or moldy housing is associated with asthma, fever, nausea, sore throats, and headaches and has been linked to anxiety and depression. Volatile organic compounds (VOCs) in paint and furniture contribute to respiratory disease, poor heating systems lead to headaches, and asbestos exposure causes lung cancer.[49] Sensitive groups such as children are disproportionately affected by these unhealthy housing conditions.

Moved to action, Hayward and his company began an initiative to help homeowners and contractors build safe and healthy homes and workplaces. He developed an approved list of safe products and created a healthy-homes tool kit for customers. Hayward argues that there are four main principles to having a healthy home: allow continuous fresh air, properly seal and insulate, minimize toxic materials, and have cleanable surfaces.

Bill Hayward's Healthy Homes program has been a valuable addition to his business, and he was featured on the cover of *Lumber/Building Material Journal* as Entrepreneur of the Year in the "over $50 million" in sales category.

In conclusion, there is a strong, natural connection between the health of our environment and our personal health. The connection between health and the environment is not always apparent to consumers, but when they connect the dots, they are usually willing to make drastic changes and switch to green products without chemicals. These epiphanies are most likely to happen during meaningful, emotional moments—the birth of a child, a national crisis, or a serious illness. At these times, consumers are ripe for communications that establish the health connection.

Thus, sustainability can be bundled with health, and the timing of the message is important. Communication strategies that seek to bundle sustainability with health will be more effective when they target consumers at the specific times of their lives when the connection is most prominent. They will be more effective with products that specifically target people in these phases. Baby products are one obvious candidate. And finally, they will also be most effective in contexts in which health is a pressing issue—for example, when air pollution is particularly bad, as is the situation in many cities in China and India.

Our energy-conservation experiment showed that the link between electricity use and its impacts on human health (via energy-related industrial emissions) remains elusive for consumers but that households—especially those with children—are likely to respond to health messaging, whereas appeals to their finances fail. And yet, in preexperiment polls, financial incentives mattered above all else. The answers to these polls show that money has a role to play in the green marketplace. So, when does money matter? And how? We will explore these questions in the next chapter.

Chapter 6

PUT MONEY IN CONTEXT

PRICE IS PROBABLY one of the first things that jumps to mind when thinking about what motivates people to make or keeps them from making a purchase. How much something costs seems like a simple, straightforward factor. This is not the case in the marketplace for environmental goods and services; it's complicated. At times, higher prices drive consumers away. At other times, higher prices draw them in. Whether people feel like they are being incentivized or penalized can make all the difference. And, of course, the number of costs and benefits is always a factor. A product might be seen as a boon or a boondoggle depending on its context. As usual, human nature plays an outsized role.

Consumerism is emotional. Buying things brings feelings of pain or discomfort, often referred to as the "pain of paying."[1] Years of research show that consumers will always claim price as the primary barrier to making a purchase. This was also the case in our experiment on household energy conservation. Despite end results that showed health considerations trumped monetary ones for electricity customers, when surveyed before the study, cost savings was listed as the most important factor in deciding to conserve energy. High prices are frequently invoked as the major impediment to buying green products. So, is saving money with green products the way to customer's hearts and wallets? Well, it depends.

In some cases, price premiums act as a deterrent. In other cases, money savings and benefits are not sufficient motivators.[2] How financial incentives are framed makes a big difference, helping consumers overcome their subconscious cognitive biases. There are mental constraints to processing information, leading many to deviate from rational decision making. This results in surprising choices: small savings framed as a tax or a loss can be quite effective, and raising a product's price might be a wise move in some situations.

Be Green and Save a Little

A common selling point for energy-efficient appliances and energy-conservation behavior is that you can be green and save money by reducing your bills. This sounds appealing, but despite such seemingly obvious benefits, many people do not invest in efficient appliances or conserve energy. This is particularly puzzling considering that efficient appliances can offer significant savings. Energy Star appliances, rated as energy efficient by the US Department of Energy, can reduce energy usage and costs by as much as 10 to 50 percent.[3] Replacing a refrigerator made in the 1980s with a new, Energy Star–rated model can save $100 a year in total energy costs. Replacing a pre-1994 washing machine saves as much as $110 a year. Multiply that by the ten- to twenty-year life span of most appliances, and it is clear that upgrading brings significant savings over time.[4] And yet 25 percent of new residential refrigerators and 31 percent of new washing machines purchased are not Energy Star rated.[5]

Psychologists note that our rationality is "bounded," or limited in ways. Instead of maximizing utility, we rely on heuristics—experience and trial and error—to choose between options. Sometimes, choices made with heuristics appear rational. At other times, they diverge significantly. People have difficulty understanding low probabilities, large amounts, and value over time—factors that feed into rational calculations of a smart appliance purchase.[6]

There are many good reasons to expect that information about cost savings will impact energy conservation. Things like turning off unused lights, unplugging charging devices, and reducing standby power are habitual or event-based actions that might require timely feedback about the associated monetary costs and benefits. The catch? Consumers rarely get good, current, or detailed information about the cost of electricity.[7] You might expect that the problem would be easily solved with better information. That is why, in our experiment, we provided real-time data to 118 households about their electricity usage at the appliance level over a year. We wanted to help them understand the energy demands of specific appliances so they could prioritize which to focus on. As previously noted, the impact of this information campaign was negligible.[8]

Households have false perceptions about energy use and the associated costs of their appliances. People think turning off lights is important in reducing energy bills, but other factors are much more important. We compared participants' energy usage by source from a baseline period with the energy use they predicted before our experiment.[9] Respondents overestimated how much energy is consumed by lighting and underestimated how much is consumed by heating and cooling. On average, the participants predicted that lights would constitute 29 percent of their usage, but the average amount was only 5 percent. They used an average of fifteen times more electricity for heating and cooling than for overhead lighting. Similar results were found in a 2010 national survey, with respondents underestimating energy use and savings by a factor of 2.8 on average—small overestimates of low-energy activities were countered by large underestimates of high-energy activities.[10]

Such erroneous beliefs could be overcome with accurate information. That is why we created a website with comprehensive, appliance-level information about electricity usage and told households how much money they could save by conserving. To make the information more tangible, we also sent them weekly messages such as, "Last week, you used $x\%$ more electricity than your neighbor; this is equivalent to x dollars of savings over a year." Still, there was no difference between the electricity consumption of these households and that of the control group, which didn't have access to such information.

The results caught us by surprise, especially because they contradicted what we were told in the survey before the experiment—that saving money was participants' primary reason for conserving energy. The most likely explanation for this discrepancy is that the cost savings were not perceived as substantial enough. When households realized how inexpensive electricity was, they remained unmotivated to conserve. The average household could save only about five dollars per month by conserving energy like their most efficient neighbors—about the price of a fast-food meal or a latte.

Using standard economic reasoning, one would predict that tailored information about private benefits would motivate rational changes toward more energy-efficient behavior. But there are a few reasons to believe that is not the case. First, as in our study, consumers may not pay attention when the savings potential is minimal.[11] In the United States, the average residential electricity spending per capita is about $750 per year, or about $60 per month.[12] The US Energy Information Administration estimates that households spent only about 3 percent of their income on energy bills.[13]

When filling out surveys, people might underestimate the various efforts needed to conserve. To reduce usage, they need to change thermostat settings, turn off lights when not in a room, run full dishwashers, and turn off or unplug other electronic devices. This group of small actions is easily lost in daily routines. The same issue comes up in other settings too. When using cell phones or debit cards, consumers who do not pay attention to past usage experience "bill shock"—that is, they unwittingly cross consumption thresholds, exceeding plans or contracts that result in usage fees or overdraft penalties.[14]

Households might also find easier ways to cut costs and find other sources of savings in the budget. That could involve choosing to eat out less often,[15] taking advantage of sales at supermarkets,[16] substituting generic for brand-name prescription drugs,[17] or making other changes that do not require paying attention to and altering their energy consumption.

In general, larger incentives lead to greater behavioral responses,[18] so savings might work when they are large enough. But it remains unclear what the threshold is for people to care about energy conservation. This problem also shows up in other situations. When gas prices go down, the premium that many pay for hybrid vehicles becomes more difficult to justify.[19] Hybrids are becoming less cost-effective relative to gas-powered cars because of lower gasoline prices and better nonhybrid fuel efficiency. This could be one reason hybrid sales declined substantially in 2016.

For our energy experiment, we attempted to boost perceptions of savings by aggregating energy-usage information on a yearly rather than a monthly basis. But it was still not enough to make a difference. The reality is probably that electricity is simply too inexpensive to make most people care. It might also be the case that by projecting savings to a more distant future, we made them seem less important.

Discounting the Future

People perceive benefits as less valuable or significant when they are further away in time (*temporal discounting*) or space (*spatial discounting*), even when those benefits have a long-term advantage.[20] People discount the future, preferring smaller immediate rewards (for example, five dollars now) over larger future rewards (for example, ten dollars next year), and they avoid actions that are costly in the short term, such as investing time and money to purchase energy-efficient appliances or making the effort to switch energy retailers. There are many scenarios, such as smoking cigarettes or undersaving for retirement, that demonstrate our tendency to neglect long-term self-interests. As prominent psychologists Maury Silver and John Sabini reported in their work on procrastination, "One of the ways of being irrational . . . is to act on rational calculations for intervals that are irrationally short."[21]

This is a problem when purchasing energy-efficient products. The savings they produce happen over time, while their up-front costs are greater than those of conventional products. Yearly savings of an energy appliance need to be multiplied by its ten- to twenty-year life span to make a significant difference. Consumers regularly forgo such purchases, even though they are cost effective at a reasonable rate of return.

Discounting future energy-cost savings is closely tied to the concept of loss aversion. Loss-averse people will not gamble even with odds of a loss or gain of equal size, preferring an assured payment to a gamble that has the same expected payoff. Future uncertainty reduces their willingness to pay. Because efficient appliances generally have higher up-front costs that are recovered only over their entire operating lives, a high implicit-discount rate and associated loss leads consumers to undervalue the future savings and choose lower-efficiency appliances.[22]

Frame Savings as a Tax

Cost savings are often perceived as too small or too far in the future, but when they are framed as a loss or penalty, they have the power to dramatically change behavior. People tend to weigh losses more heavily than equal-sized gains, particularly as stakes rise.[23] We typically focus on the risks, costs, or losses, such as the financial costs, physical-safety risks, and social costs, associated with adopting new behaviors. Simultaneously, we discount equivalent gains and benefits. When faced with a decision, we feel the pain of losses far more than the pleasure of gains. Neuroscience research based on brain imaging suggests this irrational decision-making is part of how brains function. Distinct neurological pathways anticipate gain and loss. For example, product preference activated the nucleus accumbens, while excessive prices activated the insula and deactivated the mesial prefrontal cortex before the purchase decision. Activity in these brain regions independently predicted immediately subsequent purchases.[24]

The tendency to weigh losses more heavily than equal-sized gains is also reflected in contingent valuation studies, which show that people value something much more after they own it. The maximum amount we are willing to pay for something is less than what we would demand when selling or giving something up.[25]

This is best illustrated by the issue of reusable shopping bags. While at the grocery store, nearly all of us have at some point been asked, "Paper or plastic?" Most think paper is better, but numerous studies on the subject are mixed. Generally, the answer depends on what specific environmental impact is being considered. For some impacts, such as reducing carbon emissions, plastic is less harmful. For others, such as preserving biodiversity and protecting wildlife, paper is better because it biodegrades. Both have negative impacts on the environment, and nearly everyone agrees that reusable bags are preferable. Policy makers and businesses have employed a variety of strategies to discourage the use of disposable plastic and paper bags.

A recent study examined the relative effectiveness of two policies in the Washington, DC, metropolitan area: a five-cent *tax* on single-use paper or plastic bags and a five-cent *bonus* for the use of reusable bags.[26] Both policies featured the same amount of money, but they produced vastly different outcomes. Most continued to forget their reusable bags in the incentive scenario, and most remembered them in the tax scenario. While 82 percent of customers used disposable bags before the tax, that number declined to 40 percent post-implementation. In contrast, the five-cent bonus had almost no impact at all. A tax was the far more effective tool in changing behavior. The findings were echoed by a similar study in San Francisco.[27]

These results are evidence that people react more profoundly to losses than to gains, but it also matters how losses are framed. One study showed that advertising messages focusing on "avoiding a fee" and "paying a tax" both improved the likelihood that shoppers would bring reusable bags—but calling it a tax was more effective.[28]

These results appear to be based more on emotion and feeling than on rationality. But even more confounding is the possibility that reusable bags alter consumers' in-store behavior. A 2015 study examined how the bags affected grocery shopping, analyzing data from 935,000 transactions across 6,000 households.[29] Customers who brought reusable bags were more likely to buy organic goods. Although that may not be completely surprising, researchers also found that bringing reusable bags increased the probability that customers would indulge in high-fat, -sugar and -salt foods such as desserts, candy, and chips. Notably, these shoppers seemed to treat themselves only when they brought their own bags—perhaps they felt deserving because they were doing right by the environment. In stores in which reusable bags were mandated, however, customers were less likely to spend money on organics and indulgent foods.

If framing losses as a tax is indeed more compelling, our energy experiment might have fared better with messages that presented energy information as preventing losses rather than realizing gains. In the context of energy efficiency, a message such as, "This appliance is six times less efficient than the best in class," or "You are currently losing five dollars every month by not consistently turning off your lights" may be more motivating than "This appliance is two times more efficient than the average appliance," or "You could gain five dollars every month by consistently turning off your lights."[30]

Of course, not all products and behaviors can be framed as taxes, but some of the underlying principles translate to other types of messaging. And there are other strategies to use money as a motivator too—cutting up-front costs, using decoy or reference products, and bundling with conventional products. They all take advantage of these illogical ways in which people relate to money issues in the marketplace.

Cut Cost into Small Pieces

When it comes to large purchases, consumers struggle to understand value. One easy way to overcome this is to divide the cost into smaller increments. This eases the buying pain that comes with investing in expensive goods. Customers may hesitate to buy something that costs $1,000 a year, even when that item offers them high value for the price. When the same product is broken down to $84 per month, it becomes much easier to gauge its value. This avoids sticker shock and the tendency to discount long-term value in the face of short-term costs.

A similar approach revolutionized the solar sector in 2007, when Sunrun introduced its residential solar-leasing product. Instead of up-front costs in the tens of thousands, the simple new model placed the initial cost of a solar system on the leaseholder, allowing homeowners to pay over a period of twenty years. The model was successful and quickly spread to giants like SolarCity. It has been a catalyst for growth ever since. From 2014 to 2015, the residential segment of the US solar market was the fastest growing in the industry, achieving a 66 percent increase.[31] The overall market achieved a comparatively small 17 percent increase over the same period. According to GTM Research, solar leases and similar contracts accounted for 72 percent of home solar sales in 2014.[32] Reframing the cost into smaller increments lowered the price anchor point—the cost customers keep in mind when deciding whether to commit to a purchase.

Use a Green Decoy

When consumers feel uncertain about a product's price, they look to surrounding information for guidance. Individual preferences are not fixed, but consumers do not (or cannot) seek out and process all relevant information. Instead, they "anchor" to the foremost details,[33] leading to preferences that are biased toward the status quo or default option. Anchoring, the tendency to rely heavily on the first piece of information received when making decisions,[34] leads to decisions and estimates based on familiar events or values, even when those events or values have little or no bearing on the actual situation at hand.[35]

Sellers get more money by starting negotiations with a high offer.[36] That number serves as an anchor, establishing the range upon which a final settlement is likely to be based. In retail, stocking premium products next to standard options creates a sense of value, with the less expensive options appearing to be bargains in comparison. Likewise, when consumers evaluate a list of products, they use initial prices as points of reference. Later options that are cheaper seem like better deals in comparison to the (inflated) point of reference.[37]

Tesla entered the automotive market targeting wealthy customers with its expensive Roadster, which started at $109,000. Next, they released the slightly less expensive Models S and X, which came in at around $75,000 and $85,000, respectively. Interestingly, with the high-premium prices of Roadster, Model S, and Model X, Tesla intentionally or unintentionally established a reference point for the value of their products. When Tesla set its eyes on development of its first mass-market car, the Model 3 at $35,000, the high reference point of the previous models increased perception of the new product's value.[38] CEO Elon Musk confirmed that Tesla had already received nearly 400,000 preorders for the Model 3 within a month of its unveiling.[39]

With many green products, there is a catch to this strategy. Most people have already seen the cheaper conventional option, so anchoring can have the reverse effect—it makes price premiums appear bigger than they are. But this shouldn't be seen as prohibitive. There are other factors at play. Several studies have shown that increasing price makes a product more desirable and can cause people to perceive improved benefits. Higher-priced placebo pills (at $2.50 per pill) outperformed lower-priced but authentic Prozac pills (at $2.00 per pill) in terms of the effect of both kinds of pills on emotional well-being.[40] In another study, people who were given energy drinks at a discounted price saw their performance in solving puzzles decline.[41]

Cost has psychological and even physiological powers on how products are perceived and desired. Wine might be the best example of this effect. Increasing price not only improves subjective reporting of taste but also increases activity in the medial orbitofrontal cortex of the brain, an area associated with pleasant feelings.[42] When US tax credits for the Toyota Prius subsided, sales increased 68.9 percent.[43] Perhaps the Prius had reached critical mass at the same time, but at worst the price increase did little to slow the rise in sales. It may have even stoked demand. Pundits were similarly bewildered by Lexus's decision to sell a hybrid sedan priced at more than $120,000. Yet sales of the luxurious hybrid Lexus LS600h exceeded projections by more than 300 percent.[44]

When green products are cheaper than their conventional counterparts, they are often less desired. Perhaps the products convey to peers that their owners cannot afford more expensive alternatives.[45] Cheapness undercuts the products' green social signal—saving money undermines perceived environmentalist dedication.[46]

One solution to this conundrum is to create decoy products that elevate the perceived value of a green product. The concept of decoys is well-known in marketing. In the 1990s, kitchen and home furnishing retailer Williams-Sonoma introduced its first bread maker in stores for $275. After sluggish sales, a marketing consultant recommended introducing a larger, premium model priced about 50 percent higher. With this new model on the shelves, sales of the original model took off.[47] The same principle applies to green products, especially when consumers do not yet have a perceived value or price for the product. Developing a green decoy counteracts the anchoring effects of conventional, cheaper products. Consumers have difficulties choosing between cheap, inefficient appliances or more expensive, efficient ones. Adding as a decoy a third, even more expensive option at the same efficiency makes the moderately expensive product look like a deal.[48] An energy-efficient refrigerator with a marked-up price could make all other energy-efficient refrigerators in a store look like bargains for their eco-friendly features.

The Trojan Horse 2.0?

Another way to take the pain out of paying is bundling green products with conventional products. When you offer a package deal, people have a hard time placing a dollar value on specific items within the bundle. Luxury versions of car packages, typically called "LX," are a good example of successful bundling.[49] Whereas few can stomach the pain of buying not only the vehicle but also leather seats, digital navigation, an upgraded sound system, and so on, many opt for these features when they come in a package. It is easier to justify a single upgrade than the purchase of multiple accessories.

Consumer perceptions of the magnitude of gains (or losses) is biased. Losing ten euros twice does not affect a person in the same way as losing twenty all at once, even though the total loss is identical.[50] We prefer to swallow the bitter pill all at once. When previous owners of an automobile were given the same base model with twelve optional extras, those given a price bundle option had a higher evaluation of the car than when the price was partially bundled or unbundled.[51] Numerous small losses weigh more heavily on our consciences than a single big loss, even when they amount to the same thing.

The Honest Company offers a good example of effective bundling in the green marketplace. From its Essentials Bundle to the Diapers & Wipes Bundle, the company allows customers to mix and match products into a flat-rate option. This strategy does more than create a convenient way for customers to shop, it reduces the pain of paying extra for health-conscious products. The Honest Company's website shows only prices for bundles, not for individual items. As another example, in bundling LEDs with novel functionalities such as the ability to wirelessly control bulbs from smartphones and display sixteen million colors, Philips gives its Hue LEDs value beyond energy savings and beyond what conventional products like CFLs and incandescent bulbs offer.

Hayward Lumber used its experiential knowledge and position as an industry leader to become a trusted one-stop shop for green builders.[52] Incremental environmental upgrades were always costly. But with a whole-system approach, increased capital outlays by builders could be recouped through operational efficiencies. The entire building envelope must be tightened to achieve substantial energy efficiency—premiums for highly efficient doors and windows would be lost as heat waste if walls and ceilings were not similarly insulated. Because of these interdependencies, an integrated product offering was particularly attractive to green builders. Relying on intellectual capital garnered through building and buying green, Hayward Lumber offers comprehensive, environmentally sound systems.

In conclusion, money remains an important factor, but businesses would be wise to consider their target markets and the context in which their products and services are offered. Our relationship with money is inconsistent and complicated by cognitive bias and other illogical mental effects. People complain about high prices, but higher costs can also make people feel that they are buying a better or more prestigious product. Framing small costs as losses is probably more effective than couching them as savings or gains. And, because context matters, anchoring prices and using decoys are potential tools to convince consumers to buy. Finally, bundling a green product with other products can make people more willing to bite the bullet.

In reality, economic considerations are only one factor among many in making purchasing decisions. There is even a danger that money could crowd out more powerful, intrinsic motivations.[53] Imagine you are volunteering for your local library on Saturdays. Then imagine that the library has now decided to pay you five dollars per hour for your work. How would you feel about being paid such a low wage for your contribution? Would this change your motivation to help? You might think the wage is too low, feel exploited, and decide not to work there anymore. If a person is intrinsically motivated to be altruistic, giving a piece-rate monetary reward to incentivize the desired behavior may have a counteractive effect by "crowding out" the intrinsic motivation.[54] This was the case for a subset of the households in our energy experiment. Families with children actually *increased* their energy use when exposed to the monetary message. They might have felt entitled to use as much electricity as possible, since they were paying for it and the cost was so low. People sometimes respond negatively to rewards and show loss of motivation, particularly when intrinsic motivations for the desired behavior are already strong.[55] But as we described earlier, intrinsic motivations are not sufficient to woo the convenient environmentalist. So although one should be cognizant of this possible tension, it is unlikely to be problematic for the majority of green consumers.

In this chapter, we described how cognitive biases can complicate our relationship with money and how acknowledging these biases can help us devise effective strategies to frame savings related to environmental improvement. Let's now turn to emotions, the last element of the green bundle and a powerful driver of environmentally conscious behavior.

Chapter 7

AN EMOTIONAL CONNECTION

THE LAST BUT certainly not the least piece of the green bundle is emotion. As legendary filmmaker Stanley Kubrick put it, "A film is—or should be—more like music than like fiction. It should be a progression of moods and feelings. The theme, what's behind the emotion, the meaning, all that comes later."[1] Kubrick recognized the power of emotions, even considering them more powerful than the ideas they seek to convey. While effective communications with consumers may not qualify as fine art on par with *2001: A Space Odyssey*, the same idea applies. Human emotions are powerful things, which is why poet Maya Angelou said that "people will forget what you did, but people will never forget how you made them feel."[2]

With consumption, emotion includes the full set of responses elicited by product usage or consumer experiences. Fear, anger, sadness, happiness, disgust, and surprise are all examples of feelings or affective states that a product can generate.[3] Marketers know emotion can be a strong motivating factor for consumers. When people experience emotion through consumption, they are more likely to remember and connect with the brand in the future. Like Kubrick, scholars have argued that emotions, and particularly empathetic feelings, are more important than cognitions in driving environmentally conscious behavior.[4] Empathetic feelings can be associated with products to propel us to prosocial behavior, just as empathetic feelings drive us to help someone who fell in the street. Such emotions can be experienced normally while consuming a product, but they can also be stimulated through storytelling.

Done right, storytelling engages people naturally and deeply and amplifies the benefits and cobenefits of green products. But not just any old story will do—it needs to captivate target audiences and motivate them to action. Authentic, richly detailed, human, and emotionally stirring stories can bring profound results, putting businesses above the competition and sowing the seeds of long-term positive relationships with consumers.

In a 2006 experiment, *New York Times* columnist Rob Walker had writers create stories that placed low-value items from tag sales and thrift shops in human contexts. The items and accompanying stories were then posted on eBay, with astonishing results: the price value of the objects, on average, rose a staggering 2,700 percent.[5] The context and provenance of the objects generated significant value in addition to the basic worth of the objects for sale. In other words, the value is not just contained in the objects themselves but in the story or the meaning they represent to the owner.

Unfortunately, this approach is seldom used when communicating about green products. The narrative around green products, and about the environment more generally, is either quite boring, focusing on scientific numbers, or quite frightening, emphasizing the catastrophic repercussions of our behavior. Communication that is based on scientific data usually puts people to sleep; it certainly does not entice them to act. Fear-based messages are no more effective: they lead to paralysis. The public discussion about climate change most clearly illustrates this.

Narratives of fear have dominated discourse from scientists, activists, and the media when encouraging conservation responses to climate change. They focus on the catastrophic: rising sea levels, floods, hurricanes, and more. These narratives cause people to feel despair, doubt, grief, anger, or guilt—and they have not been very effective. They may even foster apathy and indifference.

This parallels what we see in communications about potential earthquakes. Like catastrophes related to climate change, earthquakes are low-probability, high-consequence events that puzzle consumers who lack experience with them. For example, there are an estimated seven million single-family homes in California, and only 908,000 of them—13 percent—purchased insurance from the California Earthquake Authority in 2016.[6] This small number is troubling, especially considering that the US Geological Survey estimates that there is more than a 99 percent chance that a magnitude 6.7 earthquake or greater will impact California in the next thirty years. The last earthquake of such magnitude was centered in Northridge in 1994. It caused sixty deaths and damaged almost a half a million homes. Demand for earthquake insurance in California spiked after the Northridge earthquake but went down a few years later.[7]

Fear is a natural reaction to the enormity of a crisis such as climate change. But because people see resulting catastrophes as low-probability events, they cannot be scared into action, and despair also does not lead to responsible action. As research shows, people respond to fear when a danger seems real and probable and when there is an effective protective response to avoid the danger. A recent meta-analysis confirmed this, showing that the effectiveness of fear-based communications in changing attitudes, intentions, and behaviors increased when researchers included efficacy statements, depicted high susceptibility and severity, and recommended one-time only (versus repeated) behaviors.[8] The combination of negative emotions and a low-probability event breeds skepticism or causes paralysis. Psychologists have suggested that although fear can motivate us to protect ourselves, it does not motivate us to help others. Empathy, on the other hand, does.[9] And it is essential to prosocial behavior. Empathy and kindness help us build authentic relationships, understand problems through the perspectives of others, and create meaningful solutions.

Rather than promote fear, an effective narrative must generate confidence that empowers people to take radical steps.[10] The usefulness of fear narratives in the green marketplace is further complicated because of uncertainty about the exact environmental improvements of a specific purchase.

Human experience brings data, environmental issues, and eco-friendly efforts to life. Without it, people do not relate to technical issues on an emotional level. They feel disconnected. Social connections are crucial, even fundamental, to human well-being.[11] In previous chapters, we described the role these connections play, through social comparison and feedback, in self-appraisal. An even more active facet of social connection is emotional connection, which includes concern, empathy and affection.

Emotions affect consumer behavior in a variety of situations. Emotions evoked by advertisements have been shown to affect consumer attitudes toward the related brand,[12] influencing shopping behavior[13] and consumer product evaluations.[14] A similar phenomenon is observed with charitable donations. Tom Watson, writing for *Forbes* magazine, noted "strong and accurate stories from the field always bring supporters closer to a cause."[15] And the richer a story's details, the better.

Consumers can experience emotions before, during, and after use of a product. For example, ecotourism allows visitors to experience a close connection to nature and empathize with wild animals. But not all products can provide this natural connection when they are being used.

Creating a close connection with stories can also drive green purchasing behavior, as long as the stories are relatable and emotionally compatible. Communicating effectively about sustainability means telling a good story that generates an emotional response. To get people to act, these stories must also offer tangible paths to improvement.

Feel Empathy

Empathy is defined as "sharing another's feelings by placing oneself psychologically in that person's circumstance."[16] It is not about intellectually knowing; it is about feeling. Empathy has long been recognized as an important element in stimulating charitable giving or prosocial behavior.[17] When people were shown a video about highly intelligent whales as a critically endangered species and asked to imagine how the whales feel and to imagine trading places with the whales, they were more likely to want to help than people who watched the same movie without the instruction to empathize.[18]

One of our studies shows in detail the role empathy plays in willingness to purchase green products. We asked one thousand consumers to express their knowledge of and preferences for four different meat eco-labels—certified humane, antibiotic-free, USDA organic, and predator friendly. Let us review each briefly.

An Emotional Connection   129

In traditional farming, livestock may be treated poorly. The certified humane label means a farm meets standards for humane living conditions and treatment of livestock during transportation and slaughter. The goal of Humane Farm Animal Care, the nonprofit behind the "certified humane" product label, is to "improve lives of farm animals by driving consumer demand for kinder and more responsible farm animal practices."

The antibiotic-free label is used for meat and poultry products from farms that raise animals without antibiotics. In both cattle and poultry farming, farmers use antibiotics to increase the growth and size of animals. These antibiotics can cause health problems for humans when consumed.

The organic label is used for products from farms that do not use pesticides or any type of growth hormones or antibiotics, that use organic feed, and that allow their livestock outside access. In both meat production and crop farming, farmers may use pesticides and growth hormones or feed their livestock nonorganic food. Pesticides and growth hormones cause problems when consumed.

Finally, the predator friendly eco-label is used for meat that has been produced without killing or harming predators. Often, predators such as coyotes, cougars, or wolves are killed because they prey on livestock. Predators are an important part of the ecosystem, helping keep prey populations constant.

Our overall hypothesis was that consumers would prefer eco-labels that provided them some "private benefits." In the list of eco-labels presented, the organic label assures that the meat is produced without chemicals and is therefore healthier. The same can be said for the antibiotic-free label. When asked to provide one word to describe these two labels, respondents' most common answer was "healthy." Meanwhile, the predator friendly and humane labels provide benefits to animals rather than consumers.

We asked consumers, on a scale from one to seven, how likely they would be to purchase meats with these labels. In addition, we asked how much they would be willing to pay for a pound of labeled meat. (We also asked consumers if they were vegetarians, and, if so, we removed them from the analysis.) The humane label was more likely to be purchased than the organic and antibiotic-free labels, whereas predator friendly was the least preferred. In terms of stated willingness to pay, the humane label enjoyed a $1.75 premium versus $1.65 for the organic label, $1.60 for the antibiotic-free label, and $1.04 for the predator friendly label. This effect did not change with gender, income, or education. These results came as a surprise. We expected the organic and antibiotic labels to be well liked but did not expect the humane label to enjoy such preference.

Eating meat poses at least two potential moral problems. The first is the question of whether it is wrong to raise and kill animals. The second is whether it stops being wrong if the processes involved are carried out humanely. This is a complicated set of moral problems, but killing animals humanely might help consumers feel more caring. When we asked what words came to respondents' minds upon seeing the certified humane ecolabel, the most common answers were "moral," "caring," and "considerate." The label helps people maintain a positive self-image through acting in line with what they perceive to be higher moral standards. Such rationale is consistent with recent research, which suggests that engaging the public with a moral rather than economic case for sustainability is more effective in some circumstances.[19] Meat consumption may be one of those circumstances.

When asking consumers to rank their top reasons for

choosing their favorite label, the fact that the label emphasized that animals were treated humanely ranked first, followed by health benefits. The ranking was stable across age, gender, and income, except for respondents over sixty years of age, who expressed health benefits as the most important criterion.

It is therefore unsurprising that use of the Certified Humane label has grown dramatically in recent years. Starting with just 143,000 certified animals in 2003, the label reached 20 million in 2007 and 96.7 million by 2014.[20] Certified Humane currently certifies 144 different producers in five countries: Brazil, Canada, Chile, Peru, and the United States.

Empathy includes both an emotional and motivational component: the tendency to be emotionally moved by other people's situations (emotional) and the desire to help others (motivational).[21] This is why increased empathy has been shown to influence consumer prosocial behavior—the voluntary, intentional behavior that results in benefits for another. So how can sustainability be bundled with products to generate the feeling of empathy among consumers? Consumers can feel emotion through their consumption experience, and they might also feel it through the visuals or storytelling associated with a product. We describe these different avenues below.

Experience It

So far, we have focused mostly on products with environmental benefits that are difficult to evaluate during consumption. These "credence" goods have qualities that cannot be observed by a consumer after purchase, making it difficult to assess the utility of them. But not all environmental goods are credence goods. Some are experience goods. An experience good is defined in economics as a product or service with characteristics, such as quality or price, that are difficult to observe in advance but can be ascertained upon consumption. Examples include movies, concerts, meals, and holiday-related goods. The consumer pays for an intangible experience—sometimes this is embodied within a tangible product (a bottle of wine or an artwork), but other times the consumer is buying purely an experience.

Experience goods can have particularly strong emotional components. One example in which sustainability is part of the experience is ecotourism, or "responsible travel to natural areas that conserves the environment and improves the well-being of local people."[22] Sustainable tourism provides visitors an opportunity to observe and interact with protected environments without destroying or damaging the resources on which their future depends.

More and more people are opting for ecotourism. According to data from Booking.com, travelers were three times as likely to stay in "green" accommodations in 2015 versus 2014. Polling thirty-two thousand global travelers in sixteen countries, the survey also found that Americans are the world's top sustainable-travel intenders, with 53 percent saying that they are likely to choose destinations based on an intention to reduce environmental impact or to ensure their tourism has a positive impact on the local community.[23]

Some have said the resulting increase in visitation may itself cause habitat destruction and detrimental changes to the behavior, feeding patterns, and well-being of wildlife.[24] Others see ecotourism as having the potential to contribute to sustainable behavior through staging life-changing experiences.[25] It has been shown that encounters with nature, particularly those involving wildlife, have a strong emotional impact on participants.[26] Such direct experiences promote emotional affinity toward nature, which in turn leads to nature-protective behavior.[27]

Tourism expert Roy Ballantyne studied visitors' memories of wildlife to understand the emotional components of ecotourism. His research team took 240 visitors' memories of wildlife tourism, recorded four months after the experience, and analyzed them qualitatively: an aquarium visit, a marine-based theme-park visit, a turtle-viewing experience, or a whale-watching tour. The analysis revealed four levels of visitor response to the experience, implying a process involving what visitors actually saw and heard (sensory impressions), what they felt (emotional affinity), what they thought (reflective response), and, finally, what they did about it (behavioral response).

In recalling wildlife tourism experiences, participants reported vivid visual, auditory, olfactory, and tactile memories. For many, the opportunity to be physically close to the animals is what made the experiences novel or remarkable. Visitors specifically referred to emotions in their recollections, and some reported that reflecting on their sensory impressions had led to a greater understanding of the animals. Some conveyed a sense of empathy or an emotional connection with the animals, which involved understanding and identifying with the animals' "feelings" and led them to care about the animals' well-being. These feelings were particularly pronounced in the turtle-viewing experience, in which visitors identified with the animals' "struggle" to accomplish tasks. Some indicated that they had indeed taken proenvironment or conservation steps as a result of their wildlife tourism experience, and they were able to report specific actions that they had already taken or intended to take. Overall, 7 percent reported adopting a specific new proenvironmental behavior as a result of the visit. An additional 11 percent reported heightened awareness of the need for personal action, such as changing habits and purchasing practices.

The emotional experiences provoked deeper thought and led to concern and respect, not only for the specific animals encountered but for the species as a whole. Activation of empathy toward specific environmental objects led to more favorable attitudes, not just toward the objects but toward nature as a whole. This was particularly the case when visitors could actually witness the animals' struggles to survive or when information provided by commentaries or signage focused on the threats posed by human actions.[28] The study clearly demonstrated the power of wildlife to activate empathy and create lasting memories through transformative experiences.[29]

Many scholars have documented changes in visitors' environmental attitudes, proenvironmental behavior, and conservation knowledge as a measure of ecotourism's success in meeting sustainability goals.[30] This example focused on the "nature" aspect of ecotourism, but similar emotions can be triggered through connections with communities of people. Another important factor is social empathy, which stresses contextual understanding and social responsibility.[31] Research shows that successful ecotourism companies generate social empathy and a better understanding of a community's entire local situation, from geological factors to language and customs.[32]

Tourism can also trigger nostalgia, a special connection to the glory of the past. This is what heritage hotels promise. Heritage hotels are older, historic buildings that have been converted. They are particularly developed in Asia,[33] and they provide opportunities for tourists to be immersed in the history, art, culture, tastes, traditions, and sentiments of a place.[34] Like ecotourism, heritage hotels hold the promise that society at large may benefit; the practice safeguards buildings that are repositories of a destination's heritage and historic memory, and it generates income and employment beneficial to enterprise and local economies.[35]

Experience goods offer a unique, first-person opportunity to connect with sustainability. And the experience doesn't always have to be tourism: movies, documentaries, and books related to the environment are also agents of behavioral change.

Show It

Experience goods are particularly well suited to generate emotions associated with nature. But most products won't offer this opportunity. So, what are other avenues to generate empathy? Something as simple as good, human photography is one answer.

In our food experiment, when meat consumers were shown an image of a young animal such as a lamb, calf, or piglet before choosing a meat eco-label, they were even more likely to prefer the humane label focused on animal treatment. Interestingly, an image of a young child eating meat made no difference in label choice. In other words, an image of a child eating a dead animal did not elicit empathy for the animals. This may not be too surprising; most people see children as innocent beings who need protein to grow and be healthy. But consumers fell for pictures of cute baby animals that were ostensibly going to be eaten.

Pictures of faces are often used to promote charitable donations. Advertisements display photographs of the people they help to evoke a form of human sympathy that promotes giving. Research shows that expressions on faces in photographs also affect sympathy and giving. In addition to transmitting information, facial expressions elicit vicarious emotions among observers, a phenomenon dubbed "emotional contagion."[36] People are particularly sympathetic and likely to donate when they see sad expressions rather than happy or neutral ones.[37]

Human pictures can also be used to elicit responses to green products. Lotus Foods imports and sells specialty rice that is organic, heirloom, and fair trade. Based in Richmond, California, Lotus Foods was founded in 1995 by Caryl Levine and Ken Lee, who discovered rare and disappearing rice varieties on a trip to China and wanted to bring them to the world to avoid their extinction.[38]

For their supply, Lotus works with small family farmers in remote locations all over the world, including Bangladesh, Cambodia, Indonesia, Bhutan, and Madagascar. As a certified B Corporation, Lotus Foods is also committed to environmental sustainability. They acknowledge the large amount of water that rice irrigation uses and implemented a "more crop per drop" strategy that saves water and seed while reducing women's labor and methane emissions. They are also dedicated to building transparent and respectful relationships with farmers through fair trade. Fair trade allows Lotus Foods to fulfill its mission of supporting sustainable global agriculture and providing economic support to small family farmers across the globe.

After a decade of operations, however, Lotus Foods was still finding it difficult to explain their unusual business model to US consumers. As expressed by company cofounder Levine, "Consumers have great power in their purse to change the world, but it is challenging to educate them about the different varieties of rice and agricultural practices and their impact on the environment."[39]

In 2010, the company undertook a brand overhaul to do a better job of communicating publicly about its relationship with farmers. The website and packaging was redesigned to highlight the central role farmers play in producing the rice Lotus sells. The brand slogan was changed from "Lotus Foods: A World of Rice" to "Lotus Foods: Rice Is Life." Each package was also branded with the phrase "Healthier Rice for a Healthier Life," referring to the nutritious value that rice provides and the better livelihood Lotus offers farmers. Underneath the phrase, packages are adorned with images of real farmers from the source country of the rice. "We know who grows our rice," Lotus promotes. As Levin put it, "Before, we had a label that emphasized the place where the rice is grown. We decided to change it to show the people who grow the rice. People want to know the people who grow their food. The farmers are those who adopt the new practices."[40]

An image of Lanja Rajaonesilala, a rice farmer from Madagascar, was broadcast on a big screen in Times Square six times during the Summer Fancy Food Show in New York to promote the launch of a Madagascan organic red rice product line. Each package depicts a specific farmer from the region of the rice's origin and tells how Lotus's initiatives have positively affected him or her. "It's important to us to get the consumer to know their farmers," Levine said. "We're committed to changing how rice is grown around the world."

Sales of Lotus Foods have increased twenty-fold since the launch of the new campaign.

Tell the Story

Pictures provoke an initial emotional connection, but a full story brings that connection to life. In order to feel empathy, a person must understand and sympathize with other people's behaviors, perspectives, and emotional states.

Stories are illustrative and memorable and allow firms

to create stronger emotional bonds with customers.[41] When we read or listen to a story, we imagine what the characters feel—in essence, we practice a key component of empathy.

Storytelling has been used since ancient times to help people understand the world around them. The basic goal is to invoke drama that incites emotion. As business author Harrison Monarth stated, "A story can go where quantitative analysis is denied admission: our hearts."[42]

According to neuroeconomist Paul Zak, telling stories induces a physiological response in the reader or listener.[43] Tense moments cause adrenal glands to release cortisol, which increases focus, whereas cute animals cause the release of oxytocin, which increases empathy and connection. Happy endings release dopamine, resulting in hope and optimism. Studies show that individuals with higher levels of oxytocin are much more likely to donate money to a stranger.[44]

Storytelling has traditionally been used by marketers, but it is particularly vital when it comes to sustainability. The purchase encouraged goes beyond buying a product for its own purpose, beyond forging a loyal bond between company and consumer. Sustainability-focused storytelling pushes consumers to think outside of their own experiences and gives them potency to act on a global problem and help others.

A good story usually offers tension with one or more incitements, preceded by conditions or settings that initiate the unconscious/conscious identification of one or more goals. The actions of a protagonist and possibly additional actors result in an outcome; the temporary occurrences of world blocks (for example, an antagonist temporarily preventing the protagonist from achieving the main goal) or personal blocks (for example, the protagonist lacks the skill to perform an act necessary to reach the goal) intensify viewer and protagonist emotion and involvement in the story.[45] Taking steps to overcome these blocks, such as seeking and gaining help from others, occurs frequently in stories.[46] Finally, a critical element of most good stories is finding a solution.

Dawn dishwashing liquid does a nice job using storytelling to communicate about its wildlife conservation efforts. When the Exxon Valdez oil spill happened in 1989, Proctor and Gamble donated hundreds of cases of Dawn to the International Bird Rescue Research Center. In 2010, Proctor and Gamble donated thousands of bottles of Dawn to the Marine Mammal Center after the BP oil spill in the Gulf of Mexico.[47] During the last four decades, Dawn has donated more than one hundred thousand bottles of dishwashing liquid to its wildlife partners, the International Bird Rescue and the Marine Mammal Center, helping the organizations clean more than seventy-five thousand marine animals in the United States.[48] Dawn also launched an aggressive communication campaign about wildlife rescue through videos and social media.

Dawn's commercials appeal to our compassion, sensitivity, and sympathy for animals covered in oil. Dawn broadcasts images in videos of animals covered in oil and being cleaned up with Dawn products, and the company features the faces of wild animals such as ducks, seals, and penguins on their bottles.

In one of their short videos, we see a baby duck as an off-camera voice says, "These birds once affected by oil are headed back home thanks to Dawn." Then we see oil-soaked birds being washed by rescuers accompanied by the line, "Rescue workers only trust Dawn because it is tough on grease yet gentle." Finally, we see pictures of happy ducks running around, and we hear, "Dawn helps save wildlife." The final shot is a picture of a bottle of Dawn. This short clip exemplifies how storytelling can be used to illuminate the connection between a product and a cause. It provides the classic elements of storytelling: it poses a problem and then offers the solution. In doing so, it creates an empathetic connection to the animals.

Seeing animals covered in oil causes an emotional reaction for most people. After they are cleaned, viewers get to see them run back home toward the water. Finally, at the end of the commercial, those watching are provided with information about how they can help save wildlife. The message is effective, and it leaves people with a choice to do something or nothing.

Dawn also took advantage of public attention to recent oil spills, such as BP Deepwater Horizon, by advertising their product when audiences are paying the most attention. The message is not all conservation—by showing ducks being cleaned off by Dawn's detergent, it illustrates how well the product works while being gentle to animals and, by extension, people. The campaign further benefits by piggybacking on the credibility of its nonprofit partners.

Dawn took the strategy a step further, engaging audiences online by having them contribute to a mosaic of thank-you cards for volunteers. The company's Facebook page currently has more than one million likes and followers. Not bad for a dish soap. On YouTube, a nine-episode series titled "Dawn Saves Wildlife" helped the company grow an audience of more than 20,700 subscribers.

This appeal to consumer morality has proved highly effective. Dawn made a billion dollars in revenue in 2012 thanks in part to its wildlife-oriented advertising campaign.[49]

A compelling story is important to increase people's willingness to act. It is a good catalyst, but it does not complete the transaction. You do not want to get people excited and leave them with nothing to do. Customers must believe that their charitable action or green-product purchase is both important and effective.

Walk the Talk

In the world of charitable giving, efficacy refers to a donor's perception that his contribution will make a difference to the cause he supports. Efficacy is most often studied in philanthropic studies, economics, and psychology, respectively. Survey studies reveal that when people think their contribution will not make a difference, they are less likely to give[50] or leave a charitable bequest.[51] But efficacy also plays an important role in consumer purchasing.

One successful approach that connects consumers to a product emotionally and provides a clear road map to a solution is the one-for-one model. In this model, for every product a customer buys, the company gives away a free product to someone in need. TOMS shoes is probably the most famous example: for every pair of shoes a consumer buys, TOMS donates one to disadvantaged children. Others have followed suit. Nouri Bar donates a meal to a hungry child for every nutritional bar it sells; Soapbox Soaps donates a month of water, a bar of soap, or a year of vitamins for each soap product it sells; and with every Yoobi school-supply purchase, the company donates a classroom package that includes notebooks, pencils, and other stationaries to a classroom in need in the United States.

The story of TOMS began when its founder, Blake Mycoskie, embarked on a journey to Argentina in 2006. He came to a "dramatically heightened . . . awareness" of the suffering of shoeless children in Buenos Aires slums.[52] Mycoskie realized that entrepreneurship could be an effective tool to mitigate such social issues. That is where one-for-one came into being.

Since 2006, TOMS has provided over 35 million pairs of shoes to children. Mycoskie decided to expand the one-for-one model to eyewear, coffee-bean roasting, and bags. For every pair of eyeglasses purchased, TOMS helps give clearer sight to a person in need. TOMS Eyewear has restored sight to over 275,000 people since 2011, and TOMS Roasting Company has helped provide 67,000 weeks of safe water since its launching in 2014. In 2015, TOMS Bag Collection was founded with the mission to help provide training for skilled birth attendants and distribute birth kits containing items that help a woman safely deliver her baby. Today, it collaborates with more than one hundred giving partners in over seventy countries around the world. TOMS is now valued at $625 million, largely because of the one-for-one model's effectiveness at motivating consumers.

TOMS persuades potential consumers that the conspicuous act of purchasing can also be a charitable act of giving that improves a child's life in another corner of the world. TOMS promotes the idea of one-for-one in branding: as long as a consumer buys an item from TOMS, another person will be helped.

The psychological mechanism behind one-for-one's success is empathy. TOMS' website illustrates how it conveys that to its audience. It uses slogans to grab attention, such as, "Each pair of shoes you purchase = a pair of shoes for a child in need," and "See how your purchase helps others." Similar promises appear nine times on the home page alone. TOMS circumvents confusion about the influence that consumers' actions will have in the near or distant future, elaborating instead on the immediate change they will make with their purchase. With the well-being of two separate people directly juxtaposed, a clear social connection drives consumers to prosocial responses.

TOMS focuses on arousing empathy with its marketing. To demonstrate how the company improves lives, they show photos of children running happily with their shoes on and of the vision impaired looking at the camera, smiling and wearing their glasses. Such images are emotionally contagious: the delighted emotions of the people helped are conveyed to potential consumers, who share those feelings by putting themselves (in this case quite literally) in the other people's shoes. That empathy creates urgency among consumers. It tells them, "Remember the comfort and joy you feel when you wear your favorite shoes? If you buy our shoes, you will help someone in need feel the same way."

There is strong evidence that helping others creates positive psychological responses in the helper, an effect sometimes labeled "empathic joy."[53] In economic models of philanthropy, this category of motives is called "warm glow" or "joy of giving."[54] Recent studies suggest that charitable donations "elicit neural activity in areas linked to reward processing"[55] and that specific parts of the brain activate "when altruistic choices prevail over selfish material interests."[56] Humans take pleasure from giving because it alleviates feelings of guilt and makes them feel good for acting in line with a social norm or a specific, prosocial self-image.

Beyond empathy, the second element the TOMS model emphasizes is efficacy. A pair of shoes is easily defined and tangible. It helps with an everyday activity—walking. This clear benefit allows the company to close the final chapter of its story with a solution to a problem. We all want to be sure our charitable work or green purchasing has an impact, but as previously noted, it can be difficult to measure that impact because of varying metrics and uncertainty about outcomes.

In one-for-one, the measurement is simple: a pair of shoes. Of course, this model is not without its detractors—some believe giving anything is a bad idea when fighting poverty.[57] They say it creates dependency, saps local initiative, kills demand for local businesses, and makes developed-world buyers complacent about taking further action to address social needs.[58] In partial response, TOMS now works to develop local manufacturing in Haiti for its shoes.

Other companies have taken up the one-for-one model, but challenges remain in adapting it for products in which an equivalent altruistic gift does not make sense. It probably does not work for large purchases such as homes or cars. But how does it work with a bottle of water? Should you give a bottle for each one you purchase?

The mission of Ethos Water is to improve children's access to clean water. Its founder, Peter Thum, realized that children in many parts of the world lack access to clean water, so he launched the brand in August 2002, and he founded Ethos International to invest funds from the business in safe-water programs. The water costs almost two dollars per bottle, but five cents of each sale go to the Ethos Water Fund to "support water, sanitation and hygiene education programs in water-stressed countries." Starbucks acquired the company in 2005. So far, more than $12.3 million has been granted to help support water-related improvements in water-stressed countries—benefiting more than five hundred thousand people around the world.

The way Ethos operates is similar to TOMS, but Ethos is the focus of scrutiny. Because only a tiny portion of the retail price goes to charity, the company is accused of simply hiding its selfish business motives. Critics of Ethos say that it is a profit-making enterprise disguised as humanitarian relief and that it exploits the plight of Africans to sell more water in the United States without making a significant positive impact. Donating directly to a reputable charity dedicated to water projects, it is argued, might be a better way to address the issue.[59] The contribution of Ethos is not as tangible as a pair of shoes.

In addition, Ethos caught flack for using spring water from a drought county in California that was declared a natural disaster area by the US Department of Agriculture. While its customers were funding water programs in other countries, they were making a bad situation at home even worse.[60] Shortly after the criticism emerged, Starbucks announced it would be moving its California bottling operations to Pennsylvania out of concern for the drought crisis.[61] Such damage control may the last thing a company that relies on altruism wants to do.

Dramatize It

Storytelling has taken a central role in business communications, especially with the emergence of myriad new channels of communication. Increasingly, traditional advertising and marketing with top-down, one-way transmissions from companies to the masses is becoming ineffective. Consumers rely on conversational word of mouth and recommendations from trusted sources, including family and friends. Online communities provide a democratic mechanism for people to broadcast on a daily basis the details of who they are and what they care about.

The advent and rapid expansion of social media has made storytelling in real time, whether by words, audio, images, or video, much simpler and more direct. Whether it's 140 characters or a documentary film, good creative content can reach audiences across the world with little further investment—or even no investment at all. Social media also enables businesses to engage consumers in two-way conversation, elevating their sense of importance and adding a personal touch to an organization that might otherwise come across as monolithic.

With seemingly endless social-media outlets emerging and receding, keeping up might seem a Sisyphean task. Still, there are constants. Human nature and psychology are slow to evolve, and well-made content can be adapted to a variety of outlets. Most companies would love to have products and campaigns go viral and reach millions, but it's not as simple as putting out a consistent signal, even if it is well crafted. The key is to focus on the message itself and frame it in the right way.

Social-media expert James Shamshi offers tips for campaigns that seek to go viral. First, he recommends, look for existing conversations to piggyback.[62] Pay attention to trending topics and think about how your message might relate. Just as Dawn capitalized on the response to oil spills, products with environmental benefits can use social media to latch on to issues that are on people's minds at any given moment. His second recommendation is related—consider what you and your peers are talking about. That goes for individuals, businesses, and organizations alike. And of course, timing matters. Hiking goods may sell better in the spring, and Christmas decorations command poor prices in January. It also might mean waiting out times when public attention is dominated by other concerns, such as important elections or other major news events. Of course, that doesn't mean ignoring the press and other communicators. They can serve as major amplifiers if you strike a chord that is harmonious with their current interests and work. Finally, Shamshi recommends being positive, an idea we've talked about earlier in this book. Particularly with environmental issues, people—

particularly those who are not already green activists—will be more likely to share stories that offer a window of hope out of the dominant narratives of gloom, doom, and existential crises such as climate change.

With information flowing ever more easily from employees to customers, shareholders, and nonprofit organizations, there is also a higher demand for authenticity. Organizations must be true to their stories and keep the brand's promises every day, from their products to their organizational operations and even their own lifestyles—particularly the CEO. Disconnects are more easily spotted and greenwashing is more easily exposed.

The abundance and fragmentation of communication channels strains organizations that want to get their message across. Broadcasting a brand's story in today's networked world is complicated. Numerous partners are needed to create appropriate content for each medium. Breaking through noise and chatter with a coherent story has become harder.

Some now say organizations should start "thinking less about brand narrative and start thinking more about brand drama."[63] In other words, communication should be not only about what the brand says but also about what it does.

Founders and CEOs frequently find themselves at the center of these corporate dramas, and some have become real activists. Every firm seems to have its own myth describing the passion that led the founder to start the enterprise.[64] Beyond this initial role, over the past few years, chief executives—including prominent figures such as Lloyd Blankfein of Goldman Sachs and Howard Schultz of Starbucks—have taken public stances on controversial issues like race relations and gender equality that are unrelated to their core businesses.[65] Organizations and CEOs do not just tell a story: they are the story.[66] But as research shows, when CEOs speak out, they are more likely to be heard when they clearly articulate why the issue is related to the company's mission and value.[67]

Accentuate the Positive

In the previous chapters, we emphasized the need for conveying information about the functional attributes of green products and that they deliver private benefits to consumers, such as improved quality or health benefits. But this approach is limited when reduction of a product's environmental impact does not deliver individual benefits to a buyer. In such cases, the perceived benefit may be insufficient to motivate a green purchase. An alternate strategy is communicating emotional benefits.

We started by describing how the narrative on climate change tends to focus on *negative* emotions such as fear to promote behavioral change.[68] This links to the heuristics and biases literature on "loss aversion," which suggests that individuals will make larger efforts to avoid losing than they would to achieve similar gains.[69] Negative emotions might be less effective than positive emotions, however, when the probability of loss is perceived as low. In such cases, the anticipation of positive emotions can have a more profound effect on behavior.[70]

One particularly strong positive emotion is empathy—a sense of connectedness in which we feel someone's predicament and are moved to help. This emotion can be powerful, especially when there is a clear and tangible way to solve the problem. It can even create joy.

We have described three main avenues to elicit emotion related to sustainability. First, for products that include an experience, the connection with nature or communities in need can elicit powerful emotions that link consumers to the issue and favor behavioral change. Second, following the adage "a picture is worth a thousand words," we described how images can connect consumers to employees and communities associated with the products. Third, stories allow firms to create stronger emotional bonds by invoking drama.

There are multiple emotions associated with green behavior. In this chapter, we focused on empathy and the sense of connectedness, but green behavior is associated with many other positive emotions—for example, nostalgia. A recent study noted that green behavior is also associated with a positive self-identity, personal pride, sense of leadership, satisfaction, and sense of achievement.[71]

Interventions to increase green purchasing behavior should focus on these positives rather than trying to elicit negative emotions for *not* acting in a sustainable manner.[72]

In conclusion, emotion joins quality, health, money, and status as a cobenefit of sustainable products and services. As described, each of these cobenefits will likely be more suited for some products than for others. But not all products evoke the same emotional states when consumed.[73] Appeals that more closely match the specific needs satisfied by a product category will be more persuasive for consumers than appeals that address less relevant needs.[74] Each form of consumption value increases in salience depending on the main private benefits a product category offers.

The green bundle strategy is also dependent on integrity, honesty, and good faith. The strategy will fail when information presented about the environmental benefits of products is confusing or misleading. Lack of trust in environmental claims is one of the main excuses that conventional environmentalists use to explain lack of interest in green products. A related excuse is confusion regarding environmental claims and the gap between expectations and the reality of environmental impact.[75] Businesses need to better understand how to convey environmental information clearly and effectively to unleash the benefits of the green bundle. Before moving to the characteristics of effective information campaigns, let's look at examples of nefarious behaviors and the role politics and regulation have played in cover ups and scandals that have marred the word *green*.

Chapter 8

THE PITFALLS OF GREENWASHING

VOLKSWAGEN BUILT SOME of the most iconic back-to-earth vehicles in the 1960s—particularly the Beetle and the Microbus. In 2015, the magic bus lost its charm when the US EPA issued a notice of violation. The company had installed software in its "clean diesel" fleet that sensed when a vehicle was being tested and automatically reduced the amount of emissions during the test. The California Air Resources Board investigated and found in road tests that the vehicles emitted almost forty times the permitted levels of nitrogen oxides.[1]

The fallout from the intentional deception was catastrophic. In June 2016, the company agreed to pay $14.7 billion to settle claims in the United States, including $10 billion to buy back affected vehicles.[2] It was far and away the largest civil settlement ever made by an automobile company. And Volkswagen's legal woes continued—forty-two state attorneys, the Federal Trade Commission, and the Department of Justice also launched investigations. Overseas, the German state of Bavaria, Norway's sovereign-wealth fund, and a slew of individual investors filed suit.[3] The company recalled 8.5 million vehicles in Europe and estimated that 11 million vehicles would be affected worldwide.[4]

This egregious case serves as a cautionary tale, but it is an outlier. Intentional lying is the least common form of greenwashing. Nevertheless, the case of Volkswagen and of others—both high and low profile—foment distrust and add to the confusion in the green marketplace. Greenwashing also endangers the effectiveness of green bundle strategies.

So far, we have focused on the motivation pillar of the bundle—the link between environmental performance and product attributes. But how people perceive the message will depend on who sends the message and how credible it is.

One of the reasons people offer to explain their reluctance to purchase green products is general suspicion of corporate environmental claims.[5] When companies run advertisements saying how great their green credentials are, the first thought in many people's minds is that "they're hiding something." This trend affects businesses in other ways too. It affects investor confidence in environmentally friendly firms, eroding the capital market for socially responsible investing. It creates risks when consumers, nongovernmental organizations, and government entities question a firm's claims. And there's the threat of legal action. In 2012, Honda settled a class-action suit for false and misleading statements regarding the fuel efficiency of its hybrid Civic. The automaker agreed to pay $100 to $200 to every customer who had bought the car between 2003 and 2009 and to give them a $1,000 rebate on a new vehicle.[6]

You would think that businesses have every incentive to clearly communicate with consumers. Why, then, do firms continue to engage in greenwashing? First, improving and accurately measuring environmental performance is difficult. Second, there are strong incentives and market pressure to "go green"—or to appear green, even if your product really is not. Due to expanding green markets, instances of greenwashing have skyrocketed in recent years. This increase was illustrated in a series of TerraChoice Group studies. A staggering 98 percent of surveyed retail products in the United States, Canada, the United Kingdom, and Australia were linked to some form of greenwashing.[7] Third, there are many barriers to coordination within different areas of a firm. Information about environmental impacts does not always flow easily between the marketing department and other areas of the firm or the supply chain.

In addition, lax and uncertain regulation is a key driver that, in combination with other external, organizational, and individual drivers, creates a setting in which the practice becomes more likely. In this chapter, we will see how. To avoid greenwashing, one needs to recognize it and to understand its causes. But first, let's start by further defining greenwashing—in all its forms—and how to identify it.

Understanding Greenwashing

"In approximately April of 2017, Mr. Gregorio purchased Green Works® Naturally Derived Dishwashing Liquid from a Duane Reade store located in New York, New York. While shopping, Mr. Gregorio was specifically interested in purchasing natural cleaning products. Mr. Gregorio purchased the Green Works® Product based on the claim that it was 'naturally derived.' He understood this to mean that he was purchasing a natural product that did not contain any synthetic or non-natural ingredients. Mr. Gregorio believed that Defendant's 'naturally derived' claims were true and relied on them in that he would not have purchased the Green Works® Product at all, or would have been only willing to pay a substantially reduced price for the Green Works® Product, had he known that the natural representations were false."[8]

This is the basis for a class-action lawsuit against Green Works cleaning products. The suit claims the products are mislabeled to make consumers think they contain all-natural ingredients when they do not. Named plaintiffs Joseph Gregorio and Patrick Quiroz allege that The Clorox Company is taking advantage of market interest in all-natural products to make consumers purchase cleaners they wouldn't buy if they knew what was really in them. In other words, they say Clorox was greenwashing. Green Works is a line of cleaning products that is labeled as being "naturally derived." In fact, the plaintiffs claim, Green Works products contain ingredients that are "synthetic, non-natural and highly chemically processed." One ingredient that plaintiffs take issue with is boric acid, a compound used in products as an insecticide, antiseptic, or flame retardant. Another is calcium chloride, a chemical preservative used for de-icing roads, the plaintiffs noted.

When Clorox first introduced the Green Works line in 2008, it secured an endorsement from the Sierra Club and a nationwide introduction at Walmart and vowed the products would "move natural cleaning into the mainstream."[9] Sales that year topped $100 million, and several other major consumer-products companies came out with their own green cleaning supplies. Clorox had effectively bundled the environment with a powerful product. This product line did not compromise on quality, clearly targeting convenient environmentalists. Unfortunately, the company's information strategy appears to have misled consumers.

Although the practice was recognized as early as the mid-to-late 1960s, the term *greenwashing* was coined by biologist Jay Westervelt in a 1986 essay about the hotel industry's practice of placing notes in each room promoting reuse of towels—supposedly to save the environment. Most of the time, little or no effort was made to reduce energy waste. Green markets and greenwashing have continued expanding since, and analysts have focused on explaining the phenomenon more precisely with various definitions and concepts. Legal scholars, for instance, adopted a definition that is neutral with regard to intent, saying that those who engage in greenwashing are "making false or misleading claims regarding environmentally friendly products, services or practices."[10] As is often the case with the practice of law, it can be difficult to determine what intentions were or who was involved.

Let's build on this neutral definition to define greenwashing, describing it as the act of misleading consumers regarding the environmental practices of a company (firm-level greenwashing) or the environmental benefits of a product or service (product-level greenwashing).[11]

An example of firm-level greenwashing is General Electric's "Ecomagination" campaign, which advertised the company's work in the environmental arena while it lobbied against new EPA clean-air requirements. An example of product-level greenwashing is LG Electronics and its miscertified Energy Star refrigerators. Energy Star is a government-backed, third-party eco-label, indicating that a product meets a certain set of energy-efficiency guidelines. The label certified many of LG Electronics' refrigerator models. It was later discovered, however, that ten of the certified LG refrigerator models listed erroneous energy-usage measurements and did not actually meet the efficiency standards required.[12]

Since both greenwashing firms and greenwashed products begin with firm behavior, it is important to consider corporate conduct. A greenwashing firm engages in two behaviors at the same time: poor environmental performance and positive communication about its environmental performance. In other words, it does not walk the talk.

Environmental performance falls along a spectrum, but for simplification, let's bucket firms into one of two environmental-performance categories: poor environmental performers ("brown" firms) and good environmental performers ("green" firms). It would be counterproductive to communicate negatively about poor environmental performance, so brown firms typically remain silent or try to represent their bad performance in a positive light.

When it comes to communication, firms fall along a spectrum ranging from no communication to increasing degrees of positive communication. But again, for simplification, let's organize firms into two categories regarding communication about their environmental performance. Firms that positively communicate about performance, through marketing and public-relations campaigns, for example, can be described as "vocal" firms. Those that do not communicate about their environmental performance can be described as "silent" firms. Thus, firms with good environmental performance that positively communicate about it can be described as "vocal green firms," while those that do not communicate about their environmental performance can be described as "silent green firms." Among brown firms, we describe those not communicating about their environmental performance as "silent brown firms." Brown firms that positively communicate about their environmental performance are simply "greenwashing firms."

From figure 8.1, we see that there are two paths by which a company can become a greenwashing firm (and vice versa). A vocal firm can decline in environmental performance, moving it from quadrant II to quadrant I. A brown firm can

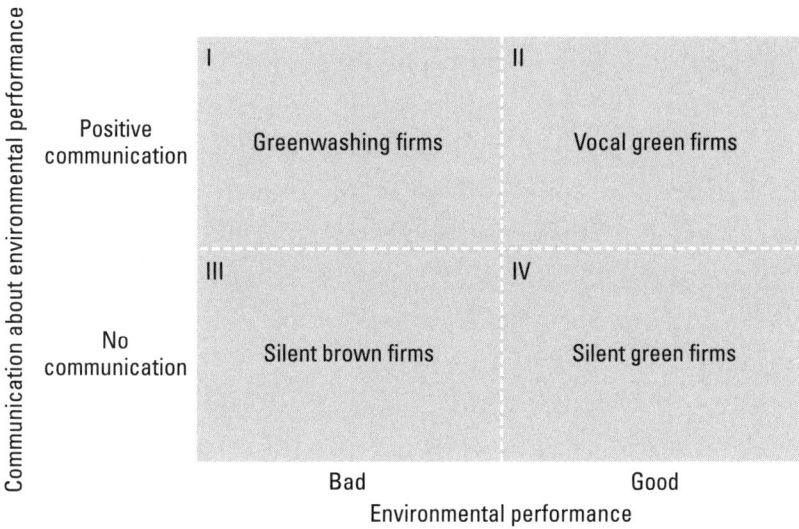

FIGURE 8.1. A Typology of Firms Based on Environmental Performance and Communication. Source: Magali A. Delmas and Vanessa Cuerel Burbano, "The Drivers of Greenwashing," *California Management Review* 54, no. 1 (2011): 64–87.

change communication about its performance, moving it from quadrant III to quadrant I.

The Many Faces of Greenwashing

For companies and other parties to understand and prevent the drift to quadrant I, they must first recognize the symptoms of greenwashing, which usually arise at the product level. Useful efforts have been made to categorize and quantify product-level greenwashing. For example, ten signs of greenwash range from "fluffy language," words or terms with no clear meaning, such as *eco-friendly*, to "outright lying," totally fabricated claims or data.[13]

The nonprofit organization Greenpeace offers a greenwashing detection kit with three main flags: (1) makes claims that are vague or seemingly unprovable, (2) overstates or exaggerates how green the product/company/service actually is, and (3) leaves out or masks important information, making the green claim sound better than it is. Greenpeace emphasizes the communication medium used to mislead consumers—whether words, visuals, or graphics. Without words, advertisers can utilize the color green or images of nature to make customers think a product or company is environmentally friendly than it is.

A more detailed categorization is provided by TerraChoice, which organizes product-level greenwashing into "seven sins." Let's review them here, considering the percentage of US firms that have committed at least one of these grievances.[14]

Sin of Hidden Tradeoff: 73 Percent Guilty

The most common sin is when a product is claimed to be green based on an unreasonably narrow set of attributes, without due attention to other important environmental issues. These claims emphasize one trait but fail to address the full impact of the product. Not usually false, the claims paint a greener picture of the product than thorough analysis supports. Examples include energy-efficient office technology that doesn't give attention to the materials it uses, and paper and lumber products that promote recycled content or sustainable-harvesting practices without addressing manufacturing impacts such as air emissions, water emissions, and global warming. Fiji water's "untouched by man" ad campaign conveys the message that the company does not touch the environment to get its water. Other aspects of the environment are "touched" during transportation of the water, however. And it is sold in single-use plastic bottles, which are oil intensive to produce and contribute four billion pounds of waste to landfills and roadside litter.[15]

Sin of No Proof: 59 Percent Guilty

In this case, a product's claim cannot be substantiated by easily accessible information or a third party. Many paper products claim to contain a certain percentage of postconsumer recycled content. This is unsubstantiated because it's not possible for consumers to check this information easily.

Sin of Vagueness: 56 Percent Guilty

Some claims are so poorly defined or broad that their real meaning is likely to be misunderstood by the intended consumer. Calling products "all-natural" is perhaps the best example of this. Arsenic, uranium, mercury, and formaldehyde are all naturally occurring but highly poisonous.

Vagueness of environmental claims triggered the class-action lawsuit against Clorox Green Works. The packaging for the products includes the words "naturally derived." According to the class-action document, "Consumers understand 'natural' and 'naturally derived' to mean 'existing in nature and not made or caused by people; coming from nature' or 'not having any extra substances or chemicals added; not containing anything artificial.' Under this definition, and the expectations of reasonable consumers, the Products cannot be considered 'natural' or 'naturally derived' because they contain ingredients that are synthetic, non-natural and highly chemically processed."[16]

Sin of Worshipping False Labels: 24 Percent Guilty

This type of claim gives a false impression of third-party certification. Windex used a Greenlist logo that looked like it was from a third party. In actuality, it was just Johnson & Johnson's own label. S. C. Johnson—whose brands include Windex, Glade, Raid, Shout, and Ziploc—created Greenlist in 2001. It included a process to bring green chemistry to its products by rating raw materials based on environmental and health impacts. It began putting the logo on products that met certain criteria in 2008. Two class-action lawsuits in California and Wisconsin argued that the use of the logo did not clearly show that it was an internal process rather than a third-party seal and that it implied products were made with environmentally friendly ingredients.[17] As Fisk Johnson, S. C. Johnson's chairman and CEO, acknowledged, "In retrospect, we could have done a better job at being more transparent and clearer with our label and what it meant."[18]

Sin of Irrelevance: 8 Percent Guilty

Environmental claims can also be irrelevant, such as the claim that a product is "phosphate-free" when it wouldn't normally include phosphate in the first place. It's the equivalent of claiming that flour is fat-free, which is always true. It is still common to see the claim "CFC-free refrigerator." CFCs are already banned by law, making the claim irrelevant.

Sin of Lesser of Two Evils: 4 Percent Guilty

This is a claim that is true for the product type but distracts consumer from the real impact. For example, organic cigarettes might avoid using chemicals in the production of tobacco, but that only distracts consumers from the fact that smoking is detrimental to their health. Cigarette butts are also the most littered item in the United States and the world.[19]

Sin of Fibbing: <1 Percent Guilty

Occasionally, a company tells outright lies about products. This brings us back to Volkswagen, although its actions can hardly be seen as fibs. Volkswagen undertook a communication campaign portraying itself as an environmental steward, with its fleet on the vanguard of a clean-energy revolution. It promoted diesel as a low-emissions alternative to gasoline and spent $77 million in 2015 to advertise its diesel cars on the American market, often proclaiming their greenness. Another famous example of this is when Lululemon Athletica, the athletic-apparel maker, claimed that its product line Vitasea contained seaweed when it didn't.[20] Lululemon further claimed that Vitasea clothes released amino acids, minerals, and vitamins into the skin. But an independent lab's analysis found no meaningful difference in mineral content between Vitasea clothing and standard cotton T-shirts. Under pressure from regulators in Canada, where Lululemon is based, the company stopped marketing the line.

As the list shows, only less than 1 percent of products are involved an intentionally false environmental claim. (This might reflect the difficulty in identifying such claims, though.) And yet the percentage of firms engaged in the first three forms of greenwashing is remarkably sizable. To understand how the practice has become so widespread, we must more deeply comprehend what drives the phenomenon.

Why Greenwash? Drivers Amid Uncertain Regulation

There are many factors that can drive a business to engage in deliberate or unintentional greenwashing. Managers must understand these factors to identify the sources of bad behavior and avoid the practice.

Greenwashing drivers are present at three levels: individual, organizational, and external (see figure 8.2).

People Are People

To understand this complex set of drivers, it helps to start with a little basic human psychology. Companies are not ma-

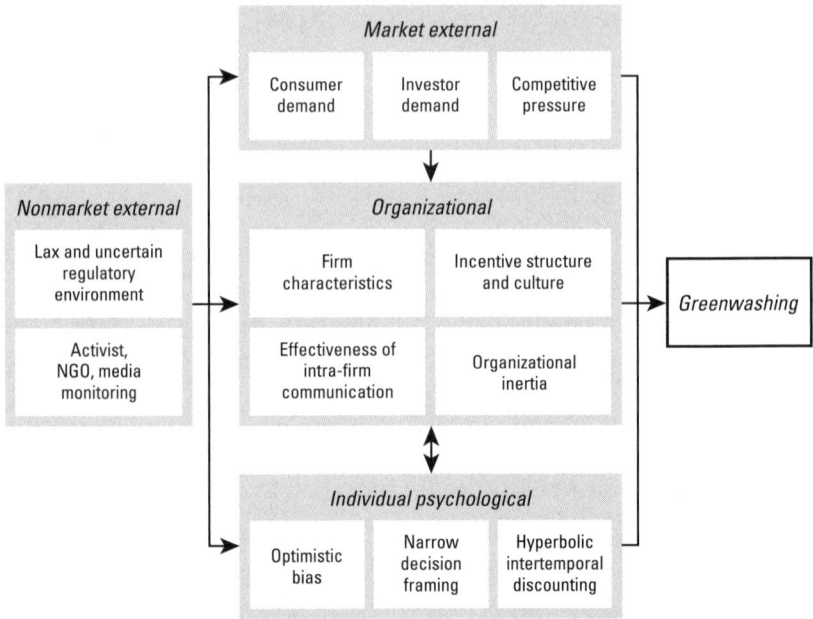

FIGURE 8.2. Drivers of Greenwashing. Source: Magali A. Delmas and Vanessa Cuerel Burbano, "The Drivers of Greenwashing," *California Management Review* 54, no. 1 (2011): 64–87.

chines operated by mindless automatons—they're made up of human beings with normal (and sometimes abnormal) tendencies. Besides, individuality and creativity can be valuable assets. Absolute control over how everyone in a firm operates is neither possible nor desirable, yet leaders and individuals play influential roles in firm behavior as they make decisions and try to keep in mind the numerous factors that affect those decisions.

Multitasking has been widely panned as something our brains simply cannot do effectively,[21] so it comes as no surprise that people have a hard time keeping every aspect of the big picture in mind. We tend to frame things narrowly, making decisions in isolation of relevant factors and considerations.[22] This can lead decision makers to communicate about a product or firm's greenness without considering what's needed to implement that greenness, thus setting themselves up to greenwash.

We also tend to focus on short-term gains over longer-term benefits. For example, when choosing between $100 today and $120 in a week, most prefer the former. In psychological studies on temptation, self-control, and procrastination, future outcomes are frequently undervalued.[23] Likewise, consumers fail to achieve "target savings" because of their desire for instant gratification. With greenwashing, managers communicate about sustainability and social responsibility with the intention of bearing the costs in the future. Alas, when that future arrives, the decision maker once again acts impatiently and fails to live up to the commitment.

Optimistic bias poses yet another problem. People overestimate the likelihood of positive events and underestimate the likelihood of negative ones. Instead of looking at past results, our forecasts become tethered to plans for success.[24] In a survey of new entrepreneurs, 80 percent perceived their chances of success as 70 percent or better, and 33 percent put their chances of success at 100 percent. These responses were unrelated to objective predictors of success such as college education, prior supervisory experience, and initial capital.[25] Of course, chances of success are much slimmer; nine out of every ten start-ups fail.[26]

As long as humans are involved in business, these factors will remain in play. But firms can take actions to limit their impact and fallout. These particular phenomena become more pronounced under conditions of uncertainty and limited information,[27] so better-informed workforces will be less prone to their effects. Meanwhile, performance evaluation and properly aligned incentive structures can also mitigate these tendencies.[28]

Business Is Business

Private enterprise comes in many shapes and sizes. Exxon-Mobil experiences greenwashing risks much differently than a mom-and-pop store in Poughkeepsie. Size, industry, profitability, and resources influence the strategies that are available, the costs and benefits associated with particular actions, and the degree to which a firm experiences external pressures. The potential benefits of greenwashing—such as increased access to green consumers and investors—also vary with these characteristics. Consumer-products firms face greater pressure to appear environmentally friendly than do service firms. Large, publicly traded firms tend to be the focus of analysis by the Socially Responsible Investing (SRI) community; as such, they face greater levels of investor pressure than do smaller, private firms.

The cost of getting caught varies too. Again, consumer products have it rough. They are the most subject to regulation under the Federal Trade Commission Act and the most likely to be targeted by campaigns seeking to generate public outrage—although social media and viral content has expanded scrutiny to a broader array of firms. Because of their ability to whip up public attention and outcry, large firms with well-known brands are popular targets for activists and the media.[29] The same goes for industries renowned for poor environmental performance, such as oil and chemical manufacturers. These companies commonly top lists such as Greenpeace's "Top Greenwashers." Mitigating this exposure is the fact that profitable firms with higher margins can better withstand bottom-line shocks from reputational damage. They also weather fines and litigation costs more easily.

In addition to these basic characteristics, incentive structures can determine firm behavior.[30] Incentives that reward managers for arbitrary financial goals often result in unethical behavior.[31] Likewise, rewarding on-time performance and punishing late performance each directly contributes to unethical behavior. This was the case in 1990 with Eastern Airlines, which was indicted for falsifying maintenance records.[32] Faulty cockpit gauges were knowingly installed, and landing gear, radar, fuel systems, and automatic pilots were improperly maintained, according to the sixty-count indictment.[33] Fortunately, no accidents resulted, but pilots reported experiencing problems in flight. "Thousands of innocent passengers may have been put at risk every day by the actions of these defendants," then attorney general Dick Thornburgh said in a statement.

Incentives to reach arbitrary marketing quotas—particularly quotas for communications that portray the firm in an environmentally friendly or socially responsible light—increase the likelihood that a firm will greenwash. Indeed, such incentives could drive managers to take shortcuts in validating the truth of communications or to "look the other way" when they have reason to question the validity of their messaging.

A firm's ethical climate—shared perceptions and beliefs that certain reasoning or behaviors are expected norms for decision making—also plays a role.[34] The ethical climate of an organization can be categorized as one of three types, based on moral judgment: In an egoistic climate, company norms support the satisfaction of self-interest; in a benevolent climate, company norms support maximization of overall well-being; and in a principled climate, company norms support following abstract principles, independent of situational outcomes such as legal mandates or codes of ethics.[35] Unethical behavior has been shown to occur more frequently at organizations in which egoistic climates dominate.[36] Ethical climates tend to be intractable and difficult to change, but implementing codes and other explicit standards of conduct can reduce unethical behavior, even within dominantly egoistic climates. To the extent that these standards include explicit directives about truthful communication and representation of firm behavior, they diminish the chances that a firm will greenwash.

Organizational inertia is another factor that influences and explains firm behavior.[37] This persistence of existing form and function is more likely to be prevalent in large, old firms than in small, new ones.[38] It hampers strategic change and can lead to a naturally occurring lag between a declaration of green intent and its implementation or between a CEO's commitment to greening the company and the company's alteration of structure and processes to make it happen.[39] This disconnect may be particularly prevalent in firms transitioning between CEOs or during mergers and acquisitions. BP's chief executive, Bob Dudley, may have engaged in greenwashing due to organizational inertia. He was criticized by the press for doing "little but talk about improving safety since he took the reins" in the wake of the Macondo well explosion.[40] Despite his declared intent to change processes and procedures to improve BP's safety, changes appear to have taken longer than anticipated to implement.

Another important characteristic is intrafirm communication. When internal communications are sticky or difficult, they hinder innovation.[41] This can lead to inadvertent greenwashing. Firms with ineffective communication between their marketing and product-development departments are more likely to greenwash. Marketers might overstate benefits by not understanding a product's reality from supply chain to packaging. Lack of direct relationships is one cause of poor knowledge sharing within a company, whereas close and frequent interactions between R&D and other functions leads to project effectiveness.[42]

The Short Arm of the Law

So what's to stop a company from greenwashing? When it comes to the law of the land, the answer is not much. The current regulatory environment may be the single factor that most encourages (or fails to discourage) greenwashing. In the United States, regulation is extremely limited, and enforcement is spotty and uncertain. Variation across countries and complexities regarding appropriate jurisdiction of cross-country practices compounds the problem, contributing to an unclear, even confusing, environment for multinational corporations. This lax and uncertain regulatory context isn't lost on consumers and investors. Demand for green products, services, and firms is influenced by information about firm greenwashing and environmental practices.

In the United States, corporate disclosure of environmental practices is not mandated, aside from a few exceptions such as toxic releases. Mandatory disclosure and third-party auditing would make it more difficult for brown firms to get away with greenwashing, even if the practices themselves were not regulated, since consumers, investors, and NGOs would be able to compare a firm's communications with reliable information about their environmental practices.

Apart from toxic releases, the only portion of a firm's greenwashing activities that is subject to federal regulation is advertising that falls under Section 5 of the Federal Trade Commission (FTC) Act. The FTC can apply Section 5 of the Act—which prohibits unfair or deceptive acts or practices—to environmental-marketing claims. If the FTC finds an advertiser violated Section 5, it can issue a cease-and-desist order. If the violator does not stop the practice, the agency may issue a fine of up to ten thousand dollars or up to one year in prison.[43] The Act also establishes criminal liability if the violation is committed with the intent to defraud or mislead. The FTC has investigated companies for environmental claims under Section 5 of the Act, but charges have been few and far between. According to the FTC website, there were just forty-one environmental cases from 2012 to 2016.[44]

From the perspective of firms, it is uncertain whether environmental claims are likely to result in charges. This is despite the FTC's issuance of Green Guides, which is designed to make it easier to understand what environmental claims the FTC may or may not find deceptive.[45] Some cases have been relatively straightforward, such as one against Perfect-Data Corporation in 1993, which challenged "ozone friendly" and "contains no ozone depleting CFCs" claims for an aerosol cleaning product that actually did contain such chemicals. Other cases are less obvious. The FTC charged Kmart in 2009 for making false and unsubstantiated claims that its American Fare brand disposable plates were biodegradable. Although the plates may have been biodegradable in compost, the FTC alleged that the defendants' products are typically disposed of in landfills, incinerators, or recycling facilities, where it is impossible for waste to biodegrade within a reasonably short period of time. But then the FTC conceded that, by these standards, even a piece of produce might not be biodegradable within a reasonably short period of time.[46]

Herein lies the challenge with Section 5. Definitions of terms such as *biodegradable* and *all-natural* remain vague, and it is unclear whether the FTC would construe their use as deceptive. Several states attempted to create their own regulations, but none have been more stringent. Given the history of these charges, firms likely perceive minimal risk.

Multinational firms operating in countries outside the United States are also subject to the regulations of host countries in which they operate. In many countries, including most developing countries, there is no regulation of environmental claims. Standards vary elsewhere. International equivalents of the FTC include the Advertising Standards Authority (ASA) in the United Kingdom, the Australian Competition and Consumer Commission (ACCC), and the Canadian Standards Association (CSA). The CSA and the Canadian Competition Bureau released "Environmental Claims: A Guide for Industry and Advertisers" in 2008. It requires companies to provide support for their environmental claims and discourages the use of vague claims such as "green." Misleading advertising by a corporation in Canada is punishable by fines, product seizure, and imprisonment. In the United Kingdom, the Department for Environment, Food, and Rural Affairs (DEFRA) issued guidelines similar to those of the FTC and CSA, but they also take into account the international standard for environment claims, ISO 14021. ISO 14201 was developed by the International Organization for Standardization. It specifies requirements for sclf-dcclarcd cnvironmental claims, listing terms commonly used, providing qualifiers for their use, and describing methodology for general evaluation and verification. Adherence to these standards is voluntary, although a handful of countries, such as Australia, France, and Norway, have backed them with enforceable fines and penalties. This is an example of moving in the right direction—more specificity, multinational backing, and repercussions in participating nations.

The current regulatory environment has profound effects on the individual and organizational drivers of greenwashing. The psychological drivers of greenwashing—including narrow framing, a focus on short-term gains, and optimistic bias—become more pronounced under conditions of uncertainty, or where there is limited or imperfect information. Firms face few incentives to develop structures and processes that would tip organizational tendencies toward being truly green. This is not to say that those organizational- and individual-level behaviors are not problematic on their own. But this depiction points again toward the importance of setting the right tone at the top (in this case, at a level that is higher than the corporations themselves).

Employees, managers, and firm leaders have limited tools to evaluate regulations. As managers in a brown firm decide whether to communicate positively about environmental performance, we can infer that they will be likely to exhibit these psychological tendencies. The regulatory context is therefore an indirect driver of firm greenwashing in that it exacerbates the individual-level drivers of greenwashing.

Effectiveness of intrafirm communication, incentive structure, and ethical climate are also affected by regulatory context. In a lax regulatory context, there is little incentive for firms to ensure that organizational characteristics such as incentive structures and ethical climate are aligned to minimize greenwashing, and there is little incentive to put processes in place to improve the effectiveness of intrafirm communication to decrease the likelihood that firms will greenwash.

The Long Arm of Public Opinion

Given the limited formal regulatory systems, activist groups and NGOs—along with and through the media—play a major role as informal monitors of firm greenwashing. By campaigning against and spreading information about negative incidents, these organizations work toward holding brown firms accountable for communicating positively about their poor environmental performance.

Nonprofit organizations employ diverse strategies to communicate their information. Greenpeace's stopgreenwash.org features articles about greenwashing firms. SourceWatch publishes a list of case studies, providing information about specific incidents. Meanwhile, sites such as GoodGuide and Environmental Working Group's Skin Deep Cosmetics Database offer product-level information to inform purchasing decisions. The Greenwashing Index, from the University of Oregon and EnviroMedia Social Marketing, created a public forum for greenwashing examples to be uploaded and rated.

Activist and NGO-led campaigns have broad reach, spreading information to larger audiences than websites relying on individuals to seek information themselves. The Coastal Alliance for Aquaculture Reform of Vancouver, British Columbia, successfully campaigned to reduce ocean pollution from salmon farms that used floating nets. They targeted a retailer that sold farmed salmon—Safeway—because of the company's self-proclamations that it is a good environmentalist and corporate citizen.[47] The group placed a large advertisement in the *New York Times* featuring dead seals and salmon feces under the heading "Ingredients for Extinction," playing on Safeway's "Ingredients for Life" campaign. The case demonstrates that active communication about green or socially responsible practices can lead to more intense activist, NGO, and media scrutiny. Access to consumers and the public has increased significantly through social media, YouTube, and other internet platforms. These tools decrease the costs and time required to share information.

Threat of exposure by activists, NGOs, and the media deters brown firms from communicating positively about their performance. As consumers and investors become more interested in environmental issues, activist groups become more powerful and exert greater influence and pressure. The media is also more likely to report greenwashing as such stories become likely to capture reader interest. But given the limited formal regulation and enforcement of greenwashing, these groups can bring about only reputational damage. Threat of exposure would be much more of a deterrent if there were legal ramifications too.

Although activists and the media may keep brown firms quiet, in the shadows, consumer and investor demand motivate them to greenwash. Socially Responsible Investing (SRI), for instance, uses environmental and social criteria to select or avoid investing in certain companies. SRI is based on the assumption that good environmental performance can be associated with good financial performance. All else being equal, the greater the perceived consumer and investor pressure to be environmentally friendly, the more likely a brown firm is to greenwash to gain access to capital, not to mention to the market share to attract future investments.[48]

The competitive landscape is another influential factor. Organizations model themselves after similar organizations that they perceive to be legitimate or successful. Research shows this also applies to the adoption of green practices.[49] Firms communicate about supposed green practices out of a fear of falling behind rivals. For instance, global financial-services company UBS adopted a more progressive climate-change policy after an internal report demonstrated that it lagged behind competitors in publicly committing to fight global warming.[50] Thus, as positive communication about green practices becomes more common within an industry or group of competitors, firms become more likely to greenwash.

Limited regulation and uncertain enforcement interacts with these external-level market drivers—specifically, consumer and investor demand. Consumers cannot be confident that a brown firm would be caught and punished if it were to falsely communicate about its environmental practices. As these practices continue to go unchecked, consumers become increasingly cynical, eroding the market for green products and services. Similarly, this creates a lack of verifiable information that challenges investors and funds following SRI and other environmental-assessment strategies.[51] Rampant, unchecked greenwashing not only erodes the market for green practices and services but also erodes the capital market for socially responsible investing.

In conclusion, the prevalence of greenwashing has skyrocketed in recent years; more and more firms have been combining poor environmental performance with positive communication about environmental performance. Our proposed simple framework that organizes drivers into external-level drivers (the regulatory and monitoring context, as well as market drivers), organizational-level drivers, and individual-level drivers shows why many brown firms choose to positively communicate about their environmental performance and greenwash in the process. Limited and imperfect information about firm environmental performance along with uncertainty about regulatory punishment for greenwashing contribute to greenwashing directly and indirectly.

Meanwhile, human cognitive tendencies such as narrow decision framing, hyperbolic intertemporal discounting, and optimistic bias are heightened when individuals make decisions based on increasingly limited or imperfect information and as uncertainty increases. Regulators and nongovernmental organizations can act to improve the availability of information and to decrease uncertainty about punishment to moderate this effect. At the same time, managers can adjust incentives and take steps to counter these cognitive tendencies as well as organizational-level drivers of greenwashing.

Greenwashing is common and complex. It is a major factor in the marketplace for environmental products and services, and it goes much deeper than the overt lies that tripped up Volkswagen. Avoiding the practice requires close attention to human realities and organizational structures. And although governments may not be watching closely, environmentally conscious consumers certainly are. Connecting with these consumers—the majority of whom are driven by factors other than protecting the environment—takes more than words. Avoiding false perceptions is a critical first step to effectively selling green products and services. The problem of greenwashing may be complicated, and a better understanding of what greenwashing is and of its driver is the first step in avoiding it. But there are also concrete steps businesses can take to go beyond avoiding mistakes and to set the stage for success with those often-fickle consumers.

Chapter 9

SENDING A CLEAR SIGNAL

CLOTHING MANUFACTURER PATAGONIA is widely considered a model of environmental responsibility in business. Founded by Yvon Chouinard, an avid surfer, alpine climber, and fly fisherman, the company has staked out the front lines of sustainable business practices since the late 1980s. It now bills itself as "The Activist Company."[1] Patagonia was the first major retailer to use all organic cotton in its clothing. It makes fleece from recycled soda bottles and pledges 1 percent of its annual sales to grassroots environmental organizations.[2]

The outdoorsy Chouinard naturally gravitated toward environmentalism while the company was still relatively small. Concerned about the cotton industry's reliance on toxic pesticides, Patagonia decided to go organic and worked directly with farmers to grow enough supply to meet its needs. The process took eighteen months, but since 1996, the company's garments have been created using only organic cotton.[3]

The talk matches the walk. Patagonia is a well-known leader in communicating about its green practices, adopting a transparency model. It developed an online, interactive map to give the public an inside look at the sustainability and workplace practices of its suppliers. Patagonia admits its missteps and limitations.[4] People for the Ethical Treatment of Animals (PETA) called the company out in 2015 for getting wool from an Argentinian farm that mistreated lambs. Within days, Patagonia CEO Rose Marcario apologized publicly and pledged to rebuild the company's wool program so that only humanely treated animals would be used and grasslands would be maintained. "We will continue to sell products made from the wool we've already purchased," Marcario said in a statement. "But Patagonia will not buy wool again until we can assure our customers of a verifiable process that ensures the humane treatment of animals."[5]

Even more radically, Patagonia has taken out ads encouraging consumers to buy less, reuse, and repair the clothing they already have.[6] Despite its commitment to sustainability, Marcario admitted that the company "still takes more from the earth than it returns."[7]

Most firms can't afford to be so aggressive with sustainability efforts, of course. Publicly traded businesses have investors to think of. Not every consumer base fits with environmentalism as well as outdoor-clothing buyers, and not every company's founder is in the midst of a decades-long love affair with wilderness. Still, there are lessons to be learned from the vanguard, lessons that reach all the way to the bottom line. By staking out early ground in the growing market for green products, Patagonia has profited immensely. Between 2008 and 2013 alone, the company's profits tripled.[8]

We have already seen the numerous ways businesses slip up and greenwash—damaging brands, eroding consumer confidence, and sometimes, incurring monster legal settlements.[9] So how can firms become more Patagonia-like? "First, do no harm" should be the mantra. There are concrete steps to take that will avoid greenwashing and position a business to take advantage of the expanding green marketplace.

To be sure, counteracting the drivers of greenwashing can involve substantial changes: altering firm structures, establishing new processes, and instituting employee incentives and training. The end goal is making it easier to communicate about environmental issues within the firm and the supply chain. Fortunately, businesses do not have to go it alone: credible reporting standards and eco-labels are the external keys to making these changes and providing easily understood environmental messages.

Beyond credibility, sending effective messages requires that the messages are received and understood by consumers. The credibility, clarity, and visibility of the messages are important. To ensure that green messages pierce the fog of communications and get heard and understood, here are a few concrete strategies to employ.

Standardize the Dialogue

It all starts at the top. The role of the CEO is supremely important in creating a culture of open communication and collaboration. The effects of a CEO's words cascade throughout an organization and have an enormous impact on transformation toward environmental responsibility.[10] Walmart is certainly no Patagonia in structure, practice, or reputation. But when former CEO Lee Scott admitted, "We're not green," to an audience of executives and marketers in Boulder, Colorado, it set the stage for refreshing modesty in the retailer's communication about its environmental performance and in the recognition that it needed to improve.[11] The company has since made improvements to its environmental footprint but has not overly bragged about it.

Such modesty is increasingly effective. Millennials have overtaken baby boomers as the largest generation in the United States. And while they generally distrust advertisements, they respond to authenticity.[12] As another example, Frito-Lay's SunChips campaign about its solar-powered chip plant has been lauded as "proud, but not overly boastful about saving the world."

> Greater transparency is an unstoppable force. It is the product of growing demands from everybody with an interest in any corporation—its stakeholder web—and of rapid technological change, above all the spread of the Internet, that makes it far easier for firms to supply information, and harder for them to keep secrets [. . .] With greater transparency will come greater accountability and better corporate behavior.[13]

The messages CEOs set forth must also move down the chain of command. Employees working on sustainability should be given C-suite access and visibility, which would show executive staff how seriously the company takes such issues and would shape environmental communications at the highest level.[14] Sustainability officers and departments should be given increased oversight of other divisions and geographic offices. This reduces the chance of miscommunications with marketing, product-development, and supply-chain management divisions. Human resources should get in on the act too. They have the capacity to implement training and ethics courses to inform employees about the risks and drivers of greenwashing, and they can give tips on how to avoid the practice. Finally, managers can institute codes and explicit standards to promote ethical firm climates.

To effectively make these changes, existing industry standards should be relied on. As the CEO of Timberland noted, "We need consistency of dialogue regarding environmental metrics."[15] To that end, firms can use the ISO 14001 Environment Management System standard, the Global Reporting Initiative's Sustainability Reporting Framework, and other established standards. These standards maintain consistency of language and guide internal information gathering and sharing.

The internationally recognized ISO 14001 was developed by the International Standards Organization. Via third parties, more than 300,000 companies in 171 countries have been certified to it. The standard provides a systematic framework for managing the immediate and long-term environmental impacts of an organization's products, services, and processes. True to the axiom, "You can't manage what you don't measure," it requires procedures for companies to "monitor and measure, on a regular basis, the key characteristics of [their] operations and activities that can have a significant impact on the environment." It also refers to ISO 14031, which provides specific indicators by which environmental performance can be evaluated based on criteria set by firm management.

The Global Reporting Initiative (GRI) offers guidelines to assist firms with reporting systems. GRI is an international, independent standards organization that helps businesses, governments, and other organizations understand and communicate how they affect issues such as climate change, human rights, and corruption. Like ISO 14001, the GRI framework enables third parties to assess the environmental impact of a company's activities and supply chain. The guidelines include performance criteria on energy, biodiversity, and emissions. Over nine thousand organizations currently report with GRI.[16]

Although these standards set the stage, managers must bear in mind the challenges and limitations of their employees and organizations when implementing changes. They should keep in mind individual tendencies to overestimate the likelihood of positive outcomes and act impatiently, and they should also carefully assess their firm's flexibility and how fast it is likely to change. In the short term, incremental changes within existing structures and processes are probably more effective than moon shots at radical transformation.

Employee incentives can counteract some of the human cognitive tendencies that inhibit change. As a start, managers should eliminate incentives likely to encourage greenwashing—for example, marketers should not be rewarded for quantity and reach of proenvironmental messaging with no regard for accuracy. Social media makes this particularly important. A post can make its way around the world in seconds. If inaccurate, it might damage a firm's credibility with the push of a button—poisoning the well for future communications. Other options include rewarding employees for identifying inaccurate claims and punishing those who play a role in greenwashing incidents.

Engage Suppliers

Getting one's own ship in order is a good start, but the challenges of going green and communicating honestly about it extend beyond four walls. Having a clear understanding of how suppliers impact the environment is frequently overlooked, but it is every bit as important. Many businesses do not even know who their suppliers are, let alone how they perform environmentally (even Patagonia got caught on this one, in the case of its inhumanely sourced wool). In many cases, firms produce much higher emissions through supply chains than they do directly. Supply chains are estimated to be responsible for nearly two-thirds of all hazardous waste generated by major US economic sectors.[17]

"Out of sight, out of mind" simply does not work these days. Businesses are held responsible for the bad actions of their suppliers, from poor working conditions to environmental damage. The rise of global, complex, multitier supply chains has only amplified these concerns. A series of recent scandals brought the supply chain to the public's attention; there was tainted milk from China, horsemeat in the ready meals of UK retailers, and the collapse of a garment factory in Bangladesh that resulted in more than 380 deaths. In the last example, workers who died were laboring under poor safety conditions to produce clothing for American and European consumers. Major corporations were caught off guard. It took time for about two dozen major retailers and apparel companies, including Walmart, Gap, and Disney, to figure out whether their garments were indeed produced at the factory.[18]

Disasters involving human casualties cause understandable public outrage, damaging firms' reputations in the process. And when regulators get involved to halt the operations of bad actors, they halt the flow of products to customers. Supply-chain disruptions lead to production and shipping delays and have long-term effects on stock prices.[19]

The same goes for bad environmental behavior. Actions such as measuring supply-chain emissions should be seen as more than mere public-relations exercises, more than risk avoidance. They pave the way for companies to cut costs and introduce product innovations. In a recent study, firms who reduced supply-chain greenhouse-gas emissions were more efficient and performed better financially.[20] New Balance Athletic Shoe reduced the number of suppliers it does business with by 65 percent based on sustainability criteria, improving supply-chain efficiency in the process.[21]

An increasing number of firms now actively seek information about suppliers' sustainability and require them to adopt better practices. This is important in facilitating the communication of environmental and social performance not only within a firm but also throughout the supply chain.

The first steps to take are to inventory suppliers, identify the most significant environmental and social challenges they have, and prioritize sustainability efforts. Getting this information can be challenging. Practices are often embedded in suppliers' organizations, and environmental improvement can be hard to assess from the outside. Frequently, no quantifiable criteria or parameters exist to measure a particular operation's environmental impact. Suppliers' inability to communicate environmental responsiveness to outside audiences makes it challenging to gauge impacts. For these reasons, suppliers tend to hold more information about their performance than do buyers, in a phenomenon known as information asymmetry.

Fortunately, there are ways to fix this problem to gather information and establish credible governance structures throughout the supply chain. Firms can ask suppliers to adopt ISO 14001, as did the "Big Three" US automakers (General Motors, Ford, and Daimler-Chrysler).[22] The organizational capabilities required to adopt such a system facilitate green supply-chain management implementation.[23] Firms can also adopt scorecards and performance-reduction requirements. Scorecards aim to systematically measure and improve sustainability. They assess environmental footprints and encourage continued improvement by measuring energy and water use, recyclable materials, waste, and greenhouse-gas emissions of the entire supply chain. Both Walmart and Procter & Gamble (P&G) used protocols from the World Resources Institute, the World Business Council for Sustainable Development, and the Carbon Disclosure Project to develop supplier sustainability scorecards.[24]

P&G launched its scorecard in 2010 to track partners' performance and improvement on key environmental metrics: carbon, energy, water, and waste. It was developed in collaboration with twenty leading global-supplier representatives and now includes about six hundred suppliers, tracking and encouraging improvement. In 2015, P&G partnered with Ecodesk, a global supply-chain sustainability database and communication platform, to launch a cloud-based supplier-assessment scorecard. It measures and rewards improvement for each of the criteria, regardless of starting point or business size. It features quantitative criteria that automatically score suppliers on comparative performance and the completeness of their sustainability-data reporting. Without intense, active scrutiny on the part of P&G, the scorecard shows whether suppliers are fully engaged with the sustainability program and whether they are driving ongoing improvements.

Not all suppliers will be willing to follow their customers' requirements. In a study of 3,152 automotive suppliers, only 24 percent adopted ISO 14001 within the deadline provided by the Big Three automakers.[25] Those most likely to adopt were younger suppliers trying to establish new business transactions and suppliers with few alternative customers. Those that resisted tended to be older and smaller and produce fewer specialized products. Resistant firms additionally included those not required to report emissions to the EPA Toxic Release Inventory, which makes them less visible to regulators and environmental NGOs.

Most corporate focus has been on the sustainable profile of the internal production process, but there is an increasing need to understand sustainability issues as they relate to the supply chain. Global supply chains are complex, interconnected, and often lack transparency—increasing the likelihood of social and environmental disasters.

Provide ethical leadership and training
- CEO emphasizes ethical behavior and honest communication
- Provide ethics courses and training to inform employees on how to avoid greenwashing

Align employee incentives
- Eliminate perverse incentives, e.g., environmental communication counts
- Reward employees for identification of greenwashing claims
- Punish employees involved in contributing to greenwashing

Improve environmental information sharing process
- Increase centralization of decisions regarding environmental communication
- Institute standards and requirements for internal gathering and sharing of information on environmental-performance indicators with communications and public relations divisions
- Implement information sharing systems and training modules with suppliers

Rely on established reporting standards
- Environmental Management Systems
- Global Reporting Initiative
- Carbon Disclosure Project

FIGURE 9.1.   Steps to Environmental Information Credibility

In conclusion, we provided recommendations to increase the credibility of the companies' information on environmental performance. We contend that there are many steps that managers can take to improve the credibility of their firms' environmental performance. They can facilitate and improve knowledge about greenwashing; effectively align intrafirm structures, processes, and incentives within the firm and its suppliers; and rely on established reporting standards. Figure 9.1 summarizes these steps.

Simplify the Message

Once firms have a clear understanding of the environmental impacts of their operations and suppliers, they can begin transparently communicating with consumers about sustainability issues.

As mentioned, it is hard for consumers to assess the environmental or social impacts of products.[26] These impacts are often unobservable when a product is consumed because they relate to the production phase of the good (for example, involvement of child labor) or to its postconsumption phase (for example, the extent to which the good can be recycled). It would be costly for consumers to obtain information related to the environmental or social impact of these products; they would have to observe the production process and its environmental and social impacts.[27] This results in information asymmetry between the producer, who has some information about these impacts, and the consumer, who does not. Communication of the environmental impact of the product by the firm or a third party can remedy this information asymmetry.

Another challenge is that information about the environmental impacts of products can be complex. The issues involved are as diverse as water usage, biodiversity loss, air quality, and climate change. Aggregation of impacts might be necessary to facilitate understanding. In addition, the issues involve facts and figures that can be difficult to comprehend. This is particularly the case when the units used in these figures are unfamiliar to readers (for example, "4.7 tons of CO_2 emitted by a car")[28] or when these figures are extreme in magnitude (for example, "last year 38.2 billion tons of carbon dioxide were released into the air from the burning of fossil fuels").[29] Most people are not familiar with what a ton of CO_2 means, and although 38.2 billion tons sounds big, how big is it really? In this case, it is important to try to use more intuitive metrics. Such information needs to be translated into simple and easily understood messages. A few basic principles can make numbers more accessible: parsimony, comparability, contextualization, translation, and sometimes, expansion.[30]

People get overwhelmed by extensive use of metrics; messages that require less cognitive effort are more effective. Parsimonious use of terminology reduces the cognitive effort needed to understand complex environmental impacts. For highly quantitative information that can be difficult for people to process because the numbers are challenging or the domain is unfamiliar, numbers become more easily evaluated if they are broken into categories, such as grades, or if they have end points clearly labeled as good. For example, in our energy experiment, when we used red dots to designate those who used above-average electricity and green dots for those with below-average usage, consumers intuitively understood better than they did when usage was presented in kilowatt-hours per week.

In order to reduce the cognitive effort needed to understand several different numbers within a message, managers can, for example, provide an aggregate number for a multitude of environmental impacts, or they can choose to focus on the most important environmental impact. One example of this strategy is the LEED standard for buildings. Projects pursuing LEED certification earn points across several areas that address sustainability issues. The areas include location and transportation, water efficiency, energy and atmosphere, materials and resources, and indoor environmental quality. Each area includes different avenues for buildings to obtain points, up to a maximum of 110. Indoor environmental quality includes minimum indoor air-quality performance, environmental tobacco-smoke control, enhanced indoor-air-quality strategies, low-emitting materials, construction indoor-air-quality management plan, indoor air-quality assessment, thermal comfort, interior lighting, daylight, quality views, and acoustic performance. Based on points achieved, a project can receive one of four LEED rating levels: certified, silver, gold, or platinum. A firm receives basic certification with 40 to 49 points, silver with 50 to 59 points, gold with 60 to 79 points, and platinum with 80 to 110. Each category signals a level of performance in easily understood terms.

Another challenge comes when consumers are asked to compare effects across scales. One way to cut through the confusion is to standardize a message. For example, there are many different greenhouse gases to keep track of: carbon dioxide, methane, nitrous oxide, hydrofluorocarbon gases, perfluorocarbon gases, and sulfur hexafluoride, for starters. Each has its own global warming potential (GWP), a measurement of how much heat the gases can trap within the atmosphere and how much of an environmental impact they are expected to have.[31] To make things easier, each gas's GWP is translated into a common unit that compares and relates all emissions so they can be reported as a single quantity. That unit is called the carbon dioxide equivalent, and it has become the standard unit for measuring carbon footprints.[32]

Context is important. Regarding energy efficiency, people have a hard time understanding what a kilowatt-hour means. More easily understood measures describe household consumption relative to neighbors. Such comparisons help consumers understand usage better than such technical metrics as kilowatt-hours.[33] This method has the added benefit of generating analogies that give numbers meaning for laypeople. For example, research has shown that adding perspective sentences that employ ratios, ranks, and unit changes to measurements can substantially improve people's ability to understand large or novel numbers.[34] For instance, 4.7 tons of CO_2 emitted by a car is roughly three times as heavy as a car, or about two times as heavy as a rhinoceros.[35] Visualization can be helpful too. For example, to understand how much gas 35 billion tons of CO_2 is, imagine the state of Connecticut

(5,500 square miles) covered in a 3,200-foot-thick blanket (a 0.6-mile-thick blanket of gas).[36]

It also helps to translate metrics into things people care about. Often, the necessary math can be too cumbersome for consumers to do themselves. For example, kilowatt-hours of electricity conserved directly correlate to dollar savings. People often fail in making the translation, however. In our second energy-conservation experiment, we sent messages to households that "translated" the electricity they used into dollar amounts or pounds of air pollutants. Most did not know what a few hundred pounds of air pollutants meant, so we told them the pollutants were known to cause childhood asthma and cancer. We translated and contextualized the numbers. We also compared their usage to their top 10 percent most efficient neighbors, making it easier for them see the wide range of electricity usage for a similar apartment.

Translation allows conversion of environmental impact into the cobenefits described in the green bundle. Of course, translating energy savings into dollars is simple. What about environmental improvements being translated into health improvements? This can be translated into more durable products, or products more convenient to use.

Finally, sometimes numbers seem too small to matter, but they can be expanded to take on meaning. This is the case with individual green purchases that might not have an impact by themselves but might have a much greater impact in the aggregate, when millions of consumers change consumption behavior. Take lights, for example. One sixty-watt incandescent bulb is equivalent to a ten-watt LED. Although the savings are tiny for an individual, they become huge when spread across millions of consumers over the life of a light bulb. It is therefore better to express the cost savings for several years of usage. The cost savings from electricity consumption can be expressed over a week, a month, or a year.

Parsimony
  • Aggregate environmental impacts
  • Break the numbers into more easily understood categories

Comparability
  • Use one scale for different impacts
  • Re-scale individual impacts for better evaluability

Contextualization
  • Use analogies
  • Provide more easily understood measures

Translation
  • Translate metrics into simpler ones
  • Translate metrics into something people care more about

FIGURE 9.2.   Principles of Message Simplification

When you look at how much each type of bulb would cost to purchase and operate over a twenty-five-thousand-hour life span (about twenty-three years at three hours per day), then the differences are significant. The total operational cost of an incandescent is $201, versus $48 for a CFL and $38 for a LED.[37] Still, these savings might not be sufficient to motivate consumers to switch lights, as we found out in our experiment. They might be better framed as a loss. Other strategies offered to make numbers seem larger include expanding the denominator so numerators are larger and thus the difference between alternatives seems larger, leading these expanded attributes to receive more weight in choice.[38]

Reliable and complex calculations of environmental impacts are important for the credibility of environmental messages. The challenge is to communicate them simply. Parsimony, comparability, contextualization, translation, and even expansion are principles that can help in message simplification (see figure 9.2). Relying on eco-labels might also be another solution.

Choose the Right Eco-Labels

Firms can communicate their product's environmental claim via two primary avenues—their internal communications team and eco-labels from outside organizations. Eco-labels identify products or services proven to be environmentally preferable within a specific product or service category. They provide easily understandable and identifiable customer information to increase demand for products perceived as environmentally favorable. Eco-labels offer more legitimacy than firms' own green labels, especially when they are third-party certified.

Not all eco-labels are successful, however. Some thrive, but most flop. Managers should be aware of the risks involved in adopting a poorly designed label. After devoting considerable resources to certifying products with UK's Carbon Trust label, British supermarket chain Tesco dropped the process, citing prohibitive costs and minimal consumer recognition.[39] Labels vulnerable to claims of greenwashing can also damage the deserving reputations of green firms and their products. Ecover—a sustainable cleaning-products company—recently boycotted the European Union (EU) Eco-label, claiming that its lax standards allowed entry to subpar performers and harmed the company's superior environmental credentials.[40]

With so many options out there, a few guidelines will help firms make the best choice from the current eco-label morass. These guidelines help raise label awareness, understanding, and credibility.[41]

Eco-labels are a useful tool for conveying information that reduces this asymmetry. But for an eco-label to do so successfully, consumers must understand what it is trying to communicate but also be aware of it.[42] How thoroughly can a consumer interpret the connection between environmental

issues, a label's meaning, and actions needed to produce results?[43] The answer to that question goes a long way toward
understanding its effectiveness.

First, consumers need to understand what the eco-label is
about. The message must be simple and clear. For example,
Blue Angel, which was established by the German government, uses a logo that is very similar to the United Nations
Environment Programme (UNEP) logo. This communicates
the similarities between Blue Angel's mission—to protect
people and provide a voice for the environment—and the
mission of UNEP. The Blue Angel logo also specifies the focus of certification with phrases such as "protects the environment and the health" or "protects the water." Clarity of
messaging allows eco-labels and firms to avoid committing
the greenwashing sin of vagueness. The public will overlook a
product's environmental virtues if they are poorly or insuffi-
ciently communicated.

Second, consumers need to be aware of the eco-label.
They need to have seen it. An eco-label's visibility is increased
when it links to websites with additional information and reviews. Trip Advisor created a label program called Green
Leaders to inform travelers about hotels participating in the
program through its website. Trip Advisor's site gets about
390 million unique visitors per month, so the label has significant visibility.[44]

Managers should also make sure a label devotes adequate
resources to communication. The Marine Stewardship Council (MSC) is one of the world's most widely recognized eco-
labels. A 2012 independent survey commissioned by the council showed that 30 percent of consumers who buy fish at least
once every two months are aware of its eco-label for sustainable and well-managed fisheries—up from 23 percent in
2010.[45] The organization devotes significant resources to com-

munication of its label, with more than six dedicated central-communication staff members and eleven local media contacts. It also puts its communication team at the disposal of newly certified organizations to help them promote it and garner media coverage.[46]

Labels that address multiple products and countries should be favored over isolated ones. Multiproduct labels benefit from greater visibility because they are seen in various markets. The organic coffee eco-label issued by the US Department of Agriculture has increased recognition compared to those from Rainforest Alliance and Smithsonian Migratory Bird Center. This is largely due to the fact that it covers a multitude of products, while the other two focus exclusively on coffee.[47] Having a presence in multiple countries also improves label recognition. The Marine Stewardship Council label is found in sixty-three different countries, while the average number of countries for fishery eco-labels is just seven.[48] (Conversely, certain eco-labels might enjoy strong local recognition but have limited potential for broader recognition.)

Managers should favor labels endorsed by governments and large retailers. Energy Star is widely recognized and understood by US consumers and is perceived as a credible standard because of support from the Department of Energy.[49] Government support can be crucial to a label program's credibility, financial stability, and long-term viability.[50] Energy-efficient products naturally save money over time, but consumers overemphasize the higher initial price and shy away.[51] Energy Star drives demand by working with state and local governments to require that agencies install compliant products in their own offices.[52] The label also works with electric utilities as part of their demand-side management programs, providing rebates to consumers who purchase certified appliances.[53]

The high recognition of MSC stems in part from its adoption by large retailers. The blue fish logo adorns the new packaging of McDonald's Filet-O-Fish sandwich and is prominently displayed at the fish counter of every Whole Foods Market. It is the label that Walmart, Costco, and Target rely on to reach their environmental goals while meeting increasing customer demand for sustainable seafood.

Credibility of the eco-labeling process is also essential for improving consumer confidence and increasing their willingness to purchase green products. For our purposes, credibility can be defined as perceptions and assumptions that the operations of an actor or agent are trustworthy, responsible, desirable, and appropriate.[54] In some cases, eco-labels are issued by independent organizations that have developed transparent criteria and are third-party verified. In other cases, they represent only the claims of a for-profit organization related to vague environmental friendliness. If a firm uses labels that lack credibility, it faces the possibility of being complicit in greenwashing.

For a label program to be credible, several elements must be present: shared governance with stakeholder involvement, stringent and transparent standards, and a credible third-party certification process.

Stakeholder involvement, in particular, has been described as a key component of eco-label credibility.[55] It is a fundamental principle in the development of the Forest Stewardship Council's standards. The organization prides itself on having a clear and accessible process for developing policies and standards, one in which no interest dominates and all are involved.[56] The board of directors includes representatives from environmental NGOs, rural-development agencies, human rights and workers organizations, industries, and consumers of forest products.[57] The council's global standards are developed and modified through a participatory process that involves environmental, social, and economic stakeholders. This provides the framework for creating standards that are tailored to distinct regions, countries, or ecosystems.[58]

When representative stakeholders are not involved, eco-labels can be criticized for lack of independence. The Marine Services Council was launched as a collaboration between Unilever, the world's largest purchaser of frozen food, and the World Wildlife Fund (WWF), the international conservation organization. This exclusive relationship caused controversy, and the organization was panned for lack of stakeholder involvement in the program's design and implementation.[59] To strengthen independence and fend off assertions of being a puppet of WWF and Unilever, MSC was restructured as a fully independent nonprofit organization in 1999.[60]

Generally, managers should prefer eco-label organizations with many partners. This balances the various opinions and perspectives that attend environmental issues, ensures broad consumer appeal, and prevents backlash from consumer segments that feel left out. Sierra Club's Green Home label is awarded based on review of a prospective company's self-declared home-product description and sustainability credentials. Gaining certification indicates that a business "makes a legitimate and meaningful effort to offer a product or service that is more sustainable than what is commonly sold."[61] Sierra Club partners with a broad range of NGOs, businesses, educational institutions, and newspapers for the program.[62]

The success of eco-labels depends on the success of these partnerships and the credibility of the partners.[63] In the case of the MSC, World Wildlife Fund strategically partnered with Unilever, a leading consumer-goods manufacturer and the largest seller of fish sticks in the world in order to address future resource scarcity. Michael Sutton, the WWF co-coordinator of the MSC, explained: "We had to change the rules of the game. People had to come to us because they needed our competence and reputation if they were looking for new ways of problem solving and substitutes for regulations." The reputation of WWF conferred credibility to the label, the success of which gave Unilever a strong tool to protect market share and long-term viability.[64] Often NGOs or the government are perceived as credible partners.

Of course, the standards themselves matter too. Credibility depends on having standards stringent enough to identify exemplary environmental performance. Consumers quickly lose confidence in labels that fail to differentiate the good performers from the bad ones. Compare two forest certification programs: the Sustainable Forestry Initiative and the Forest Stewardship Council. The Sustainable Forestry Initiative uses a widespread scheme with no minimum level of performance. In 2001, the environmental organization Forest Ethics attacked the initiative for its lack of stringency and described it as a "green façade."[65] Following this, seven companies, including four from the Fortune 500—Aetna, Allstate, Office Depot, and Symantec—said they would phase out use of the label. The Forest Stewardship Council, though, has widespread support because it mandatcs spccific levels of performance and results.[66]

Stringency of standards is important to credibility, which translates into trust, brand loyalty, and willingness to pay.[67] One way to assess it is by measuring scope. Do the label's standards include supply-chain impact? Does it cover social issues as well as environmental ones? What other retailers use it? Consumers are more likely to trust organic eco-labels that are sold by retailers considered to be socially responsible. Thus, a brand like McDonald's benefits from the fact that the same label on its Filet-O-Fish is found in the eco-conscious Whole Foods Market.

When partnering with stakeholders with expertise in environmental assessment, managers should stay involved in the assessment and labeling process. Whenever possible, they should run independent analyses to ensure coherent results and compliant suppliers. An overlooked mistake in the evaluation of a product's environmental or social impact can harm consumer confidence. Lululemon—a popular yoga-apparel brand—launched a product line they claimed was made from a seaweed fiber with myriad health benefits. But an independent investigation revealed no difference between the apparel and regular cotton (that is, the material contained no evidence of seaweed). Lululemon's executives admitted to not testing the materials themselves and relying solely on information from suppliers.[68] The day the information was made public in the *New York Times*, Lululemon's stock price dropped 8 percent and continued to decline for several weeks.[69]

Eco-labeled products often come from novel materials and processes, so managers should ensure supply-chain availability. Consumer confidence can be lost when a green product is available only intermittently or when growing demand cannot be met. Many companies found it difficult to rely primarily on eco-labeled seafood because of limited supply.[70] To boost supplies from sustainable fisheries, Unilever had to develop its own system for approving products and producers until the supply of MSC products increased to meet its needs.[71]

Another important feature to look for is third-party certification, which is "a procedure by which a third party provides written assurance that a product, process, or service conforms to specified standards, on the basis of an audit conducted to agreed procedures."[72] The MSC certification program accredits independent certifiers that assess fisheries against the standard.[73] Third-party certification is the most effective mechanism to guarantee improved environmental and social performance[74] as well as credibility in the eyes of the consumer.[75]

Eco-label visibility	Clarity of message	Shared governance	Standard stringency	Credible certification process	Standard transparency
Strong commitment to label communication	Simple and clear message to consumers	Eco-labels with multiple partners	Standards address supply chain	Third-party certification	Results of eco-label audit communicated
Multi-products and international labels			Standards cover environmental and social issues	Verification of accreditors	Mutual recognition of standards
Endorsements from large retailers	Logo recognizable	Government and/or NGO participation	Eco-label conducts studies to assess its impact	Field visits	Chain of custody

FIGURE 9.3.   Eco-Label Awareness, Understanding and Confidence

Effective eco-labels are not reluctant to share relevant information with the public. Consumer confidence is sensitive to the transparency of the certification process, standards, and product-performance evaluations. Organizations with a culture of secrecy foster skepticism about possible greenwashing and overall credibility, making competing products with transparent labels more attractive.

Transparency gives external parties access to information regarding the sustainable practices and governance adopted by the eco-label scheme. Consumers should be able to trace green products through a transparent "chain of custody." The Forest Stewardship Council implements such a system, tracking timber from certified forest to consumer. It requires certification bodies to create reports on forest-management audits and risk assessments for controlled wood that are publicly available on the internet. In contrast, the Programme for the Endorsement of Forest Certification provides only public summaries of audit reports and suffers from weaknesses in the reporting process.[76]

Choosing the right eco-label will increase consumer awareness, understanding, and confidence. Figure 9.3 out-

lines some specific variables that managers could use to select eco-labels. To increase consumer awareness, they should
choose eco-labels with strong commitment to label communication, and they should prefer multiproduct labels. To ensure consumer understanding of the label, they should favor
simple, clear messages and a recognizable logo. To gain consumer confidence, they need to check the credibility of the
eco-label organization and its partners and favor eco-label organizations with multiple partners, including the government
and nonprofit organizations. They should also prefer more
stringent standards and choose transparent eco-label organizations. Of course, these different elements we described can
interact with each other. For example, the presence of open
and consensus-based standard-setting from an eco-label has
been shown to increase the media coverage of the eco-label
and therefore its visibility.[77]

There are many challenges in setting businesses up to be
transparent, avoid greenwashing, and have market success,
but tested, legitimate eco-labels and standards take a lot of
the pain out of the process. Companies no longer have to
green themselves like Patagonia. Having the will to make
changes is a necessary first step, and a firm's internal dialogue should be standardized from the top down. After that,
external tools ease the process significantly.

REACHING THE CONVENIENT ENVIRONMENTALIST

HUMAN CONSUMPTION IS a primary driver of environmental problems. But our urge to consume is encoded in survival—it is clearly not going away. That urge can also be harnessed to solve problems, though. Information is a powerful tool to enable and move consumers toward sustainable behavior, and it is more readily available than ever before. With information about the environmental impacts of products at their fingertips, consumers can make informed choices, driving a revolution of sustainability for whole corporate sectors.

So far, the revolution has moved slowly. Many companies have failed to translate green into gold. Firms tend to be idealistic about consumer behavior, underestimating their level of sophistication or relying too much on rational decision-making models that don't account for biases in human decision-making. Furthermore, many have taken a piecemeal approach that decouples green messages from actual organizational practices, leading to inconsistencies and fomenting distrust.

People care increasingly about the environment but are busier and more skeptical about environmental claims. Products are usually not purchased simply because they are better for the environment, and product quality cannot be sacrificed for sustainable goals. Largely, today's consumers are convenient environmentalists—they will buy green, but it needs to be on their own terms. Complicating matters has been a steady stream of firms getting exposed for greenwashing and making other false representations. This has made consumers distrustful of green messages. And they are confused about what is really good for the environment in the first place. So, how do you reach these people—a majority of consumers—and convince them to buy green?

The answer lies in the green bundle. Messaging that pairs sustainability with private benefits creates a win-win for consumers. They are not only doing right by the world but also doing the right thing for their own lives. In a sense, they get to have their cake and eat it too—they benefit psychologically from their altruism and benefit in a more tangible sense from added value.

Of course, to change consumer behavior, firms first need to get their message right. This goes beyond communications. It requires adopting a culture of transparency and framing authentic messages that resonate with consumers. At a time when information zooms around the world in an instant from any handheld device, transparency is an unyielding force. In most cases, the cost of resisting is greatly outweighed by the benefits of embracing this force before competition. We propose a holistic approach that begins with the firm and ends with the consumer.

We explained how to convert green intentions to purchases using evidence-based approaches rooted in behavioral principles. There are two pillars to effective information strategies: (1) awareness and understanding (which engenders confidence) and (2) willingness to pay. These are depicted in

Sustainable Information Strategies	
Consumer awareness, understanding, and confidence	Consumer willingness to pay
• Leadership dedication • Tangible environmental impacts • Genuine communication throughout the organization • Supplier engagement • Credible third party eco-certification	• Private benefits: • Quality • Health • Status • Money • Emotion

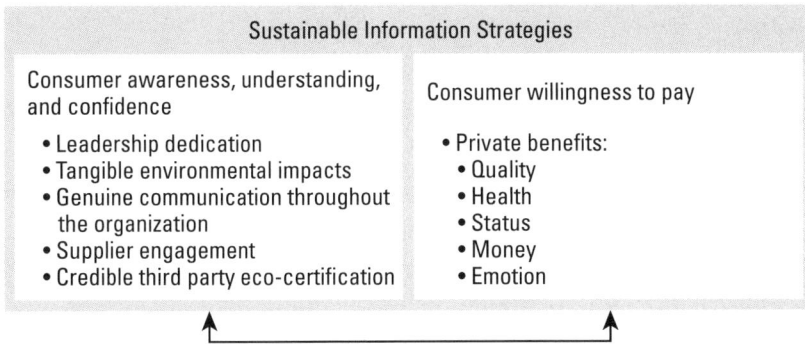

FIGURE C.1.   Pillars of Effective Information Strategies

figure C.1. We now provide more specific strategies that firms can use to follow these steps.

To reach customers, green messages must pierce a busy cloud of green information. The message must be clear and credible. These may seem like simple imperatives, but many companies fail to hit all of the notes.

Practice green modesty and transparency. CEOs are pivotal to developing clarity and credibility. Rightly seen as figureheads for the companies they manage, they must exemplify a sustainable ethos in their personal and professional lives or risk damaging the credibility of the firm's efforts. Going green cannot be delegated to a marketing department or PR firm. Fortunately, managers do not need to reinvent the wheel to get a credible message across. They can use external tools such as eco-labels to develop a sound, credible information strategy. These tools give firms clarity about environmental impact while allowing them to remain modest in their claims and thus resist the temptation to overpromote eco-friendliness.

Indeed, one challenge that often arises (and leads to inadvertent greenwashing) is lack of coordination among different units of an organization. This can cause marketers, for example, to overstate environmental benefits because they do not understand the complexity or impacts of a new product from R&D. To avoid this pitfall, CEOs need to set the tone by clearly stating their green modesty, instituting proper incentives, and relying on codes and standards that promote an ethical climate. These standards can bring about consistency of dialogue regarding environmental metrics. The ISO 14001 international environmental-management-system standard and the Global Reporting Initiative can be helpful tools for initiating this process. The risk of misunderstanding a product's green impact becomes even more likely when several organizations are involved, such as when a supplier is not forthcoming about the environmental impacts of its materials. Although this may come as a surprise, even today many firms do not know the environmental and social impacts of their suppliers. Supply-chain environmental-sustainability scorecards are one way that companies can begin to take charge of this information.

Once firms better understand the environmental impact of their products, they face the challenge of translating this information not only into a clear signal that can be understood by consumers but also into something that consumers care about.

Firms can communicate about sustainability to consumers through two avenues: their own communications and eco-labels. Eco-labels identify products or services that have proven environmental advantages within a specific product or service category. They provide more legitimacy than firms' own communications, especially when they are third-party certified. But not all eco-labels offer the same credibility and recognition, so care should be taken when choosing them. It is also important that a label is recognized by consumers, transparent about its certification systems, and clear in communications about the environmental benefits.

Most information strategies stop here and thus generate only a small number of responsive consumers. The steps just described, though necessary, are insufficient to make consumers go green. Again, there is little willingness to pay for environmental benefits or the public good alone. Moreover, research shows that if there is any perceived trade-off in quality, even fewer people are willing to pay.

Consumers' willingness to pay is a less explored piece of the puzzle for green markets, but it is the key to developing effective informational strategies. This is where the green bundle comes in. Consumers will translate aspirational beliefs into actions when they see green products as being bundled with private benefits, such as health benefits or improved quality. Firms need to bundle environmental or public-good benefits with private benefits, including better performance, enhanced status, improved health, money savings, and even emotional returns.

Emphasize increased quality. Few are willing to pay a premium without some measure of private benefit. Conversely, with certain goods, such as cleaning products, consumers may confuse or associate eco-labeling with poor quality. It is therefore important to communicate quality alongside environmental virtue. The Clorox Company promotes the view that natural cleaners are at least as good as their conventional counterparts by boasting that products with the Green Works label "clean with the power you expect." In many cases, there is a natural overlap between quality and greenness. Performance, functionality, usability, durability, comfort, and convenience are all attributes that can be effectively bundled with sustainability.

Leverage peer pressure. Most of us care what others think, and we like to display the good things we are doing. The unusual appearance of the Toyota Prius became a selling point after the car was used to bring Hollywood stars to the red carpet of the Academy Awards. Suddenly, this strange-looking vehicle could make people look like stars themselves. Status is a powerful tool to compel behavior in the marketplace, and it is particularly effective when consumption is highly visible. Not all products are as conspicuous as a car, however. Using information technologies and social media, less visible products such as energy consumption can be made more conspicuous and therefore subject to social pressure.

Promote health benefits. Research shows that the most important reason we buy green is for our health and the health of our families. Health is the main reason people choose organic products that are produced without chemicals. Thus, it was not surprising to see that, over a ten-year period, the organic-food market grew 238 percent, from $8.6 billion to $29 billion, while the overall food market grew 33 percent.

Health attributes are an important private benefit that can be associated with green products. In our field experiment on energy conservation, we found that messages on the health impact of electricity-generation successfully led households to reduce energy consumption.[1] But people do not always make the connection between environmental and health benefits. Information campaigns are one way to close that link, and there are critical times when consumers will be more receptive to campaigns about environment and health. These include national health crises, such as the water contamination in Flint, Michigan, which raise awareness and lead consumers seek strategies to protect their health. They also include personal times in individuals' lives, such as when they start a family or face health problems.

Unravel monetary returns. Money is the most cited reason to avoid or embrace green products and services. Premiums often scare consumers away, whereas monetary savings associated with saving energy or resources are appealing. But perceptions of premiums or savings vary widely depending on context or reference point. How financial incentives are framed makes a big difference; framing can help consumers overcome their subconscious cognitive biases. Small savings framed as a tax or a loss can be quite effective, and raising a product's price can even help in some situations. Context matters, so anchoring prices and decoys are potential tools that can convince consumers to buy.

Stimulate empathy. The final piece of the green bundle is the emotional connection between the consumer and the sustainable products. Consumers will empathize with a cause when the story is told the right way. In addition, they need to believe their purchases will make a tangible difference. Communications about green products must be both relatable and emotionally compatible. A wise company will invest in marketing that does this effectively and legitimately.

It is imperative to bridge the distance between green consumption and impact, making the benefits of consumption tangible by showing how they help a specific person. TOMS shoes has successfully established that kind of connection with their concept of one-for-one donations based on consumption.

When to Bundle?

Under what conditions should managers use the green bundle strategy? When should they emphasize greenness, and when should they emphasize private cobenefits? Product attributes and situational context are important elements to consider when implementing green bundle strategies.

Appeals that closely match the specific needs satisfied by a product category will be more persuasive for consumers than appeals that address less-relevant needs. For example, emotional value will be highly salient for consumers when purchasing items with experiential characteristics because of the complementarity between the emotionally driven purchase experience and the value source. For product categories that are functional, rational thoughts and functional attributes dominate the decision-making process, so complementarities will be best when the environmental attributes enhance the performance of a product (for example, increased efficiency).

Sometimes the different elements of the bundle interact. For example, performance and status are often related. This is the case with Tesla, in which the car's high performance increases the owners' status. Similarly, functionality, comfort, and health are cobenefits that have been found in green buildings. More comfortable and functional environments can lead to lower stress and better health. People working in green buildings report improved air quality, odors, noise, lighting, and thermal comfort and ergonomics; they also experience fewer health symptoms.[2] Firms can focus on developing cobenefits that will trigger the most additional benefits.

The relevance of these benefits will vary according to context. Situational aspects moderate perceptions of the functional, social, health, or emotional benefits associated with sustainability. This is the case with health benefits from environmental improvements. The importance of the connection between environmental damage and health tends to be most salient at critical junctures in the lives of consumers: when starting a family, having children, or getting sick and wanting to understand why.

Social and cultural contexts are important too. People care greatly about how they are perceived by their social groups.

When others in our social groups care about the environment, we will be more likely to purchase green products to
be seen positively by friends and neighbors. This is not to say
that "brown" consumers can't be reached but that the message must to be tailored to their values. Otherwise, the strategy may backfire, as it does with men who don't see greenness
as masculine.

Most of the examples in this book come from developed
countries, but many of the innovations described have relevance for other economic and cultural contexts. Monetary
savings and durability are two attributes that are particularly
relevant for consumers in developing countries. As demonstrated, however, stated motivations are not always what drives
conservation behavior—we need to be careful with overgener-
alizations. For example, we asked about two thousand Indians
living in urban areas what motivated them to conserve energy.
Money was the most frequently cited motivation. Health was
among the least common motivations. Overall, for respondents who stated they engage in energy conservation behaviors, 84 percent cited saving money and only 9 percent of respondents cited either their health or their family's health as
motivating factors for engaging in energy conservation.[3] But
when we provided Indian households with real-time information about their electricity usage framed in terms of cost savings, they didn't conserve energy. When the issue was framed
in terms of air pollution, however, they reduced usage significantly.[4] Despite statements to the contrary, the health benefits
of saving energy were a better motivator. Similar results were
seen in the United States, showing that similar motivations
sometimes work across cultures.[5] The context matters, but it
needs to be carefully assessed in each information campaign.

In the conditions just described, a vocal green bundle
communication strategy would be most effective. It is advan-

tageous to emphasize environmental benefits and their connections to private benefits. Sometimes, however, even when environmental benefits sync up with private cobenefits, it might be more effective to emphasize the private benefits while remaining silent about the environment.

The Silent Green Bundle

In some situations, greening products does not offer clear private cobenefits. And, as we know, emphasizing environmental benefits alone leads only a small number of committed consumers to buy green. It is still possible to use a silent green bundle strategy, however. For example, a company can bundle green products with conventional ones to increase their appeal. This was achieved by the Hayward Lumber Company. Some of its certified green lumber wasn't of a different quality than conventional lumber, but it still commanded a price premium. Hayward Lumber offered a bundle of home products, including sustainable lumber, that provided operational efficiency and appealed to homeowners.[6]

In cases in which environmental benefits are difficult to communicate and are likely to confuse consumers, managers should avoid mentioning them. This is what two-thirds of eco-certified wineries in California have done so far. They let the quality of the wine speak for itself. This is also what Tesla did by emphasizing performance rather than environmental benefits. When people started to criticize electric cars, saying they might emit more carbon than gasoline cars in states that rely on coal for electricity generation, it did not impact Tesla's sales because environmental benefits were not emphasized in the marketing of the car.

With the silent green bundle, consumers can be sustainable without knowing it. This is the Trojan Horse strategy, in which sustainable features are embedded in a product without fanfare while other features such as usability and efficiency appeal to the convenient environmentalist.

Where to Start?

There are concrete steps you can take to start implementing a green bundle strategy. The strategy works best for products in which environmental attributes are bundled with private benefits. This means that companies that want to address environmental issues and get consumers to purchase their greener products need to explore whether these two elements are currently bundled in their products. If the connection is not there yet, they need to think about designing products with both private benefits and reduced environmental impact. This is why a successful green-information strategy starts not in the marketing department but rather in the research department: with sustainable design.

By incorporating environmental impacts into design tactics, sustainable design takes into consideration the entire life cycle of the product, making effective products that minimize resource use.[7] The application of sustainable design can greatly reduce the environmental and social impacts of these products and services. Designers are in a position to plan and shape the way in which consumption occurs as well as to bridge the considerable intention-behavior gap.[8] Most of our daily consumption patterns are routine behavior. We do things the way we are used to, and it is hard to break habits. Better design can help us change.

The way users interact with a product may strongly influence its environmental impact. This means, for example, that technical improvements to product efficiency are not necessarily turned into energy savings during the use stage. As we found in our energy-conservation experiment, consumer behaviors and practices have a significant impact on energy use and account for a significant variation by a factor of two to four in identical apartments with different occupants.[9] For example, we found that the heaviest users of the heating and cooling system in their apartments used as much as four times the electricity as the lightest users in similar apartments. This was also the case with refrigerators—the heaviest users consumed up to three times the electricity of the lightest ones.[10] Designers can try to influence this behavior[11] by creating products with user experience in mind.[12] By having a better understanding of the complexity of consumers' everyday interactions with products, services, and environments, designers can set the stage for radical changes in consumption.[13]

Likewise, communications strategies need to understand and account for how people use products. It is possible that the information pillar of the bundle strategy is well articulated: customers are aware of the information, and they understand and trust it. They even want to act on it. But the information will not be effective at influencing behavior if product usability hampers their ability to act. This was the case in our energy-conservation experiment as well. We sent messages to the households about electricity usage at the appliance level. The fridge consisted of an average of about 20 percent of usage, an important share. People attempted to reduce consumption by turning the temperature dial of their fridge to what they thought would result in lower energy use. Unfortunately, most of them misunderstood the dial, decreased the temperature, and therefore increased their electricity usage. We provided information about the total use of the fridge but not clear guidance on how to reduce energy usage.

Sustainable design can focus on product mismatching

functionalities, in which the delivered functions fail to match with the user's desired functionality,[14] or the unintended use of the product, service, or system, in which consumers use features in a manner unexpected by the designers.[15] A user-centered approach to sustainable design can help reduce environmental impact.[16]

Green bundle information strategies need to ensure a good flow of information between different areas of firms to avoid miscommunication about environmental benefits. They also need to integrate information about consumers' real use of the product to build better green products that customers value.

Our focus has been on the convenient environmentalist. We believe environmental education is key to moving toward sustainability, but it is not enough. Companies need to consider the realities of human behavior, and they need to design products that not only have a lower environmental impact but also are focused on usability.

Lobby for Transparency

Our focus has been on firm behavior at a time when government intervention to mitigate environmental problems is low and declining. Conscious consumption can help mitigate the negative environmental impacts that consumerism is having on our world. This is not to say that government does not have an important role to play in changing consumption behavior—only that businesses and sustainability advocates cannot rely solely on it. When governments do step up with increased regulations and legislation, businesses that have effectively put in place green bundle strategies will have an even greater strategic advantage.

Some have argued that the notion of a socially responsible

corporation is a possible oxymoron because of natural conflict within and among corporations.[17] They say it is not realistic to rely solely on consumers' voluntary actions to move toward sustainability, that so far voluntary approaches to environmental protection have had relatively modest impacts on environmental improvement. They say that green companies, including Tesla, benefit greatly from government subsidies for consumer purchases of green products or from government research and development. In the face of these criticisms, we believe business leadership in market transformations toward transparency is not only possible but essential.

Undeniably, government has a critical role to play in promoting transparency. Its support can be crucial to a label program's credibility, financial stability, and long-term viability. Corporations can support that role by pushing for more and clearer standards, which helps their own communication strategies in the process.

The environmental policies of developed nations have evolved substantially over the past several decades. Early pollution-control programs involved command-and-control approaches. Later policies frequently included pollution charges, tradable permits, and other market-based instruments. More recently, a third wave of environmental policy has emerged that emphasizes providing information as an integral part of risk-mitigation strategies. Here, government regulation is replaced or augmented by publicly provided information presumed to assist more cost-effective private market and legal forces. Common examples include the toxics-release inventory, lead-paint disclosures, drinking-water-quality notices, and eco-labels.[18]

But few governments mandate corporate disclosure, with a few exceptions such as toxic releases. Mandatory disclosure of environmental practices and third-party auditing would make it more difficult for brown firms to get away with green-washing, even if greenwashing practices themselves were not regulated, since consumers, investors, and nongovernmental organizations would be able to compare a firm's communications with reliable information about its environmental practices.

Corporations can play important role in working with government to promote transparency. Those who seek to develop a culture of transparency can even gain competitive advantages by doing so. Our research shows greater lobbying activity among greener firms within high-polluting industries such as energy, perhaps because those firms can leverage new regulations to gain competitive advantages over their rivals.[19]

A World of Green Transparency?

Being green is not just for tree huggers, but we need to be realistic about human behavior—people are complex and self-interested, driven by forces other than pure altruism. There are many reasons to believe that sustainable information strategies can change the marketplace and move convenient environmentalists to action. But most people need to see a public good that also brings private benefits such as status, savings, health, quality, and emotional connectedness. That is how we can close the gap between intention and action. Consumers have not yet been given the choices they need to truly be green. When the marketplace provides them, you will see a sustainability revolution.

NOTES

Introduction

1. https://www.inc.com/magazine/20061101/green50_integrators.html.

2. http://www.bloomberg.com/bw/magazine/content/09_25/b4136 056155092.htm.

3. Organic Trade Association, "U.S. Organic Industry Survey 2017," https://ota.com/resources/organic-industry-survey; US Census, "Retail and Food Services Sales 1992–2016," https://www.census.gov/retail/index .html.

4. McGraw-Hill Construction, "The Green Outlook 2012," http:// biggreenopportunity.org/wp-content/uploads/2013/05/Big-Green -Opportunity-Report-FINAL-WEB.pdf.

5. TerraChoice Group Inc., "Greenwashing Report 2010," http://sins ofgreenwashing.com/findings/greenwashing-report-2010/index.html.

Chapter 1

1. Martin Miller, "The Oil Spill That Sparked the Green Revolution," *Los Angeles Times*, November 30, 1999, http://articles.latimes.com/1999 /nov/30/local/me-38862; Ari Phillips, "How a Massive Oil Spill in 1969 Changed Everything," *Think Progress*, June 30, 2014, https://thinkprogress .org/how-a-massive-oil-spill-in-1969-changed-everything-c4da7ecd5038 #.22b3cd9nf; Christine Mai-Duc, "The 1969 Santa Barbara Oil Spill That Changed Oil and Gas Exploration Forever," *Los Angeles Times*, May 20, 2015, http://www.latimes.com/local/lanow/la-me-ln-santa-barbara-oil-spill -1969-20150520-htmlstory.html. Jennifer Latson, "The Burning River That Sparked a Revolution," June 22, 2015, http://time.com/3921976 /cuyahoga-fire/.

2. *Consumer boycott* means a boycott adopted by consumers of a product or service to express their displeasure with the seller, manufacturer, or provider. https://definitions.uslegal.com/c/consumer-boycott/.

3. Monroe Friedman, "Consumer Boycotts in the United States,

1970–1980: Contemporary Events in Historical Perspective," *Journal of Consumer Affairs* 19, no. 1 (1985): 96–117.

4. Ibid.

5. "United States Consumers Boycott Tuna to Protect Dolphins, 1988–1990," Global Nonviolent Action Database, http://nvdatabase .swarthmore.edu/content/united-states-consumers-boycott-tuna-protect -dolphins-1988-1990.

6. Anthony Ramirez. "'Epic Debate' Led to Heinz Tuna Plan," *New York Times*, April 16, 1990, http://www.nytimes.com/1990/04/16/business /epic-debate-led-to-heinz-tuna-plan.html?pagewanted=all.

7. David P. Baron, "Private Politics," *Journal of Economics & Management Strategy* 12, no. 1 (2003): 31–66.

8. Wallace N. Davidson III, Dan L. Worrell, and Abuzar El-Jelly, "Influencing Managers to Change Unpopular Corporate Behavior through Boycotts and Divestitures: A Stock Market Test," *Business & Society* 34, no. 2 (1995): 171–96.

9. Yael Wolinsky-Nahmias, ed., *Changing Climate Politics: US Policies and Civic Action* (Thousand Oaks, CA: CQ Press, 2014): 198.

10. Jill Gabrielle Klein, N. Craig Smith, and Andrew John, "Why We Boycott: Consumer Motivations for Boycott Participation," *Journal of Marketing* 68, no. 3 (2004): 92–109.

11. Sankar Sen, Zeynep Gürhan-Canli, and Vicki Morwitz, "Withholding Consumption: A Social Dilemma Perspective on Consumer Boycotts," *Journal of Consumer Research* 28, no. 3 (2001): 399–417.

12. Ibid.

13. Organic Trade Association, "US Organic: State of the Industry," 2017, https://www.ota.com/resources/organic-industry-survey; US Census Bureau, "Total Retail and Food Services Sales in the United States from 1992 to 2016," https://www.census.gov/retail/index.html.

14. "Ecolabel Index," Big Room Inc., 2017, http://www.ecolabelindex .com/.

15. US Green Building Council, "LEED," http://www.usgbc.org/leed.

16. Russ Gaskin, "The Big Green Opportunity for Small Business in the U.S.," Green America, Association for Enterprise Opportunity, Ecoventures International, 2013, http://biggreenopportunity.org/wp-content /uploads/2013/05/Big-Green-Opportunity-Report-FINAL-WEB.pdf.

17. "The Sins of Greenwashing: Home and Family Edition 2010," TerraChoice, 2010, http://sinsofgreenwashing.com/index35c6.pdf.

18. Mindy Fetterman, "Wal-Mart Grows 'Green' Strategies," *USA Today*, September 24, 2006, http://usatoday30.usatoday.com/money/indus tries/retail/2006-09-24-wal-mart-cover-usat_x.htm.

19. Byron Pope, "Automotive R&D Spending Down Last Year, Study Shows," Wards Auto, November 9, 2010, http://wardsauto.com/news-analysis/automotive-rd-spending-down-last-year-study-shows.

20. "The Most Innovative Companies of 2011," Fast Company, 2011, https://www.fastcompany.com/most-innovative-companies/2011.

21. "Good Guide Ratings," Good Guide Inc., 2017, https://www.goodguide.com/#/.

22. "Seafood Watch," Monterey Bay Aquarium Foundation, 2017, http://www.seafoodwatch.org/.

23. "The Environment: Public Attitudes and Individual Behavior—A Twenty-Year Evolution," SC Johnson, 2011, http://www.scjohnson.com/Libraries/Download_Documents/SCJ_and_GfK_Roper_Green_Gauge.sflb.ashx.

24. Riley E. Dunlap, Kent D. Van Liere, Angela G. Mertig, and Robert Emmet Jones, "New Trends in Measuring Environmental Attitudes: Measuring Endorsement of the New Ecological Paradigm: A Revised NEP Scale," *Journal of Social Issues* 56, no. 3 (2000): 425–42.

25. Magali A. Delmas and Robert Clements, "Green Products Recognition, Understanding, and Preference: The Case of Coffee Eco-Labels," December 21, 2017, available at SSRN: https://ssrn.com/abstract=3091882.

26. "Green Generation: Millennials Say Sustainability Is a Shopping Priority," 2015, http://www.nielsen.com/us/en/insights/news/2015/green-generation-millennials-say-sustainability-is-a-shopping-priority.html; Robert D. Straughan and James A. Roberts, "Environmental Segmentation Alternatives: A Look at Green Consumer Behavior in the New Millennium," *Journal of Consumer Marketing* 16, no. 6 (1999): 558–75.

27. Morley Winograd and Michael Hais, "How Green Are Millennials?," 2013, http://www.newgeography.com/content/003455-how-green-are-millennials.

28. Ibid.; Ann P. Minton and Randall L. Rose, "The Effects of Environmental Concern on Environmentally Friendly Consumer Behavior: An Exploratory Study," *Journal of Business Research* 40, no. 1 (1997): 37–48; Andrew Gilg, Stewart Barr, and Nicholas Ford, "Green Consumption or Sustainable Lifestyles? Identifying the Sustainable Consumer," *Futures* 37, no. 6 (2005): 481–504.

29. Emma Rex and Henrikke Baumann, "Beyond Ecolabels: What Green Marketing Can Learn from Conventional Marketing," *Journal of Cleaner Production* 15, no. 6 (2007): 567–76.

30. Stanislas Dupré, *Talk the Walk: Advancing Sustainable Lifestyles through Marketing and Communications* (New York: UNEP/Earthprint, 2005).

31. Timothy M. Devinney, Pat Auger, and Giana M. Eckhardt, *The Myth of the Ethical Consumer* (Cambridge, UK: Cambridge University Press, 2010).

32. Walter Coddington, *Environmental Marketing: Positive Strategies for Reaching the Green Consumer* (New York: McGraw-Hill, 1993).

33. Ibid.

34. Jacquelyn Ottman, *The New Rules of Green Marketing: Strategies, Tools, and Inspiration for Sustainable Branding* (Oakland, CA: Berrett-Koehler, 2011).

35. Morven G. McEachern and Paulin McClean. "Organic Purchasing Motivations and Attitudes: Are They Ethical?," *International Journal of Consumer Studies* 26, no. 2 (2002): 85–92.

36. Andrew Gilg, Stewart Barr, and Nicholas Ford, "Green Consumption or Sustainable Lifestyles? Identifying the Sustainable Consumer," *Futures* 37, no. 6 (2005): 481–504.

37. David Tiltman, "Who Is the Ethical Consumer?," *Marketing* 11 (2007): 28–30.

38. K. Chitra, "In Search of the Green Consumers: A Perceptual Study," *Journal of Services Research* 7, no. 1 (2007): 173–91.

39. Scott Bearse et al., "Finding the Green in Today's Shoppers: Sustainability Trends and New Shopper Insights," *GMA/Deloitte Green Shopper Study Research Report* (2009): 1–28.

40. Michel Laroche, Jasmin Bergeron, and Guido Barbaro-Forleo, "Targeting Consumers Who Are Willing to Pay More for Environmentally Friendly Products," *Journal of Consumer Marketing* 18, no. 6 (2001): 503–20.

41. The Nielsen Company, "The Sustainability Imperative," October 12, 2015, http://www.nielsen.com/us/en/insights/reports/2015/the-sustainability-imperative.html.

42. Jacquelyn Ottman, *The New Rules of Green Marketing: Strategies, Tools, and Inspiration for Sustainable Branding* (Oakland, CA: Berrett-Koehler, 2011).

43. The Nielsen Company, "The Sustainability Imperative."

44. Based on 842 responses.

45. Leon Kaye, "The SunChips Compostable Bag Claim Combusts," *Triple Pundit*, July 2010, http://www.triplepundit.com/2010/07/the-sun chips-compostable-bag-claim-combusts/.

46. Amy Guittard, "How Frito-Lay Can Take Their Compostable Packaging Failure Out of the Dumps," *Triple Pundit*, December 2012, http://www.triplepundit.com/2010/12/frito-lay-compostable-packaging-failure/.

47. European Commission, "EU Ecolabel Facts and Figures," http:// ec.europa.eu/environment/ecolabel/facts-and-figures.html.

48. Marketing Week, "Eco Group Fights Boycott of Green Labelling Scheme," *Marketing Week*, November 23, 1995, https://www.marketingweek .com/1995/11/23/eco-group-fights-boycott-of-green-labelling-scheme/.

49. "Emission Control and Exhaust," AutoZone, http://www.auto zone.com/parts/emission-control-and-exhaust.

50. "The Home Depot: A Deep Commitment to FSC," Forest Stewardship Council, https://us.fsc.org/en-us/newsroom/newsletter/id/711.

51. Magali A. Delmas, Erica Plambeck, and Monifa Porter, "Environmental Product Differentiation by the Hayward Lumber Company" (unpublished case study, Stanford Graduate School of Business, Stanford, CA, 2004).

52. Magali A. Delmas and Vanessa Cuerel Burbano, "The Drivers of Greenwashing," *California Management Review* 54, no. 1 (2011): 64–87.

53. "Farmed Fish Eco-Labels Fall Short of Protecting Environment, Says Report," December 7, 2011, Sustainable Food News, https://www .sustainablefoodnews.com/story.php?news_id=14719.

54. Dan Ackman, "WorldCom, Tyco, Enron—R.I.P.," *Forbes*, July 1, 2002, https://www.forbes.com/2002/07/01/0701topnews.html.

55. Harry Stevens, "Bitter Fruit: Dole Sued for Greenwashing Guatemalan Banana Operations," Triple Pundit, November 2012, http://www .triplepundit.com/2012/11/bitter-fruit-dole-sued-greenwashing-guate malan-banana-operations/.

56. Paul Nastu, "Fiji Water Targeted in 'Greenwashing' Class Action Suit," *Environmental Leader*, December 2012, https://www.environmental leader.com/2010/12/fiji-water-targeted-in-greenwashing-class-action -suit/.

57. Karina Basso, "Huggies Maker Sued in Natural Label Class Action Lawsuit," Top Class Actions, August 11, 2015, https://topclassactions .com/lawsuit-settlements/lawsuit-news/94041-huggies-maker-sued-in -natural-label-class-action-lawsuit/; Jennifer Chait, "Huggies Goes Green! Well, at Least Goes Greenwashing," Alloy, August 24, 2009, http://www .alloy.com/well-being/huggies-goes-green-well-at-least-goes-green washing/.

58. Magali A. Delmas and Vanessa Cuerel Burbano, "The Drivers of Greenwashing," *California Management Review* 54, no. 1 (2011): 64–87.

59. Karl Moore, "Authenticity: The Way to the Millennial's Heart," *Forbes*, August 14, 2014, https://www.forbes.com/sites/karlmoore/2014 /08/14/authenticity-the-way-to-the-millennials-heart/#6f49d4b94531; Erik Martin, "How to Use Authenticity, Brands, and Visuals to Engage

Millennials," *EContent*, October 26, 2015, http://www.econtentmag.com /Articles/News/News-Feature/How-to-Use-Authenticity-Brands-and -Visuals-to-Engage-Millennials-106455.htm.

60. Raz Godelnik, "How White Polar Bear Cans Upset Coca-Cola's Cause Marketing Campaign," Triple Pundit, December 2011, http://www .triplepundit.com/2011/12/coca-cola-failed-white-polar-bear-cans/.

61. Magali A. Delmas and Neil Lessem, "Saving Power to Conserve Your Reputation? The Effectiveness of Private versus Public Information," *Journal of Environmental Economics and Management* 67, no. 3 (2014): 353–70.

62. Magali A. Delmas, "Perception of Eco-Labels: Organic and Bio-dynamic Wines," *UCLA Institute of the Environment* (2010): 9–10.

63. Ibid.

Chapter 2

1. Chiara Longoni, Peter M. Gollwitzer, and Gabriele Oettingen, "A Green Paradox: Validating Green Choices Has Ironic Effects on Behavior, Cognition, and Perception," *Journal of Experimental Social Psychology* 50 (2014): 158–65.

2. Jenny Van Doorn and Peter C. Verhoef, "Willingness to Pay for Organic Products: Differences between Virtue and Vice Foods," *International Journal of Research in Marketing* 28, no. 3 (2011): 167–80; Shih-Chang Tseng and Shiu-Wan Hung, "A Framework Identifying the Gaps between Customers' Expectations and Their Perceptions in Green Products," *Journal of Cleaner Production* 59 (2013): 174–84.

3. M. Giana Eckhardt, Russell Belk, and Timothy M. Devinney, "Why Don't Consumers Consume Ethically?," *Journal of Consumer Behaviour* 9, no. 6 (2010): 426–36.

4. Nicola Power, Geoffrey Beattie, and Laura McGuire, "Mapping Our Underlying Cognitions and Emotions about Good Environmental Behavior: Why We Fail to Act Despite the Best of Intentions," *Semiotica* 2017, no. 215 (2017): 193–234.

5. Icek Ajzen, "The Theory of Planned Behavior," *Organizational Behavior and Human Decision Processes* 50, no. 2 (1991): 179–211.

6. Michal J. Carrington, Benjamin A. Neville, and Gregory J. Whitwell, "Why Ethical Consumers Don't Walk Their Talk: Towards a Framework for Understanding the Gap between the Ethical Purchase Intentions and Actual Buying Behaviour of Ethically Minded Consumers," *Journal of Business Ethics* 97, no. 1 (2010): 139–58.

7. Rosemary Robin Charlotte McEachan, Mark Conner, Natalie Jayne Taylor, and Rebecca Jane Lawton, "Prospective Prediction of Health-

Related Behaviours with the Theory of Planned Behaviour: A Meta-Analysis," *Health Psychology Review* 5, no. 2 (2011): 97–144.

8. Falko F. Sniehotta, Justin Presseau, and Vera Araújo-Soares, "Time to Retire the Theory of Planned Behaviour," *Health Psychology Review* 8, no. 1 (2014): 1–7.

9. Ibid.

10. Paschal Sheeran, Peter M. Gollwitzer, and John A. Bargh, "Non-conscious Processes and Health," *Health Psychology* 32, no. 5 (2013): 460.

11. Mark Conner, Gaston Godin, Paschal Sheeran, and Marc Germain, "Some Feelings Are More Important: Cognitive Attitudes, Affective Attitudes, Anticipated Affect, and Blood Donation," *Health Psychology* 32, no. 3 (2013): 264.

12. McEachan, Conner, Taylor, and Lawton, "Prospective Prediction of Health-Related Behaviours."

13. Carrington, Neville, and Whitwell, "Ethical Consumers."

14. Tilde Herrera, "Want to Sell a Green Product? Don't Call It Green," *Green Biz* (blog), January 30, 2012, https://www.greenbiz.com/blog/2012/01/30/want-sell-green-product-dont-call-it-green.

15. Marco Perugini and Richard P. Bagozzi, "The Role of Desires and Anticipated Emotions in Goal-Directed Behaviours: Broadening and Deepening the Theory of Planned Behaviour," *British Journal of Social Psychology* 40, no. 1 (2001): 79–98.

16. Judith I. M. De Groot and Linda Steg, "Mean or Green: Which Values Can Promote Stable Pro-Environmental Behavior?," *Conservation Letters* 2, no. 2 (2009): 61–66.

17. Don A. Moore and George Loewenstein, "Self-Interest, Automaticity, and the Psychology of Conflict of Interest," *Social Justice Research* 17, no. 2 (2004): 189–202; Siegwart Lindenberg and Linda Steg, "Normative, Gain and Hedonic Goal Frames Guiding Environmental Behavior," *Journal of Social Issues* 63, no. 1 (2007): 117–37.

18. Andreas Diekmann and Peter Preisendörfer, "Green and Greenback: The Behavioral Effects of Environmental Attitudes in Low-Cost and High-Cost Situations," *Rationality and Society* 15, no. 4 (2003): 441–72; Gebhard Kirchgässner, "Towards a Theory of Low-Cost Decisions," *European Journal of Political Economy* 8, no. 2 (1992): 305–20.

19. Emmanuel K. Yiridoe, Samuel Bonti-Ankomah, and Ralph C. Martin, "Comparison of Consumer Perceptions and Preference toward Organic versus Conventionally Produced Foods: A Review and Update of the Literature," *Renewable Agriculture and Food Systems* 20, no. 4 (2005): 193–205.

20. G. Turco, "Organic Food—an Opportunity at Who's Expense?," *Industry Note* (2002).

21. Pat Auger, Paul Burke, Timothy M. Devinney, and Jordan J. Louviere, "What Will Consumers Pay for Social Product Features?," *Journal of Business Ethics* 42, no. 3 (2003): 281–304; Wen-Hsien Tsai, Sin-Jin Lin, Ya-Fen Lee, Yao-Chung Chang, and Jui-Ling Hsu, "Construction Method Selection for Green Building Projects to Improve Environmental Sustainability by Using an MCDM Approach," *Journal of Environmental Planning and Management* 56, no. 10 (2013): 1487–1510; Ken Peattie, "Golden Goose or Wild Goose? The Hunt for the Green Consumer," *Business Strategy and the Environment* 10, no. 4 (2001): 187–99; Emma Rex and Henrikke Baumann, "Beyond Ecolabels: What Green Marketing Can Learn from Conventional Marketing," *Journal of Cleaner Production* 15, no. 6 (2007): 567–76.

22. Freya Williams, "Charge Less, Sell More: How to Price Green Products," *Green Biz* (blog), May 5, 2011, https://www.greenbiz.com/blog /2011/05/10/charge-less-sell-more-how-to-price-green-products.

23. De Groot and Steg, "Mean or Green."

24. Ken Peattie, "Green Consumption: Behavior and Norms," *Annual Review of Environment and Resources* 35 (2010): 195–228.

25. James Andreoni, "Giving with Impure Altruism: Applications to Charity and Ricardian Equivalence," *Journal of Political Economy* 97, no. 6 (1989): 1447–58; James Andreoni, "Impure Altruism and Donations to Public Goods—a Theory of Warm-Glow Giving," *Economic Journal* 100 (June 1990): 464–77; Alice M. Isen, "Success, Failure, Attention and Reaction to Others: The Warm Glow of Success," *Journal of Personality and Social Psychology* 15 (August 1970): 294–301.

26. Daniel Kahneman and Jack L. Knetsch, "Valuing Public Goods: The Purchase of Moral Satisfaction," *Journal of Environmental Economics and Management* 22 (January 1992): 57–70.

27. Jacquelyn A. Ottman, Edwin R. Stafford, and Cathy L. Hartman, "Avoiding Green Marketing Myopia: Ways to Improve Consumer Appeal for Environmentally Preferable Products," *Environment: Science and Policy for Sustainable Development* 48, no. 5 (2006): 22–36.

28. Peattie, "Golden Goose or Wild Goose?"

29. Valarie A. Zeithaml, "Consumer Perceptions of Price, Quality, and Value: A Means-End Model and Synthesis of Evidence," *The Journal of Marketing* 52, no. 3 (1988): 2–22.

30. Kent B. Monroe, *Pricing: Making Profitable Decisions* (New York: McGraw-Hill, 1990), 46.

31. Jillian Sweeney, Geoffrey Soutar, Alma Whiteley, and Lester Johnson, "Generating Consumption Value Items: A Parallel Interviewing Process Approach," in *AP—Asia Pacific Advances in Consumer Research*, eds. Russel Belk and Ronald Groves, vol. 2 (Provo, UT: Association for Consumer Research, 1996), 108–15.

32. James C. Anderson and James A. Narus, "Business Marketing: Understand What Customers Value," *Harvard Business Review* 76 (1998): 53–67.

33. Jagdish N. Sheth, Bruce I. Newman, and Barbara L. Gross, "Why We Buy What We Buy: A Theory of Consumption Values," *Journal of Business Research* 22, no. 2 (1991): 159–70.

34. Jillian Sweeney and Geoffrey Soutar, "Consumer Perceived Value: The Development of a Multiple Item Scale," *Journal of Retailing* 77, no. 2 (2001): 203–20.

35. Ibid.

36. Ibid.

37. Ibid.

38. Ibid.

39. Ottman, Stafford, and Hartman, "Avoiding Green Marketing Myopia."

40. *Oxford Living Dictionaries*, s.v. "complementarity," https://en.oxforddictionaries.com/definition/complementarity.

41. Sharon Shavitt, "The Role of Attitude Objects in Attitude Functions," *Journal of Experimental Social Psychology* 26, no. 2 (1990): 124–48.

42. Olli T. Ahtola, "Hedonic and Utilitarian Aspects of Consumer Behavior: An Attitudinal Perspective," *ACR North American Advances* 12 (1985): 7–10; Barry J. Babin, William R. Darden, and Mitch Griffin, "Work and/or Fun: Measuring Hedonic and Utilitarian Shopping Value," *Journal of Consumer Research* 20, no. 4 (1994): 644–56; Elizabeth C. Hirschman and Morris B. Holbrook, "Hedonic Consumption: Emerging Concepts, Methods and Propositions," *The Journal of Marketing* 46, no. 3 (1982): 92–101; Morris B. Holbrook and Elizabeth C. Hirschman, "The Experiential Aspects of Consumption: Consumer Fantasies, Feelings, and Fun," *Journal of Consumer Research* 9, no. 2 (1982): 132–40; Brian Lofman, "Elements of Experiential Consumption: An Exploratory Study," *ACR North American Advances* 18 (1991): 729–35.

43. Michal Strahilevitz and John G. Myers, "Donations to Charity as Purchase Incentives: How Well They Work May Depend on What You Are Trying to Sell," *Journal of Consumer Research* 24, no. 4 (1998): 434–46.

44. C. Whan Park, Bernard J. Jaworski, and Deborah J. MacInnis,

"Strategic Brand Concept-Image Management," *The Journal of Marketing* 50, no. 4 (1986): 135–45.

45. J. Brock Smith and Mark Colgate, "Customer Value Creation: A Practical Framework," *Journal of Marketing Theory and Practice* 15, no. 1 (2007): 7–23.

46. Sharon Shavitt, "The Role of Attitude Objects in Attitude Functions," *Journal of Experimental Social Psychology* 26, no. 2 (1990): 124–48.

47. John Peloza and Jingzhi Shang, "How Can Corporate Social Responsibility Activities Create Value for Stakeholders? A Systematic Review," *Journal of the Academy of Marketing Science* 39, no. 1 (2011): 117–35.

48. Michal Strahilevitz and John G. Myers, "Donations to Charity as Purchase Incentives: How Well They Work May Depend on What You Are Trying to Sell," *Journal of Consumer Research* 24, no. 4 (1998): 434–46.

49. Ibid.

50. Erica Mina Okada, "Justification Effects on Consumer Choice of Hedonic and Utilitarian Goods," *Journal of Marketing Research* 42, no. 1 (2005): 43–53.

51. Sweeney, Soutar, Whiteley, and Johnson, "Generating Consumption Value Items."

52. Ottman, Stafford, and Hartman, "Avoiding Green Marketing Myopia."

53. Paul Bennett, *Psychology and Health Promotion* (London: McGraw-Hill, 1997).

54. Daniel C. Esty, "Environmental Protection in the Information Age," *New York University Law Review* 79 (2004): 115.

55. Kahneman and Knetsch, "Valuing Public Goods."

56. R. Julie Irwin and Joan Scattone Spira, "Anomalies in the Values for Consumer Goods with Environmental Attributes," *Journal of Consumer Psychology* 6, no. 4 (1997): 339–63.

57. Lise Magnier, Jan Schoormans, and Ruth Mugge, "Judging a Product by Its Cover: Packaging Sustainability and Perceptions of Quality in Food Products," *Food Quality and Preference* 53 (2016): 132–42.

58. Iris Vermeir and Wim Verbeke, "Sustainable Food Consumption: Exploring the Consumer 'Attitude–Behavioral Intention' Gap," *Journal of Agricultural and Environmental Ethics* 19, no. 2 (2006): 169–94; Peter C. Verhoef, "Explaining Purchases of Organic Meat by Dutch Consumers," *European Review of Agricultural Economics* 32, no. 2 (2005): 245–67; Yeonshin Kim and Sejung Marina Choi, "Antecedents of Green Purchase Behavior: An Examination of Collectivism, Environmental Concern, and PCE," *ACR North American Advances* 32 (2005): 592–99.

59. Nancy Furlow, "Greenwashing in the New Millennium," *Journal of Applied Business and Economics* 10, no. 6 (2009): 22–25.

60. Ken Peattie and Martin Charter, "Green Marketing," in *The Marketing Book*, ed. Michael J. Baker, 5th ed. (Oxford and Burlington, MA: Butterworth-Heinemann, 2003), 726–56.

61. James Wimbush, Jon Shepard, and Steven Markham, "An Empirical Examination of the Relationship between Ethical Climate and Ethical Behavior from Multiple Levels of Analysis," *Journal of Business Ethics* 16, no. 16 (1997): 1705–16.

62. Jaap Jelsma and Marjolijn Knot, "Designing Environmentally Efficient Services: A 'Script' Approach," *The Journal of Sustainable Product Design* 2, no. 3 (2002): 119–30; Dan Lockton, David Harrison, and Neville Stanton, "Making the User More Efficient: Design for Sustainable Behaviour," *International Journal of Sustainable Engineering* 1, no. 1 (2008): 3–8; Ida Nilstad Pettersen and Casper Boks, "The Ethics in Balancing Control and Freedom When Engineering Solutions for Sustainable Behaviour," *International Journal of Sustainable Engineering* 1, no. 4 (2008): 287–97; Tracy Bhamra, Debra Lilley, and Tang, "Design for Sustainable Behaviour: Using Products to Change Consumer Behaviour," *The Design Journal* 14, no. 4 (2011): 427–45.

63. Joseph Zammit-Lucia, "Why Green Brands Are Failing to Capture Public Attention," *The Guardian*, July 5, 2013, https://www.theguardian.com/sustainable-business/green-brands-fail-public-appeal?goback=.gde_145633_member_265867854#.

Chapter 3

1. Mike Monticello, "Car Brands Ranked by Owner Satisfaction," *Consumer Reports*, December 22, 2016, http://www.consumerreports.org/car-reliability-owner-satisfaction/car-brands-ranked-by-satisfaction/; Stephen Edelstein, "Tesla Tops Consumer Reports' Customer Satisfaction Index," Green Car Reports, December 23, 2016, http://www.greencarreports.com/news/1107982_tesla-tops-consumer-reports-customer-satisfaction-index.

2. Mark Rechtin, "Tesla Model S P85d Earns Top Road Test Score," *Consumer Reports*, October 20, 2015, http://www.consumerreports.org/cro/cars/tesla-model-s-p85d-earns-top-road-test-score.

3. Ibid.

4. David A. Garvin, "What Does 'hltoduct Quality' Really Mean?," *Sloan Management Review* (Fall 1984): 25–43.

5. Maria K. Magnusson, Anne Arvola, Ulla-Kaisa Koivisto Hursti,

Lars Åberg, and Per-Olow Sjödén, "Attitudes towards Organic Foods among Swedish Consumers," *British Food Journal* 103, no. 3 (2001): 209–27; Renée Shaw Hughner, Pierre McDonagh, Andrea Prothero, Clifford J. Shultz, and Julie Stanton, "Who Are Organic Food Consumers? A Compilation and Review of Why People Purchase Organic Food," *Journal of Consumer Behaviour* 6, no. 2–3 (2007): 94–110; Helene Hill and Fidelma Lynchehaun, "Organic Milk: Attitudes and Consumption Patterns," *British Food Journal* 104, no. 7 (2002): 526–42.

6. Laurence Fillion and Stacey Arazi, "Does Organic Food Taste Better? A Claim Substantiation Approach," *Nutrition & Food Science* 32, no. 4 (2002): 153–57.

7. Aurelice B. Oliveira, Carlos F. H. Moura, Enéas Gomes-Filho, Claudia A. Marco, Laurent Urban, and Maria Raquel A. Miranda, "The Impact of Organic Farming on Quality of Tomatoes Is Associated to Increased Oxidative Stress during Fruit Development," *PLoS One* 8, no. 2 (2013): e56354.

8. Alfred A. Marcus, *Innovations in Sustainability* (Cambridge, UK: Cambridge University Press, 2015): 137.

9. Magali A. Delmas, Matthew E. Kahn, and Stephen L. Locke, "The Private and Social Consequences of Purchasing an Electric Vehicle and Solar Panels: Evidence from California," *Research in Economics* 71, no. 2 (2017): 225–35.

10. This could be because BMW makes an expensive, high-performance hybrid vehicle (i8) and a more moderately priced all-electric vehicle (i3). If the sample contains mostly buyers of the i3, we would not expect vehicle performance to be a motivating factor.

11. "Forums," Tesla, https://forums.tesla.com/forums.

12. John Rudolf, "A Bear Hug? Nissan Ad Raises Eyebrows," *New York Times*, September 10, 2010, https://green.blogs.nytimes.com/2010/09/10/hugged-by-a-polar-bear-nissan-ad-raises-eyebrows/.

13. Joe Romm, "Wow! Watch the Nissan Leaf's Provocative, Irreverent Polar Bear Ad, Which Markets Global Warming," ThinkProgress, September 11, 2010, https://thinkprogress.org/wow-watch-the-nissan-leafs-provocative-irreverent-polar-bear-ad-which-markets-global-warming-7028945a4450/.

14. John Voelcker, "2018 Nissan Leaf Teaser: Electric Car Will 'Amaze Your Senses,'" Green Car Reports, August 23, 2017, http://www.greencarreports.com/news/1112268_2018-nissan-leaf-teaser-electric-car-will-amaze-your-senses.

15. Paul Dourish, *Where the Action Is: The Foundations of Embodied Interaction* (Cambridge, MA: MIT Press, 2004).

16. "LED Basics," Office of Energy Efficiency and Renewable Energy, US Department of Energy, https://www.energy.gov/eere/ssl/led-basics.

17. Omar Isaac Asensio and Magali A. Delmas, "The Effectiveness of US Energy Efficiency Building Labels," *Nature Energy* 2, article no. 17033 (2017): 1–8.

18. S. Abbaszadeh et al., "Occupant Satisfaction with Indoor Environmental Quality in Green Buildings," Center for the Built Environment (2006): 365–70.

19. William J. Fisk, "Health and Productivity Gains from Better Indoor Environments and Their Relationship with Building Energy Efficiency," *Annual Review of Energy and the Environment* 25, no. 1 (2000): 537–66.

20. Juan Ren and Yu Liu, "Study on High-Performance Office Buildings" (paper presented at the Applied Mechanics and Materials Conference, 2012): 1025–28.

21. Piet M. A. Eichholtz, Nils Kok, and John M. Quigley, "Ecological Responsiveness and Corporate Real Estate," *Business & Society* 55, no. 3 (2016): 330–60.

22. Carole Jacques, "Driven by Higher Rents and Values, Green Buildings Market Grows to $260 Billion," Lux Research Inc., October 29, 2014, http://www.luxresearchinc.com/news-and-events/press-releases /read/driven-higher-rents-and-values-green-buildings-market-grows-260.

23. Stephen A. Jones and John Mandyck, *World Green Building Trends 2016* (New York: Dodge Data & Analytics, 2016).

24. Franz Fuerst and Patrick McAllister, "Green Noise or Green Value? Measuring the Effects of Environmental Certification on Office Values," *Real Estate Economics* 39, no. 1 (2011): 45–69.

25. J. K. Gershenson, G. J. Prasad, and Y. Zhang, "Product Modularity: Definitions and Benefits," *Journal of Engineering Design* 14, no. 3 (2003): 295–313.

26. John McManus, "Kb Home, KTGY, and Builder to Team on Innovation Program," Builder Online, April 21, 2016, http://www.builder online.com/builder-100/strategy/kb-home-builder-to-team-on-innovation -program_o.

27. The KB team sees modularity, componentization, and a carefully engineered real-time and over-time interplay between the envelope and a home's systems as its strategic pathway to learning how a house can be a home of the future in 2020, 2050, and beyond. John McManus, "A Modular Site-Built Hybrid," *Builder Online*, September 9, 2016, http://www .builderonline.com/greenbuild-kb-home-projekt-sponsor-pavilion/a -modular-site-built-hybrid_o.

28. Jennifer Castenson, "The Flexible Space of the Future: Green-build KB Home ProjeKt Partner Virginia Tech Demonstrates Its Movable Wall," *Builder Online*, November 1, 2016, http://www.builderonline.com/design/the-flexible-space-of-the-future_o.

29. Jennifer Castenson, "How One Home Speaks to Today's Buyer," *Builder Online*, November 14, 2016, http://www.builderonline.com/design/projects/how-one-home-speaks-to-todays-buyer_o.

30. Brian Shackel, "Usability—Context, Framework, Definition, Design and Evaluation," in *Human Factors for Informatics Usability*, ed. B. Shackel and S. Richardson (Cambridge, UK: Cambridge University Press, 1991), 21–38.

31. https://removeandreplace.com/2015/03/04/refrigerator-temperature-control-dial-what-do-the-numbers-relate-to-cold-colder-coldest/.

32. Willett Kempton, "Two Theories of Home Heat Control," *Cognitive Science* 10, no. 1 (1986): 75–90.

33. Sharon A. Davison and Marc M. Sebrechts, "Why Can't I Adjust My Refrigerator's Temperature?: Or What's Wrong with My Mental Model?," in *Posters and Short Talks of the 1992 SIGCHI Conference on Human Factors in Computing Systems* (New York: ACM, 1992), pp. 8-8.

34. Tracy Bhamra, Debra Lilley, and Tang Tang, "Design for Sustainable Behaviour: Using Products to Change Consumer Behaviour," *The Design Journal* 14, no. 4 (2011): 427–45.

35. "EcoFridge Saves Time and Money," Autodesk, https://sustainabilityworkshop.autodesk.com/project-gallery/ecofridge-saves-time-and-energy.

36. Ibid.

37. Renee Wever, Jasper Van Kuijk, and Casper Boks, "User-Centred Design for Sustainable Behaviour," *International Journal of Sustainable Engineering* 1, no. 1 (2008): 9–20.

38. Ibid.

39. Ibid.

40. Several units may be used to measure the durability of a product according to its field of application, such as years of existence, hours of use, and operational cycles. Tim Cooper, *Beyond Recycling: The Longer Life Option* (London: The New Economics Foundation, 1994).

41. http://corporate.ppg.com/Media/Newsroom/2014/Architects-cite-durability-as-most-important-green; Jessica Lyons Hardcastle, "Durability 'Most Important Green Building Product Attribute,'" Environmental Leader, October 24, 2014, https://www.environmentalleader.com/2014/10/durability-most-important-green-building-product-attribute/.

42. Alex Wilson, "Durability: A Key Component of Green Building," Building Green, November 1, 2005, https://www.buildinggreen.com /feature/durability-key-component-green-building.

43. Macaela Mackenzie, "The Puffer Coat Gets a Stylish Update Thanks to Patagonia and Reformation," *Allure*, October 6, 2016, http:// www.allure.com/story/patagonia-reformation-collaboration.

44. "Patagonia's Mission Statement," Patagonia, http://www.patago nia.com/company-info.html.

45. Rosie Dalton, "Here Are Some Tips from Patagonia Which Will Make You a More Conscious Shopper," http://wellmadeclothes.com/arti cles/HereAreSomeTipsFromPatagoniaWhichWillMakeYouAMoreCon sciousShopper/.

46. Kate Fletcher, "Durability, Fashion, Sustainability: The Processes and Practices of Use," *Fashion Practice* 4, no. 2 (2012): 221–38.

47. Nathan McAlone, "This Chart Shows Exactly How Insane Air-bnb's Growth Has Been over the Past 5 Years," Business Insider, September 8, 2015, http://www.businessinsider.com/airbnbs-summer-reach-has -grown-by-353-times-in-5-years-2015-9.

48. Lauren Sherman, "Why Fashion Insiders Are Buzzing about Patagonia," *Wall Street Journal*, January 9, 2015, https://www.wsj.com/articles /why-fashion-insiders-are-buzzing-about-patagonia-1420825704.

49. Elizabeth Cline, "The Power of Buying Less by Buying Better," *The Atlantic*, February 16, 2016, https://www.theatlantic.com/business /archive/2016/02/buying-less-by-buying-better/462639/.

50. Kelsey Ryan, "The Bottom Line: Patagonia, North Face, and the Myth of Green Consumerism," Groundswell, July 31, 2014, https:// groundswell.org/the-bottom-line-patagonia-north-face-and-the-myth-of -green-consumerism/.

51. "Patagonia Repair & Care Guides," Patagonia, http://www.pata gonia.com/worn-wear-repairs/.

52. PYMNTS, "Retail Growth by Not Growing," PYMNTS, December 2, 2015, http://www.pymnts.com/in-depth/2015/retail-growth-by-not -growing/.

53. "Product Groups and Criteria," Environment, European Commission, http://ec.europa.eu/environment/ecolabel/products-groups-and -criteria.html.

54. "American Time Use Survey," Bureau of Labor Statistics, US Department of Labor, https://www.bls.gov/tus/.

55. Julie B. Herbstman, Andreas Sjödin, Matthew Kurzon, Sally A. Lederman, Richard S. Jones, Virginia Rauh, Larry L. Needham et al.,

"Prenatal Exposure to PBDEs and Neurodevelopment," *Environmental Health Perspectives* 118, no. 5 (2010): 712.

56. Juho Hamari, Mimmi Sjöklint, and Antti Ukkonen, "The Sharing Economy: Why People Participate in Collaborative Consumption," *Journal of the Association for Information Science and Technology* 67, no. 9 (2016): 2047–59.

57. Koen Frenken, "Sustainability Perspectives on the Sharing Economy," *Environmental Innovation and Societal Transitions* (2017): 1–2.

58. Harald Heinrichs, "Sharing Economy: A Potential New Pathway to Sustainability," *Gaia* 22, no. 4 (2013): 228.

59. Rachel Botsman and Roo Rogers, *What's Mine Is Yours: The Rise of Collaborative Consumption* (New York: HarperCollins, 2011).

60. David Spiegel, "Uber's Books Still Top Secret, but Its Biggest Weakness Isn't," CNBC, June 8, 2016, http://www.cnbc.com/2016/06/08/ubers-66-billion-valuation-may-ride-on-shaky-foundation.html.

61. Sara Ashley O'Brien, "Airbnb's Valuation Soars to $30 Billion," CNN, August 8, 2016, http://money.cnn.com/2016/08/08/technology/airbnb-30-billion-valuation/.

62. Julia, "5-Year Anniversary Remarks from Uber Ceo Travis Kalanick," Uber, June 4, 2015, https://newsroom.uber.com/5-years-travis-kalanick/; Anne Brice, "Uber and Lyft to Get Environmental Scrutiny," Berkeley News, November 20, 2015, http://news.berkeley.edu/2015/11/20/environmental-impacts-uber-lyft/.

63. "New Study Reveals a Greener Way to Travel: Airbnb Community Shows Environmental Benefits of Home Sharing," Airbnb, July 31, 2014, https://www.airbnb.com/press/news/new-study-reveals-a-greener-way-to-travel-airbnb-community-shows-environmental-benefits-of-home-sharing.

64. Tracey Lien, "Uber Is on Growth Fast Track, Leaked Document Shows," *Los Angeles Times*, August 21, 2015, http://www.latimes.com/business/la-fi-0822-uber-revenue-20150822-story.html.

65. McAlone, "This Chart Shows."

66. Lisa Goetz, "4 Reasons Why Riders Choose Uber," Investopedia, June 30, 2014, http://www.investopedia.com/articles/markets/063016/4-reasons-why-riders-choose-uber.asp.

67. Jean Folger, "The Pros and Cons of Using Airbnb," Investopedia, March 28, 2014, http://www.investopedia.com/articles/personal-finance/032814/pros-and-cons-using-airbnb.asp.

68. Juliet Schor, "Debating the Sharing Economy," *Journal of Self-Governance and Management Economics* 4, no. 3 (2016): 7–22.

69. Hans Nijland and Jordy van Meerkerk, "Mobility and Environmental Impacts of Car Sharing in the Netherlands," *Environmental Innovation and Societal Transitions* 23 (2017): 84–91.

70. Elliot W. Martin and Susan A. Shaheen, "Greenhouse Gas Emission Impacts of Carsharing in North America," *IEEE Transactions on Intelligent Transportation Systems* 12, no. 4 (2011): 1074–86.

71. Juho Hamari, Mimmi Sjöklint, and Antti Ukkonen, "The Sharing Economy: Why People Participate in Collaborative Consumption," *Journal of the Association for Information Science and Technology* 67, no. 9 (2016): 2047–59; Lars Böcker and Toon Meelen, "Sharing for People, Planet or Profit? Analysing Motivations for Intended Sharing Economy Participation," *Environmental Innovation and Societal Transitions* 23 (2017): 28–39.

72. Yuliya Voytenko Palgan, Lucie Zvolska, and Oksana Mont, "Sustainability Framings of Accommodation Sharing," *Environmental Innovation and Societal Transitions* 23 (2017): 70–83.

73. Ibon Galarraga Gallastegui, "The Use of Eco-Labels: A Review of the Literature," *Environmental Policy and Governance* 12, no. 6 (2002): 316–31; Ken Peattie and Andrew Crane, "Green Marketing: Legend, Myth, Farce or Prophesy?," *Qualitative Market Research: An International Journal* 8, no. 4 (2005): 357–70.

74. Magali A. Delmas, Olivier Gergaud, and Jinghui Lim, "Does Organic Wine Taste Better? An Analysis of Experts' Ratings," *Journal of Wine Economics* 11, no. 3 (2016): 329–54.

75. Magali A. Delmas and Laura E. Grant, "Eco-Labeling Strategies and Price-Premium: The Wine Industry Puzzle," *Business & Society* 53, no. 1 (2014): 6–44.

76. Ibid.

77. George E. Newman, Margarita Gorlin, and Ravi Dhar, "When Going Green Backfires: How Firm Intentions Shape the Evaluation of Socially Beneficial Product Enhancements," *Journal of Consumer Research* 41, no. 3 (2014): 823–39.

78. Tilde Herrera, "Want to Sell a Green Product? Don't Call It Green," *GreenBiz* (blog), January 30, 2012, https://www.greenbiz.com/blog/2012/01/30/want-sell-green-product-dont-call-it-green.

Chapter 4

1. Alex Taylor III, "The Birth of the Prius," *Fortune*, March 6, 2006, http://archive.fortune.com/magazines/fortune/fortune_archive/2006/03/06/8370702/index.htm.

2. Kelly Carter, "'Hybrid' Cars Were Oscars' Politically Correct Ride,"

USA Today, March 30, 2003, http://usatoday30.usatoday.com/life/2003 -03-30-hybrids_x.htm.

3. Daniel Miller, "How the Oscars and Hollywood Turned Their Backs on Green Cars," *The Hollywood Reporter,* http://www.hollywood reporter.com/news/oscars-2012-arrivals-hollywoods-green-cars-chevy -volt-fisker-karma-294814.

4. "The Top-10 Bestselling Cars in California in 2014," *Los Angeles Times,* http://www.latimes.com/business/autos/la-fi-hy-top-10-best-sell ing-cars-california-2014-pictures-photogallery.html.

5. Jeremy S. Brooks and Charlie Wilson, "The Influence of Contextual Cues on the Perceived Status of Consumption-Reducing Behavior," *Ecological Economics* 117 (2015): 108–17.

6. Ibid.

7. Tian Zhang, "China Slaps 10 Percent Tax on Luxury Cars to Curb Conspicuous Consumption," *Financial Review,* http://www.afr.com /business/transport/automobile/china-slaps-10-per-cent-tax-on-luxury -cars-to-curb-conspicuous-consumption-20161130-gt1d3c#ixzz4RjU MT2zD.

8. Steven E. Sexton and Alison L. Sexton, "Conspicuous Conservation: The Prius Halo and Willingness to Pay for Environmental Bona Fides," *Journal of Environmental Economics and Management* 67, no. 3 (2014): 303–17.

9. Pat Barclay, "Trustworthiness and Competitive Altruism Can Also Solve the "Tragedy of the Commons," *Evolution and Human Behavior* 25, no. 4 (2004): 209–20.

10. Vladas Griskevicius, Joshua M. Tybur, Jill M. Sundie, Robert B. Cialdini, Geoffrey F. Miller, and Douglas T. Kenrick, "Blatant Benevolence and Conspicuous Consumption: When Romantic Motives Elicit Strategic Costly Signals," *Journal of Personality and Social Psychology* 93, no. 1 (2007): 85; Shari Miller, Jennifer E. Lansford, Philip Costanzo, Patrick S. Malone, Megan Golonka, and Ley A. Killeya-Jones, "Early Adolescent Romantic Partner Status, Peer Standing, and Problem Behaviors," *The Journal of Early Adolescence* 29, no. 6 (2009): 839–61.

11. Charlie L. Hardy and Mark Van Vugt, "Nice Guys Finish First: The Competitive Altruism Hypothesis," *Personality and Social Psychology Bulletin* 32, no. 10 (2006): 1402–13; Herbert Gintis, Eric Alden Smith, and Samuel Bowles, "Costly Signaling and Cooperation," *Journal of Theoretical Biology* 213, no. 1 (2001): 103–19; Pat Barclay and Robb Willer, "Partner Choice Creates Competitive Altruism in Humans," *Proceedings of the Royal Society of London B: Biological Sciences* 274, no. 1610 (2007): 749–53.

12. François Rabelais, *Gargantua and Pantagruel, Fourth Book, Chapter VIII* (Overland Park, KS: Digireads, 2011).

13. Noah J. Goldstein, Robert B. Cialdini, and Vladas Griskevicius, "A Room with a Viewpoint: Using Social Norms to Motivate Environmental Conservation in Hotels," *Journal of Consumer Research* 35, no. 3 (2008): 472–82.

14. Ibid.

15. Richard Conniff, "Using Peer Pressure as a Tool to Promote Greener Choices," Yale Environment 360, April 16, 2009, http://e360 .yale.edu/features/using_peer_pressure_as_a_tool__to_promote _greener_choices.

16. Adam Corner, "Peer Pressure Plays a Key Role in Low-Carbon Living," *The Guardian*, March 30, 2010, https://www.theguardian .com/environment/cif-green/2010/mar/30/green-peer-pressure; Adam Vaughan, "Shoppers Choose Green Products to Improve Social Status, Says Study," *The Guardian*, March 29, 2010, https://www.theguardian .com/environment/2010/mar/29/green-products-social-status.

17. Per Espen Stoknes, *What We Think About When We Try Not to Think About Global Warming: Toward a New Psychology of Climate Action* (White River Junction, VT: Chelsea Green Publishing, 2015).

18. Carter, "Politically Correct Ride"; Taylor, "The Birth of the Prius"; "On Oscar Night, It's Not What You Wear, It's What You Drive; Celebrities to Arrive at Red Carpet in Alternative Fuel Vehicles," Business Wire, March 18, 2003, http://www.businesswire.com/news/home /20030318005302/en/Oscar-Night-Wear-Drive-Celebrities-Arrive -Red; Jim Henry, "Oscar Night Star Power Provides Priceless Publicity for the Prius," *Automotive News*, October 29, 2007, http://www.autonews.com /article/20071029/ANA09/710290321/oscar-night-star-power-provides -priceless-publicity-for-the-prius.

19. Henry, "Priceless Publicity for the Prius." The main person who made Priuses available for the first time at the 2003 Oscars was Mike Sullivan, a Toyota dealer. Erin Courtenay, "Red Carpet-Green Cars Campaign Wins Big at the Emmy Awards," Tree Hugger, http://www .treehugger.com/culture/red-carpet-green-cars-campaign-wins-big-at -the-emmy-awards.html. In addition, Toyota partnered with Global Green, which used Priuses to transport celebrities to their green-carpet events during the Academy Awards. As reporter Jim Henry said, "The publicity from that Oscar night and from several similar efforts at other Hollywood photo opportunities helped put the previously obscure Toyota Prius on the nation's radar screen, even though the Prius had vir-

tually no conventional national advertising." "Priceless Publicity for the Prius."

20. Lisa Pickoff-White, "Stars Take Hybrid Cars to the Red Carpet," UPI, February 27, 2005, http://www.upi.com/Stars-take-hybrid-cars-to-the-red-carpet/95141109526517/.

21. Ibid.

22. Marty Padgett, "Toyota Prius: A Brief History in Time," Green Car Reports, http://www.greencarreports.com/news/1014178_toyota-prius-a-brief-history-in-time; Pickoff-White, "Stars Take Hybrid Cars"; "Toyota Prius," Carsalesbase.com, http://carsalesbase.com/us-car-sales-data/toyota/toyota-prius/; US sales doubled to 53,991 in 2004 and nearly doubled again to 107,897 the following year—about 60% of global Prius sales.

23. "Six Celebrities and Places That Chose Artificial Grass," Artificial Grass Superstore, http://artificialgrasssuperstore.com/6-celebrities-and-famous-places-who-chose-artificial-grass/.

24. Synthetic Turf Council, "Synthetic Turf Becomes Latest Celebrity Trend," PR Newswire, http://www.prnewswire.com/news-releases/synthetic-turf-becomes-latest-celebrity-trend-122861104.html.

25. "Why Artificial Grass Is a Must Have for Celebrities!," Artificial Grass Direct, April 27, 2016, https://www.artificialgrass-direct.com/why-artificial-grass-is-a-must-have-for-celebrities/.

26. John Koblin, "Reformation, an Eco Label the Cool Girls Pick," *New York Times*, December 17, 2014, https://www.nytimes.com/2014/12/18/style/reformation-an-eco-label-the-cool-girls-pick.html.

27. Elizabeth Zelesney, "Net-a-Porter Seeks Eco-Halo with Runway to Green Collaboration," *Luxury Daily*, April 1, 2011, https://www.luxurydaily.com/net-a-porter-seeks-eco-halo-with-runway-to-green-collaboration/.

28. Haya El Nassar, "What's in Style: Eco-Friendly, Green Fashion," *USA Today*, April 28, 2013, http://www.usatoday.com/story/money/business/2013/04/28/the-rise-of-green-fashion/1996773/.

29. Imran Amed, "Stella McCartney: Change Agent," *The Business of Fashion*, March 29, 2015, https://www.businessoffashion.com/articles/people/stella-mccartney-change-agent.

30. Ingrid Schmidt, "Reformation's Yael Aflalo Brings Cachet of Cool to Eco-Friendly Fashion," *Los Angeles Times*, April 19, 2015, http://www.latimes.com/fashion/la-ig-reformation-20150419-story.html.

31. Chavie Lieber, "Reformation Founder Yael Aflalo on Sustainable Fashion and Starting Over," Racked, November 26, 2014, http://www.racked.com/2014/11/26/7567391/yael-aflalo-reformation.

32. Lieber, "Reformation Founder Yael Aflalo."

33. "Sustainable Practices," Reformation, https://www.thereformation
.com/whoweare#factoryLife.

34. Chantel Fernandez, "Reformation Debuts a Lower-Price Line,"
Fashionista, January 26, 2015, http://fashionista.com/2015/01/reformation
-lower-price-line-obviously.

35. Lieber, "Reformation Founder Yael Aflalo."

36. Ibid.

37. Carren Jao, "How One Apparel Brand Is Bringing Style to Sustainable Clothing," *Entreprenuer*, May 26, 2015, https://www.entrepreneur
.com/article/245918.

38. Fernandez, "Reformation Debuts."

39. Emily Holt, "Meet the Woman Behind Cool Ethical Label Reformation," *Vogue*, November 4, 2015, http://www.vogue.com/article/refor
mation-eco-fashion-ethical-label.

40. Holt, "Meet the Woman"; Sarah Wasilak, "The 1 Label the Stars
Have Been Wearing All Summer Long," PopSugar, August 3, 2015,
https://www.popsugar.com/fashion/Celebrities-Wearing-Reformation
-37897488?stream_view=1#opening-slide; Adrianna Barrionuevo, "See
the Latest Celebrity Bridesmaid to Look Stunning in Reformation," Who
What Wear, September 13, 2016, http://www.whowhatwear.com/dianna
-agron-reformation-bridesmaid-dress/.

41. "Red Carpet Green Dress," Red Carpet Green Dress, https://red
carpetgreendress.com/home/.

42. Stephanie Chon, "Reformation's RefRecycle Program Just Made
Donating Clothes Easy & Rewarding," *Bustle*, July 28, 2015, https://www
.bustle.com/articles/100565-reformations-refrecycle-program-just-made
-donating-clothes-easy-rewarding.

43. Margaret Badore, "Reformation Has Made Recycling Clothing
Insanely Easy," TreeHugger, August 27, 2015, http://www.treehugger.com
/sustainable-fashion/reformation-has-made-recycling-clothing-insanely
-easy.html.

44. Their online store really helped their sales pick up: "If there is
one place where Reformation really picked up steam in the last year, it
is its online store. As late as February 2013, Reformation did only about
$19,000 in sales online. John Koblin, "Reformation, an Eco Label the
Cool Girls Pick," *New York Times*, December 17, 2014, https://www.nytimes
.com/2014/12/18/style/reformation-an-eco-label-the-cool-girls-pick
.html; Barrionuevo, "See the Latest Celebrity Bridesmaid."

45. Manfred Milinski, Dirk Semmann, and H. Krambeck, "Donors
to Charity Gain in Both Indirect Reciprocity and Political Reputation,"

Proceedings of the Royal Society of London B: Biological Sciences 269, no. 1494 (2002): 881–83; Pat Barclay, "Trustworthiness and Competitive Altruism Can Also Solve the 'Tragedy of the Commons,'" *Evolution and Human Behavior* 25, no. 4 (2004): 209–20; Charlie L. Hardy and Mark Van Vugt, "Nice Guys Finish First: The Competitive Altruism Hypothesis," *Personality and Social Psychology Bulletin* 32, no. 10 (2006): 1402–13.

46. David Plotz, "Competitive Philanthropy," *Slate*, February 20, 2006, http://www.slate.com/articles/life/the_slate60/2006/02/competitive _philanthropy.html.

47. "The Giving Pledge," The Giving Pledge, https://givingpledge .org/.

48. Nic Phillips, "Best New Design: BMW's i-Series Are No Concept Cars—the Future Is Already Here (and Reasonably Priced)," CultureMap, January 20, 2014, http://houston.culturemap.com/news/innovation/01 -20-14-best-new-design-bmws-i-series-are-no-concept-cars-the-future-is -already-here-and-reasonably-priced/#slide=0.

49. Steven E. Sexton and Alison L. Sexton, "Conspicuous Conservation: The Prius Halo and Willingness to Pay for Environmental Bona Fides," *Journal of Environmental Economics and Management* 67, no. 3 (2014): 303–17.

50. Stephen Dubner, "Hey Baby, Is That a Prius You're Driving?," July 7, 2011, in *Freakonomics Radio*, podcast audio, http://freakonomics .com/podcast/hey-baby-is-that-a-prius-youre-driving/.

51. Michael S. Delgado and Neha Khanna, "Voluntary Pollution Abatement and Regulation," *Agricultural and Resource Economics Review* 44, no. 1 (2015): 1–20.

52. Matthew E. Kahn, "Do Greens Drive Hummers or Hybrids? Environmental Ideology as a Determinant of Consumer Choice," *Journal of Environmental Economics and Management* 54, no. 2 (2007): 129–45.

53. Bryan Bollinger and Kenneth Gillingham, "Peer Effects in the Diffusion of Solar Photovoltaic Panels," *Marketing Science* 31, no. 6 (2012): 900–912.

54. Ibid.

55. Ibid.

56. Samuel R. Dastrup et al., "Understanding the Solar Home Price Premium: Electricity Generation and 'Green' Social Status," *European Economic Review* 56, no. 5 (2012): 961–73.

57. Robert H. Frank, *Luxury Fever: Why Money Fails to Satisfy in an Era of Excess* (New York: Simon and Schuster, 2001).

58. Micheline Maynard, Nick Bunkley, and M. M. Chapman, "Say

'Hybrid' and Many People Will Hear 'Prius,'" *New York Times,* July 4, 2007, http://www.nytimes.com/2007/07/04/business/04hybrid.html.

59. Vladas Griskevicius, Joshua M. Tybur, and Bram Van den Bergh, "Going Green to Be Seen: Status, Reputation, and Conspicuous Conservation," *Journal of Personality and Social Psychology* 98, no. 3 (2010): 392.

60. Magali A. Delmas and Neil Lessem, "Saving Power to Conserve Your Reputation? The Effectiveness of Private versus Public Information," *Journal of Environmental Economics and Management* 67, no. 3 (2014): 353–70.

61. Corinna Fischer, "Feedback on Household Electricity Consumption: A Tool for Saving Energy?," *Energy Efficiency* 1, no. 1 (2008): 79–104.

62. Ayelet Gneezy, Alex Imas, Amber Brown, Leif D. Nelson, and Michael I. Norton, "Paying to Be Nice: Consistency and Costly Prosocial Behavior," *Management Science* 58, no. 1 (2012): 179–87.

63. Simon Gaechter and Ernst Fehr, "Fairness and Retaliation: The Economics of Reciprocity," *Critical Studies in Economic Institutions* 14, no. 3 (2003): 285–307; Simon Gaechter, Elke Renner, and Martin Sefton, "The Long-Run Benefits of Punishment," *Science* 322, no. 5907 (2008): 1510.

64. Sharon Bernstein, "Beverly Hills Fined for Not Conserving Enough Water in Drought," Reuters, October 30, 2015, http://www.reuters.com/article/us-california-drought-fines-idUSKCN0SO2IY2015 1031.

65. Matt Stevens, "Beverly Hills Put a Spotlight on Its Celebrity Water Wasters—and It Worked," *Los Angeles Times,* March 14, 2016, http://www.latimes.com/local/westside/la-me-beverly-hills-water-20160314-story.html.

66. Degen Pener, "Drought Panic, Guilt, Finger-Pointing Put Hollywood to the Test," The Hollywood Reporter, September 24, 2015, http://www.hollywoodreporter.com/features/drought-panic-guilt-finger-pointing-826081. A 2014 UCLA study showed that wealthier neighborhoods typically consume three times more water than less-affluent ones (Stevens, "Beverly Hills Put a Spotlight"). The same study also found that "when it came to voluntary cuts in water usage, residents who use less water responded more than users of more water" Pener, "Drought Panic, Guilt, Finger-Pointing."

67. Stevens, "Beverly Hills Put a Spotlight."

68. The letters covered a two-month billing cycle that generally ran from June to August.

69. Adrian Kudler, "The Rich and Famous Water Wasters of Beverly Hills," Curbed, March 14, 2016, http://la.curbed.com/2016/3/14/11223022/beverly-hills-celebrity-water-wasters.

70. Lance Williams and Katharine Mieszkowski, "The Wet Prince of Bel Air: Who Is California's Biggest Water Guzzler?," Reveal, October 1, 2015, https://www.revealnews.org/article/the-wet-prince-of-bel-air-who-is-californias-biggest-water-guzzler/; at the average of 17.2 gallons per shower, 11.8 million gallons of water is equal to 1,879.5 showers per day! "Showers," Home Water Works, http://www.home-water-works.org/indoor-use/showers.

71. Matt Hickman, "The Biggest Water Hogs in Beverly Hills Have Been Outed," Mother Nature Network, March 17, 2016, http://www.mnn.com/your-home/at-home/blogs/beverly-hills-outs-its-biggest-water-wasters.

72. Stevens, "Beverly Hills Put a Spotlight."

73. Sam Sanders, "In California, Technology Makes Droughtshaming Easier Than Ever," NPR, May 25, 2015, http://www.npr.org/sections/thetwo-way/2015/05/25/409522056/in-california-technology-makes-droughtshaming-easier-than-ever.

74. Javier Panzar, "Smartphone App Lets Neighbors Report Water Wasters," *Los Angeles Times*, October 3, 2014, http://www.latimes.com/local/la-me-water-waster-app-20141003-story.html.

75. Aaron R. Brough, James E. B. Wilkie, Jingjing Ma, Mathew S. Isaac, and David Gal, "Is Eco-Friendly Unmanly? The Green-Feminine Stereotype and Its Effect on Sustainable Consumption," *Journal of Consumer Research* 43, no. 4 (2016): 567–82.

76. Lynnette C. Zelezny, Poh-Pheng Chua, and Christina Aldrich, "New Ways of Thinking about Environmentalism: Elaborating on Gender Differences in Environmentalism," *Journal of Social Issues* 56, no. 3 (2000): 443–57.

77. Ibid.

78. Robert B. Cialdini, Raymond R. Reno, and Carl A. Kallgren, "A Focus Theory of Normative Conduct: Recycling the Concept of Norms to Reduce Littering in Public Places," *Journal of Personality and Social Psychology* 58, no. 6 (1990): 1015.

79. Riitta Räty and Annika Carlsson-Kanyama, "Energy Consumption by Gender in Some European Countries," Energy Policy 38, no. 1 (2010): 646–49.

80. Riley E. Dunlap, Kent D. Van Liere, Angela G. Mertig, and Robert Emmet Jones, "New Trends in Measuring Environmental Attitudes: Measuring Endorsement of the New Ecological Paradigm: A Revised NEP Scale," *Journal of Social Issues* 56, no. 3 (2000): 425–42.

81. Aaron R. Brough, James E. B. Wilkie, Jingjing Ma, Mathew S. Isaac, and David Gal, "Is Eco-Friendly Unmanly? The Green-Feminine

Stereotype and Its Effect on Sustainable Consumption," *Journal of Consumer Research* 43, no. 4 (2016): 567–82.

82. Ibid.

83. Ibid.

84. Dale T. Miller and D. A. Prentice, "Psychological Levers of Behavior Change," *The Behavioral Foundations of Public Policy* (2013): 301–9.

85. Dena M. Gromet, Howard Kunreuther, and Richard P. Larrick, "Political Ideology Affects Energy-Efficiency Attitudes and Choices," *Proceedings of the National Academy of Sciences* 110, no. 23 (2013): 9314–19.

86. Ibid.

87. Dora L. Costa and Matthew E. Kahn, "Energy Conservation 'Nudges' and Environmentalist Ideology: Evidence from a Randomized Residential Electricity Field Experiment," *Journal of the European Economic Association* 11, no. 3 (2013): 680–702.

88. "Arnold Schwarzenegger Says Plenty of Space for Big Cars and Jacuzzis in Green Movement," *The Daily Telegraph*, June 24, 2013, http://www.dailytelegraph.com.au/entertainment/celebrity/arnold-schwarzenegger-says-plenty-of-space-for-big-cars-and-jacuzzis-in-green-movement/news-story/fb7c19db9e5fecdda7f6d63fdcf2039e.

89. Ibid.

Chapter 5

1. Irma T. Elo and Samuel H. Preston, "Effects of Early-Life Conditions on Adult Mortality: A Review," *Population Index* (1992): 186–212; Douglas Almond and Janet Currie, "Killing Me Softly: The Fetal Origins Hypothesis," *The Journal of Economic Perspectives* 25, no. 3 (2011): 153–72.

2. Jane McMillan, "The Best Organic Crib Mattress Is Safe and Non-Toxic for Your Baby," Healthy Child, October 30, 2015, https://www.healthychild.com/safe-non-toxic-organic-crib-mattresses/.

3. "Faststats: Cancer," National Center for Health Statistics, Centers for Disease Control and Prevention, http://www.cdc.gov/nchs/fastats/cancer.htm.

4. John R. Pleis and Margaret Lethbridge-Çejku, "Summary Health Statistics for Us Adults: National Health Interview Survey, 2005," *Vital and Health Statistics, Series 10*, no. 232 (2006).

5. "Cancer Facts & Figures 2014," American Cancer Society, 2014, https://www.cancer.org/research/cancer-facts-statistics/all-cancer-facts-figures/cancer-facts-figures-2014.html. The 75 percent number includes all nongenetic factors. Pesticides and air would be more like 6 percent.

6. US Cancer Statistics Working Group, *United States Cancer Statistics:*

1999–2014 Incidence and Mortality Web-Based Report (Atlanta: Centers for Disease Control and Prevention and National Cancer Institute, 2016).

7. "Faststats: Asthma," National Center for Health Statistics, Centers for Disease Control and Prevention, http://www.cdc.gov/nchs/fastats /asthma.htm; Jeanne E. Moorman et al., "National Surveillance for Asthma—United States, 1980–2004," *MMWR Surveillance Summaries* 56, no. 8 (2007).

8. "Facts About Autism Spectrum Disorders," Autism Spectrum Disorder (ASD), Centers for Disease Control and Prevention, http://www .cdc.gov/ncbddd/autism/addm.html.

9. Paul Bennett, *Psychology and Health Promotion* (Buckingham, UK: Open University Press, 1997).

10. John Stevens-Garmon, Chung L. Huang, and Biing-Hwan Lin, "Organic Demand: A Profile of Consumers in the Fresh Produce Market," *Choices* 22, no. 2 (2007): 109–16; Desmond A. Jolly and Kim Norris, "Marketing Prospects for Organic and Pesticide-Free Produce," *American Journal of Alternative Agriculture* 6, no. 4 (1991): 174–79.

11. "9 Amazing Benefits of Organic Food," Organic Facts, https:// www.organicfacts.net/organic-products/organic-food/health-benefits -of-organic-food.html.

12. Anne Davies, Albert J. Titterington, and Clive Cochrane, "Who Buys Organic Food? A Profile of the Purchasers of Organic Food in Northern Ireland," *British Food Journal* 97, no. 10 (1995): 17–23; A. Tregear, J. B. Dent, and M. J. McGregor, "The Demand for Organically Grown Produce," *British Food Journal* 96, no. 4 (1994): 21–25; Margareta Wandel and Annechen Bugge, "Environmental Concern in Consumer Evaluation of Food Quality," *Food Quality and Preference* 8, no. 1 (1997): 19–26.

13. "Organic Industry Survey 2017," Organic Trade Association, http://ota.com/resources/organic-industry-survey.

14. Ibid.

15. Siqi Zheng, Cong Sun, and Matthew E. Kahn, "Self-Protection Investment Exacerbates Air Pollution Exposure Inequality in Urban China," *Ecological Economics* 131 (2015): 468–74; Junjie Zhang and Quan Mu, "Air Pollution and Defensive Expenditures: Evidence from Particulate-Filtering Facemasks," *Journal of Environmental Economics and Management* (2017), https://doi.org/10.1016/j.jeem.2017.07.006.

16. Ibid.

17. Bert Brunekreef and Stephen T. Holgate, "Air Pollution and Health," *The Lancet* 360, no. 9341 (2002): 1233–42.

18. National Research Council, *Hidden Costs of Energy: Unpriced Consequences of Energy Production and Use* (Washington, DC: National Academies Press, 2010).

19. Richard H. Thaler and Cass R. Sunstein, "Nudge: Improving Decisions About Health, Wealth, and Happiness," *Constitutional Political Economy* 19, no. 4 (2008): 356–60.

20. Thomas Dietz, Amy Fitzgerald, and Rachael Shwom, "Environmental Values," *Annual Review of Environment and Resources* 30 (2005): 335–72; Niklas Fransson and Tommy Gärling, "Environmental Concern: Conceptual Definitions, Measurement Methods, and Research Findings," *Journal of Environmental Psychology* 19, no. 4 (1999): 369–82; Shahzeen Z. Attari, Michael L. DeKay, Cliff I. Davidson, and Wändi Bruine De Bruin, "Public Perceptions of Energy Consumption and Savings," *Proceedings of the National Academy of Sciences* 107, no. 37 (2010): 16054–59.

21. Omar I. Asensio and Magali A. Delmas, "Nonprice Incentives and Energy Conservation," *Proceedings of the National Academy of Sciences* 112, no. 6 (2015): E510–E515.

22. Victor L. Chen, Magali A. Delmas, William J. Kaiser, and Stephen L. Locke, "What Can We Learn from High-Frequency Appliance-Level Energy Metering? Results from a Field Experiment," *Energy Policy* 77 (2015): 164–75.

23. "Efficient neighbor" in this context means households in the top tenth percentile of household weekly average kWh consumption (lowest users of electricity) for similar-size apartments in the community.

24. Households were provided with factual, evidence-based numbers that depended on their weekly kWh electricity consumption. Equivalent cost savings were calculated using household consumption data and the published Los Angeles Department of Water and Power (LADWP) electric-rate schedules for residential customers. LADWP is the nation's largest public utility. Equivalent nonbaseload emissions were calculated using emission factors from the Emissions & Generation Resource Integrated Database (eGRID) database maintained by the US EPA.

25. For these equivalencies, we used nameplate wattages for typical household consumer appliances compiled by the US Department of Energy. "Estimating Appliance and Home Electronic Energy Use," Electricity & Fuel, Energy.gov, https://energy.gov/energysaver/estimating-appliance -and-home-electronic-energy-use.

26. Olga Naldenko, "Nobody Should Drink Water with Lead, Especially Kids. EWG's Guide for Parents Can Help," *EWG News and Analysis* (blog), Environmental Working Group, October 26, 2016, http://www

.ewg.org/enviroblog/2016/10/nobody-should-drink-water-lead-especially-kids-ewg-s-guide-parents-can-help.

27. Merrit Kennedy, "Lead-Laced Water in Flint: A Step-by-Step Look at the Makings of a Crisis," NPR, April 20, 2016, http://www.npr.org/sections/thetwo-way/2016/04/20/465545378/lead-laced-water-in-flint-a-step-by-step-look-at-the-makings-of-a-crisis.

28. Erik Olson and Kristi Fedinick, "What's in Your Water? Flint and Beyond," Our Work, NRDC, June 28, 2016, https://www.nrdc.org/resources/whats-your-water-flint-and-beyond.

29. Erin Brockovich, "Community Healthbook," https://www.communityhealthbook.com/map.

30. "Bottled Water Market," International Bottled Water Association, http://www.bottledwater.org/economics/bottled-water-market.

31. There is a continued increase in per capita consumption of bottled water. Sales revenues for the US bottled water market in 2015 were $14.2 billion in wholesale dollars, an 8.7 percent increase over the previous year. "Bottled Water—the Nation's Healthiest Beverage—Sees Accelerated Growth and Consumption," International Bottled Water Association, http://www.bottledwater.org/bottled-water-%E2%80%93-nation%E2%80%99s-healthiest-beverage-%E2%80%93-sees-accelerated-growth-and-consumption. Nearly all of the bottled water sold in the United States is sourced domestically. In fact, imported bottled water accounts for only 1 percent of the US market. The vast majority of bottled water companies in the United States are small, community-based companies using local water sources and distributing their products within an average radius of three hundred miles from their bottling facilities. "US Bottled Water Market—Statistics & Facts," Statista, https://www.statista.com/topics/1302/bottled-water-market/.

32. Jennifer Kaplan, "Bottled Water to Outsell Soda for First Time This Year," Bloomberg, August 2, 2016, https://www.bloomberg.com/news/articles/2016-08-02/bottled-water-to-outsell-soda-for-first-time-with-nod-to-flint; Sy Mukherjee, "The Depressing Reason Bottled Water Is about to Outsell Soda for the First Time," *Fortune*, August 2, 2016, http://fortune.com/2016/08/02/bottled-water-outsell-soda/.

33. Laura Newcomer, "Bottled Water Costs Us 2,000 Times More Than Tap. Is It Worth It?," The Daily Beast, September 18, 2016, http://www.thedailybeast.com/articles/2016/09/18/bottled-water-costs-us-2-000-times-more-than-tap-is-it-worth-it.html.

34. "Brita," https://www.brita.com/news/brita-filters-to-flint-mi.

35. Sarah Schuch, "Debunking That Social Media Rumor on Flint

Water Filters," M Live, October 7, 2015, http://www.mlive.com/news/flint/index.ssf/2015/10/debunking_that_social_media_ru.html.

36. "Prevention Is the Best Medicine," Preventative Health, Brita, https://www.brita.com/why-brita/health/preventative-health/.

37. "Brita Builds a City of Sugar Cubes in TV Ad," Brita, https://www.brita.com/news/brita-offers-221314-reasons-to-say-no-to-sugary-beverages/.

38. "Choose Better. Choose Healthier. Choose Filtered.," Brita, https://www.brita.com/why-brita/#tjpiPph6uBf07VSG.99.

39. Jessica Wohl, "Brita Hopes to Make a Big Splash with Stephen Curry," *Advertising Age*, March 10, 2016, http://adage.com/article/cmo-strategy/brita-ready-a-big-splash-stephen-curry/303046/.

40. Diane Mastrull, "In Lead Crises, a Maker of Water-Filtration Pitchers Sees Opportunity Clearly," *The Philadelphia Inquirer*, March 27, 2016, http://www.philly.com/philly/business/20160327_In_lead_crises__a_maker_of_water-filtration_pitchers_sees_opportunity_clearly.html.

41. Christopher Gavigan, *Healthy Child Healthy World: Creating a Cleaner, Greener, Safer Home* (New York: Penguin, 2008).

42. Clare O'Connor, "How Jessica Alba Built a $1 Billion Company, and $200 Million Fortune, Selling Parents Peace of Mind," *Forbes*, May 27, 2015, https://www.forbes.com/sites/clareoconnor/2015/05/27/how-jessica-alba-built-a-1-billion-company-and-200-million-fortune-selling-parents-peace-of-mind/#6168258942b4.

43. The mission of the company is "to help people live happy, healthy lives by providing products that families everywhere can trust. Tess Townsend, "Customers Say Honest Company Not So Honest about Subscriptions," *Inc.*, http://www.inc.com/tess-townsend/honest-company-ftc-complaints-subscriptions.html.

44. Devika Kumar, "It's a Diaper War," Business Insider, January 25, 2015, http://www.businessinsider.com/r-diaper-wars-kimberly-to-take-on-pg-through-innovation-higher-ad-spend-2015-1.

45. Lawrence Pines, "How Much Is the Honest Company Worth?," Investopedia, July 6, 2016, http://www.investopedia.com/articles/company-insights/070616/honest-company-whats-next-jessica-albas-darling.asp. The nearly five-year-old Honest Company will pull in a reported $250 million in sales in 2016 of its nontoxic baby, home, and personal-care products. To date, the company has raised $222 million. Lindsay Blakely, "Jessica Alba's Honest Company Reportedly Considering a Sale to Unilever," *Inc.*, http://www.inc.com/lindsay-blakely/jessica-albas-honest-company-reportedly-considering-a-sale-to-unilever.html.

46. Kathryn Vasel, "The Honest Company Gets Sued . . . Again," CNN Money, April 27, 2016, http://money.cnn.com/2016/04/27/news /companies/honest-company-lawsuit-organic-baby-formula/.

47. Townsend, "Customers Say Honest."

48. Neil E. Klepeis et al., "The National Human Activity Pattern Survey (NHAPS): A Resource for Assessing Exposure to Environmental Pollutants," *Journal of Exposure Science and Environmental Epidemiology* 11, no. 3 (2001).

49. James Krieger and Donna L Higgins, "Housing and Health: Time Again for Public Health Action," *American Journal of Public Health* 92, no. 5 (2002).

Chapter 6

1. Drazen Prelec and George Loewenstein, "The Red and the Black: Mental Accounting of Savings and Debt," *Marketing Science* 17, no. 1 (1998): 4–28.

2. Magali A. Delmas, Miriam Fischlein, and Omar I. Asensio, "Information Strategies and Energy Conservation Behavior: A Meta-Analysis of Experimental Studies from 1975 to 2012," *Energy Policy* 61 (2013): 729–39.

3. HomeAdvisor, "Pros, Cons and Costs: Energy Star Appliances," HomeAdvisor, http://www.homeadvisor.com/r/energy-star-appliances /#.WNh-lXTyvVp.

4. Lou Carlozo, "How Much Money Will You Save with Energy Star Appliances?," Deal News, http://dealnews.com/features/How-Much-Money -Will-You-Save-With-Energy-Star-Appliances/558643.html. For example, replacing incandescent light bulbs with energy-efficient halogens, CFLs, or LEDs saves 30 to 80 percent on energy bills. That adds up to annual savings from $50 to more than $100.

5. Twenty-five percent of residential refrigerators are not energy star, 50 percent of the room air conditioners are not Energy Star, 31 percent of the purchase of new clothes washers are not Energy Star, 8 percent of dishwashers are not Energy Star. "Energy Star Unit Shipment and Market Penetration Report Calendar Year 2014 Summary," Energy Star, https:// www.energystar.gov/ia/partners/downloads/unit_shipment_data/2014 _USD_Summary_Report.pdf?6d2e-c6c5.

6. Colin F. Camerer, "Strategizing in the Brain," *Science* 300, no. 5626 (2003): 1673–75.

7. Katrina Jessoe and David Rapson, "Knowledge Is (Less) Power: Experimental Evidence from Residential Energy Use," *The American Economic Review* 104, no. 4 (2014): 1417–38; Koichiro Ito, "Do Consumers Re-

spond to Marginal or Average Price? Evidence from Nonlinear Electricity Pricing," *The American Economic Review* 104, no. 2 (2014): 537–63.

8. Omar I. Asensio and Magali A. Delmas, "Nonprice Incentives and Energy Conservation," *Proceedings of the National Academy of Sciences* 112, no. 6 (2015): E510–E515.

9. Magali A. Delmas and Neil Lessem, "Saving Power to Conserve Your Reputation? The Effectiveness of Private versus Public Information," *Journal of Environmental Economics and Management* 67, no. 3 (2014): 353–70.

10. Shahzeen Z. Attari, Michael L. DeKay, Cliff I. Davidson, and Wändi Bruine De Bruin, "Public Perceptions of Energy Consumption and Savings," *Proceedings of the National Academy of Sciences* 107, no. 37 (2010): 16054–59.

11. Hunt Allcott and Michael Greenstone, "Is There an Energy Efficiency Gap?," *The Journal of Economic Perspectives* 26, no. 1 (2012): 3–28.

12. Lou Carlozo, "How Much Money Will You Save with Energy Star Appliances?," Deal News, http://dealnews.com/features/How-Much-Money-Will-You-Save-With-Energy-Star-Appliances/558643.html.

13. For households in the lowest 20 percent of income (before taxes), energy bills average 6 percent of total expenditures, whereas for those in the highest 20 percent of income (before taxes), energy bills average only 3 percent of total expenditures. "Lower Residential Energy Use Reduces Home Energy Expenditures as Share of Household Income," US Energy Information Administration, https://www.eia.gov/todayinenergy/detail.php?id=10891.

14. Michael D. Grubb, "Overconfident Consumers in the Marketplace," *The Journal of Economic Perspectives* 29, no. 4 (2015): 9–35.

15. Sondra G. Beverly, Amanda Moore McBride, and Mark Schreiner, "A Framework of Asset-Accumulation Stages and Strategies," *Journal of Family and Economic Issues* 24, no. 2 (2003): 143–56.

16. Margaret S. Sherraden, Amanda Moore, and Philip Hong, "Savers Speak: Case Studies of Ida Participants" (paper presented at the Society for Social Work Research Annual Conference, Charleston, SC, 2000).

17. Jennifer S. Haas, Kathryn A. Phillips, Eric P. Gerstenberger, and Andrew C. Seger, "Potential Savings from Substituting Generic Drugs for Brand-Name Drugs: Medical Expenditure Panel Survey, 1997–2000," *Annals of Internal Medicine* 142, no. 11 (2005): 891–97.

18. P. Wesley Schultz, "Strategies for Promoting Proenvironmental Behavior," *European Psychologist* (2014): 107–17.

19. "Hybrid Analysis," Vincentric, http://vincentric.com/Home/In

dustry-Reports/Hybrid-Analysis-2016; Danny King, "Most Hybrid Vehicles Don't Make Financial Sense for Buyers," Auto Blog, August 25, 2016, http://www.autoblog.com/2016/08/25/hybrid-car-financial-sense-study/.

20. George Loewenstein and Richard H. Thaler, "Anomalies: Intertemporal Choice," *The Journal of Economic Perspectives* 3, no. 4 (1989): 181–93; Richard Thaler, "Some Empirical Evidence on Dynamic Inconsistency," *Economics Letters* 8, no. 3 (1981): 201–7; John G. Lynch Jr. and Gal Zauberman, "When Do You Want It? Time, Decisions, and Public Policy," *Journal of Public Policy & Marketing* 25, no. 1 (2006): 67–78; Thomas S. Critchfield and Scott H. Kollins, "Temporal Discounting: Basic Research and the Analysis of Socially Important Behavior," *Journal of Applied Behavior Analysis* 34, no. 1 (2001): 101–22.

21. Maury Silver and John Sabini, "Procrastinating," *Journal for the Theory of Social Behaviour* 11, no. 2 (1981): 207–21.

22. Richard G. Newell and Juha Siikamäki, "Nudging Energy Efficiency Behavior: The Role of Information Labels," *Journal of the Association of Environmental and Resource Economists* 1, no. 4 (2014): 555–98.

23. Daniel Kahneman, "A Psychological Perspective on Economics," *The American Economic Review* 93, no. 2 (2003): 162–68; Daniel Kahneman, Jack L. Knetsch, and Richard H. Thaler, "Anomalies: The Endowment Effect, Loss Aversion, and Status Quo Bias," *The Journal of Economic Perspectives* 5, no. 1 (1991): 193–206.

24. Brian Knutson, Scott Rick, G. Elliott Wimmer, Drazen Prelec, and George Loewenstein, "Neural Predictors of Purchases," *Neuron* 53, no. 1 (2007): 147–56.

25. Jason F. Shogren and Laura O. Taylor, "On Behavioral-Environmental Economics," *Review of Environmental Economics and Policy* 2, no. 1 (2008): 26–44; Daniel Kahneman, Jack L. Knetsch, and Richard H. Thaler, "Experimental Tests of the Endowment Effect and the Coase Theorem," *Journal of Political Economy* 98, no. 6 (1990): 1325–48.

26. Tatiana A Homonoff, *Can Small Incentives Have Large Effects?: The Impact of Taxes Versus Bonuses on Disposable Bag Use* (Princeton, NJ: Princeton University, Industrial Relations Section, 2013).

27. Rebecca L. Taylor and Sofia B. Villas-Boas, "Bans vs. Fees: Disposable Carryout Bag Policies and Bag Usage," *Applied Economic Perspectives and Policy* 38, no. 2 (2016): 351–72.

28. Sidharth Muralidharan and Kim Sheehan, "'Tax' and 'Fee' Message Frames as Inhibitors of Plastic Bag Usage Among Shoppers: A Social Marketing Application of the Theory of Planned Behavior," *Social Marketing Quarterly* 22, no. 3 (2016): 200–217.

29. Uma R. Karmarkar and Bryan Bollinger, "BYOB: How Bringing Your Own Shopping Bags Leads to Treating Yourself and the Environment," *Journal of Marketing* 79, no. 4 (2015): 1–15.

30. Sebastien Houde and Annika Todd, "List of Behavioral Economics Principles that Can Inform Energy Policy," *Work in Progress* 19 (2010).

31. https://www.seia.org/research-resources/solar-market-insight -2015-q4.

32. https://www.greentechmedia.com/articles/read/72-of-us -residential-solar-installed-in-2014-was-third-party-owned.

33. Amos Tversky and Daniel Kahneman, "Heuristics and Biases: Judgement under Uncertainty," *Science* 185 (1974): 1124–30; Dan Ariely, George Loewenstein, and Drazen Prelec, "'Coherent Arbitrariness'": Stable Demand Curves without Stable Preferences," *The Quarterly Journal of Economics* 118, no. 1 (2003): 73–106.

34. Noel T. Brewer and Gretchen B. Chapman, "The Fragile Basic Anchoring Effect," *Journal of Behavioral Decision Making* 15, no. 1 (2002): 65–77.

35. "Anchoring," Investopedia, http://www.investopedia.com/terms /a/anchoring.asp.

36. Adam D. Galinsky and Thomas Mussweiler, "First Offers as Anchors: The Role of Perspective-Taking and Negotiator Focus," *Journal of Personality and Social Psychology* 81, no. 4 (2001): 657.

37. Kwanho Suk, Jiheon Lee, and Donald R. Lichtenstein, "The Influence of Price Presentation Order on Consumer Choice," *Journal of Marketing Research* 49, no. 5 (2012): 708–17.

38. "Model 3," Tesla, https://www.tesla.com/model3.

39. Ina Herlihy, "9 Ways Behavioral Economics Can Help Increase Conversion, Retention and Roi," Medium, November 17, 2015, https:// medium.com/@inaherlihy/9-ways-behavioral-economics-can-help -increase-conversion-retention-and-roi-3e245a2604e3#.8o9gc56wy.

40. Baba Shiv, Ziv Carmon, and Dan Ariely, "Placebo Effects of Marketing Actions: Consumers May Get What They Pay For," *Journal of Marketing Research* 42, no. 4 (2005): 383–93.

41. Ibid.

42. Hilke Plassmann, John O'Doherty, Baba Shiv, and Antonio Rangel, "Marketing Actions Can Modulate Neural Representations of Experienced Pleasantness," *Proceedings of the National Academy of Sciences* 105, no. 3 (2008): 1050–54.

43. "Toyota Prius," Carsalesbase.com, http://carsalesbase.com/us-car

-sales-data/toyota/toyota-prius/; "Toyota Prius," Electric Vehicles News, http://electricvehiclesnews.com/Cars/HEV/Toyota_Prius_HEV.htm.

44. Joey T. Cheng, Jessica L. Tracy, and Cameron Anderson, *The Psychology of Social Status* (New York: Springer, 2014).

45. Vladas Griskevicius, Joshua M. Tybur, and Bram Van den Bergh, "Going Green to Be Seen: Status, Reputation, and Conspicuous Conservation," *Journal of Personality and Social Psychology* 98, no. 3 (2010): 392.

46. Vladas Griskevicius, Stephanie M. Cantú, and Mark van Vugt, "The Evolutionary Bases for Sustainable Behavior: Implications for Marketing, Policy, and Social Entrepreneurship," *Journal of Public Policy & Marketing* 31, no. 1 (2012): 115–28.

47. Dan Ariely, *Predictably Irrational* (New York: HarperCollins, 2008).

48. Stefanie Heinzle, "Behavioural Models of Decision Making and Implications for Green Marketing" (working paper, St. Gallen, Germany, 2010).

49. Stephen J. Hoch and George F. Loewenstein, "Time-Inconsistent Preferences and Consumer Self-Control," *Journal of Consumer Research* 17, no. 4 (1991): 492–507.

50. Paul Chiambaretto and Hervé Dumez, "The Role of Bundling in Firms' Marketing Strategies: A Synthesis," *Recherche et Applications en Marketing (English Edition)* 27, no. 2 (2012): 91–105.

51. Michael D. Johnson, Andreas Herrmann, and Hans H. Bauer, "The Effects of Price Bundling on Consumer Evaluations of Product Offerings," *International Journal of Research in Marketing* 16, no. 2 (1999): 129–42.

52. Monifa Porter, Magali A. Delmas, and Erica Plambeck, "Environmental Product Differentiation by the Hayward Lumber Company," in *Environmental Management: Readings and Cases*, ed. Michael V. Russo (Thousand Oaks, CA: Sage, 2008).

53. Bruno S. Frey and Felix Oberholzer-Gee, "The Cost of Price Incentives: An Empirical Analysis of Motivation Crowding-Out," *The American Economic Review* 87, no. 4 (1997): 746–55; Dan Ariely, Anat Bracha, and Stephan Meier, "Doing Good or Doing Well? Image Motivation and Monetary Incentives in Behaving Prosocially," *American Economic Review* 99, no. 1 (Mar. 2009), pp. 544–55; Uri Gneezy, Stephan Meier, and Pedro Rey-Biel, "When and Why Incentives (Don't) Work to Modify Behavior," *The Journal of Economic Perspectives* 25, no. 4 (2011): 191–209.

54. Bruno S. Frey and Reto Jegen, *Motivation Crowding Theory: A Survey of Empirical Evidence* (Zurich: Institute for Empirical Research in Economics, University of Zurich, 1999); Edward L. Deci, "Effects of Exter-

nally Mediated Rewards on Intrinsic Motivation," *Journal of Personality and Social Psychology* 18, no. 1 (1971): 105; Edward L. Deci, Richard Koestner, and Richard M. Ryan, "A Meta-Analytic Review of Experiments Examining the Effects of Extrinsic Rewards on Intrinsic Motivation" (1999): 627; Michel J. J. Handgraaf, Margriet A. Van Lidth de Jeude, and Kirstin C. Appelt, "Public Praise vs. Private Pay: Effects of Rewards on Energy Conservation in the Workplace," *Ecological Economics* 86 (2013): 86–92.

55. Mark R. Lepper, David Greene, and Richard E. Nisbett, "Undermining Children's Intrinsic Interest with Extrinsic Reward: A Test of the 'Overjustification' Hypothesis," *Journal of Personality and Social Psychology* 28, no. 1 (1973): 129; Anna C. Merritt, Daniel A. Effron, and Benoît Monin, "Moral Self-Licensing: When Being Good Frees Us to Be Bad," *Social and Personality Psychology Compass* 4, no. 5 (2010): 344–57; Benoit Monin and Dale T. Miller, "Moral Credentials and the Expression of Prejudice," *Journal of Personality and Social Psychology* 81, no. 1 (2001): 33; Deci, "Effects of Externally Mediated Rewards."

Chapter 7

1. https://www.goodreads.com/quotes/177138-a-film-is---or-should-be---more-like.

2. "Maya Angelou," Wikiquote, https://en.wikiquote.org/wiki/Maya_Angelou.

3. Paul Ekman, "Expression and the Nature of Emotion," *Approaches to Emotion* 3 (1984): 19–344.

4. Julie Ann Pooley and Moira O'Connor, "Environmental Education and Attitudes: Emotions and Beliefs Are What Is Needed," *Environment and Behavior* 32, no. 5 (2000): 711–23.

5. Ty Montague, "If You Want to Raise Prices, Tell a Better Story," *Harvard Business Review*, July 31, 2013, https://hbr.org/2013/07/want-to-raise-prices-tell-a-be.

6. "California Earthquake Authority Sees Surge in New Policies Purchased," California Earthquake Authority, https://www.earthquakeauthority.com/press-room/press-release/cea-sees-surge-in-new-policies-purchased.

7. Prior to the Loma Prieta earthquake (1989), only 22.4 percent of the homes had earthquake insurance. Four years later, 36.6 percent had purchased earthquake insurance—a 72 percent increase. One year after the Northridge earthquake of 1994, more than two-thirds of the homeowners surveyed in Cupertino County had purchased earthquake insurance.

8. Melanie B. Tannenbaum, Justin Hepler, Rick S. Zimmerman, Lindsey Saul, Samantha Jacobs, Kristina Wilson, and Dolores Albarracín, "Appealing to Fear: A Meta-Analysis of Fear Appeal Effectiveness and Theories," *Psychological Bulletin* 141, no. 6 (2015): 1178–1204.

9. Ibid.

10. Nicola Power, Geoffrey Beattie, and Laura McGuire, "Mapping our Underlying Cognitions and Emotions about Good Environmental Behavior: Why We Fail to Act Despite the Best of Intentions," *Semiotica* 2017, no. 215 (2017): 193–234.

11. Abraham H. Maslow, "A Theory of Human Motivation," *Psychological Review* 50, no. 4 (1943): 370; Emma Seppala, Timothy Rossomando, and James R. Doty, "Social Connection and Compassion: Important Predictors of Health and Well-Being," *Social Research* 80, no. 2 (2013): 411–30. Countless psychological researches have verified the importance of positive social connections on "health, well-being and survival"; Debra Umberson and Jennifer Karas Montez, "Social Relationships and Health: A Flashpoint for Health Policy," *Journal of Health and Social Behavior* 51, no. 1 suppl. (2010): S54–S66.

12. Marian Chapman Burke and Julie A. Edell, "The Impact of Feelings on Ad-Based Affect and Cognition," *Journal of Marketing Research* (1989): 69–83; Morris B. Holbrook and Rajeev Batra, "Assessing the Role of Emotions as Mediators of Consumer Responses to Advertising," *Journal of Consumer Research* 14, no. 3 (1987): 404–20.

13. Donovan Robert and John Rossiter, "Store Atmosphere: An Environmental Psychology Approach," *Journal of Retailing* 58, no. 1 (1982): 34–57.

14. Robert A. Westbrook and Richard L. Oliver, "The Dimensionality of Consumption Emotion Patterns and Consumer Satisfaction," *Journal of Consumer Research* 18, no. 1 (1991): 84–91.

15. Tom Watson, "What Makes People Generous: Charity, Empathy, and Storytelling," *Forbes*, June 30, 2014, https://www.forbes.com/sites /tomwatson/2014/06/30/what-makes-people-generous-charity-empathy -and-story-telling/#7b22f7847cba.

16. Richard S. Lazarus, *Emotion and Adaptation* (Oxford, UK: Oxford University Press on Demand, 1991).

17. Mitch Griffin, Barry J. Babin, Jill S. Attaway, and William R. Darden, "Hey You, Can Ya Spare Some Change? The Case of Empathy and Personal Distress as Reactions to Charitable Appeals," *ACR North American Advances* (1993): 508–14.

18. Mary Lou Shelton and Ronald W. Rogers, "Fear-Arousing and

Empathy-Arousing Appeals to Help: The Pathos of Persuasion," *Journal of Applied Social Psychology* 11, no. 4 (1981): 366–78.

19. J. W. Bolderdijk, L. Steg, E. S. Geller, P. K. Lehman, and T. Postmes, "Comparing the Effectiveness of Monetary versus Moral Motives in Environmental Campaigning," *Nature Climate Change* 3, no. 4 (2013): 413–16.

20. Jessica Shaw, "What You Really Get for the High Price of 'Humanely Raised' Meat," Market Watch, November 19, 2015, http://www.marketwatch.com/story/what-you-really-get-for-the-high-price-of-humanely-raised-meat-2015-11-19.

21. Charles Daniel Batson, *Altruism in Humans* (New York: Oxford University Press, 2011); Nancy Eisenberg and Paul A. Miller, "The Relation of Empathy to Prosocial and Related Behaviors," *Psychological Bulletin* 101, no. 1 (1987): 91; Walter C. Borman, Louise A. Penner, Tammy D. Allen, and Stephan J. Motowidlo, "Personality Predictors of Citizenship Performance," *International Journal of Selection and Assessment* 9, no. 1–2 (2001): 52–69; Sara Konrath, Emily Falk, Andrea Fuhrel-Forbis, Mary Liu, James Swain, Richard Tolman, Rebecca Cunningham, and Maureen Walton, "Can Text Messages Increase Empathy and Prosocial Behavior? The Development and Initial Validation of Text to Connect," *PloS One* 10, no. 9 (2015): e0137585.

22. "What Is Ecotourism?," The International Ecotourism Society, http://www.ecotourism.org/what-is-ecotourism; Josh Lew, "Can Eco-Tourism Help Underdeveloped Countries?," *Forbes*, September 12, 2011, https://www.forbes.com/sites/eco-nomics/2011/09/12/can-eco-tourism-help-underdeveloped-countries/#475691585ab4.

23. "Sustainable Travel in 2016," Booking.com, https://globalnews.booking.com/sustainable-travel-in-2016/; Alexandra Talty, "In 2015, Travel Is All About Eco-Tourism, Charity," *Forbes*, June 18, 2015, https://www.forbes.com/sites/alexandratalty/2015/06/18/in-2015-travel-is-all-about-eco-tourism-charity/#68d838cb6038.

24. Brian Wheeller, "Tourism's Troubled Times: Responsible Tourism Is Not the Answer," *Tourism Management* 12, no. 2 (1991): 91–96.

25. Frans Melissen, "Ecotourism's Potential to Stage Life Changing Experiences," in CAUTHE 2012: *The New Golden Age of Tourism and Hospitality*, book 2 (proceedings of the 22nd annual conference, La Trobe University, 2012), p. 407.

26. Roy Ballantyne, John Fien, and Jan Packer, "Program Effectiveness in Facilitating Intergenerational Influence in Environmental Education: Lessons from the Field," *The Journal of Environmental Education* 32, no. 4 (2001): 8–15.

27. Elisabeth Kals, Daniel Schumacher, and Leo Montada, "Emotional Affinity toward Nature as a Motivational Basis to Protect Nature," *Environment and Behavior* 31, no. 2 (1999): 178–202.

28. Roy Ballantyne, Jan Packer, and Lucy A. Sutherland, "Visitors' Memories of Wildlife Tourism: Implications for the Design of Powerful Interpretive Experiences," *Tourism Management* 32, no. 4 (2011): 770–79.

29. Ibid.

30. James R. Kimmel, "Ecotourism as Environmental Learning," *The Journal of Environmental Education* 30, no. 2 (1999): 40–44; Won Hee Lee and Gianna Moscardo, "Understanding the Impact of Ecotourism Resort Experiences on Tourists' Environmental Attitudes and Behavioural Intentions," *Journal of Sustainable Tourism* 13, no. 6 (2005): 546–65; Robert B. Powell and Sam H. Ham, "Can Ecotourism Interpretation Really Lead to Pro-Conservation Knowledge, Attitudes and Behaviour? Evidence from the Galapagos Islands," *Journal of Sustainable Tourism* 16, no. 4 (2008): 467–89; Clem Tisdell and Clevo Wilson, "Perceived Impacts of Ecotourism on Environmental Learning and Conservation: Turtle Watching as a Case Study," *Environment, Development and Sustainability* 7, no. 3 (2005): 291–302.

31. Kate Groch, Karen E. Gerdes, Elizabeth A. Segal, and Maureen Groch, "The Grassroots Londolozi Model of African Development: Social Empathy in Action," *Journal of Community Practice* 20, no. 1–2 (2012): 154–77.

32. Ibid.

33. Maurizio Peleggi, "Consuming Colonial Nostalgia: The Monumentalisation of Historic Hotels in Urban South-East Asia," *Asia Pacific Viewpoint* 46, no. 3 (2005): 255–65.

34. Woojin Lee and Deepak Chhabra, "Heritage Hotels and Historic Lodging: Perspectives on Experiential Marketing and Sustainable Culture," *Journal of Heritage Tourism* 10, no. 2 (2015): 103–10.

35. Joan C. Henderson, "Selling the Past: Heritage Hotels," *Turizam: znanstveno-stručni časopis* 61, no. 4 (2013): 451–54.

36. Elaine Hatfield, John T. Cacioppo, and Richard L. Rapson, "Primitive Emotional Contagion," *Review of Personality and Social Psychology* 14 (1992): 151–77; Elaine Hatfield, John T. Cacioppo, and Richard L. Rapson, "Emotional Contagion," *Current Directions in Psychological Science* 2, no. 3 (1993): 96–100; Roland Neumann and Fritz Strack, "'Mood Contagion': The Automatic Transfer of Mood between Persons," *Journal of Personality and Social Psychology* 79, no. 2 (2000): 211.

37. Deborah A., Small and Nicole M. Verrochi, "The Face of Need:

Facial Emotion Expression on Charity Advertisements," *Journal of Marketing Research* 46, no. 6 (2009): 777–87.

38. "Company Overview of Lotus Foods, Inc.," Bloomberg, http://www.bloomberg.com/research/stocks/private/snapshot.asp?privcapid=232404758.

39. Caryl Levine, interview by Magali A. Delmas, March 2, 2017.

40. Ibid.

41. Lury Giles, "Leading with Narrative," Impact Information Plain Language Services, http://www.impact-information.com/impactinfo/newsletter/plwork51.htm.

42. Harrison Monarth, "The Irresistible Power of Storytelling as a Strategic Business Tool," *Harvard Business Review*, March 11, 2014, https://hbr.org/2014/03/the-irresistible-power-of-storytelling-as-a-strategic-business-tool.

43. Paul Zak, "Why Your Brain Loves Good Storytelling," *Harvard Business Review*, October 2014, https://hbr.org/2014/10/why-your-brain-loves-good-storytelling.

44. Ibid.

45. Robert McKee and Bronwyn Fryer, "Storytelling That Moves People," *Harvard Business Review* 81, no. 6 (2003).

46. Arch Woodside, Suresh Sood, and Kenneth E. Miller, "When Consumers and Brands Talk: Storytelling Theory and Research in Psychology and Marketing," *Psychology & Marketing* 25, no. 2 (2008).

47. Mara Einstein, *Compassion, Inc.: How Corporate America Blurs the Line between What We Buy, Who We Are, and Those We Help* (Berkeley: University of California Press, 2012).

48. "Adding Multimedia Dawn® and Shedd Aquarium Inspire Next Generation of Wildlife Enthusiasts," P&G, http://news.pg.com/press-release/pg-corporate-announcements/adding-multimedia-dawn-and-shedd-aquarium-inspire-next-gene.

49. Caeleigh Warburton, March 28, 2015, Company Appeals, http://blogs.stlawu.edu/greenwashingcritiques/company-appeals/; Associated Press, "Glance: Procter & Gamble's 'Billion-Dollar Brands,'" Yahoo Finance, http://finance.yahoo.com/news/glance-procter-gambles-billion-dollar-214306330.html.

50. Ana Maria Arumi et al., *The Charitable Impulse* (New York: Public Agenda, 2005); William D. Diamond and Rajiv K. Kashyap, "Extending Models of Prosocial Behavior to Explain University Alumni Contributions," *Journal of Applied Social Psychology* 27, no. 10 (1997): 915–28; Brian Duncan, "A Theory of Impact Philanthropy," *Journal of Public Economics*

88, no. 9 (2004): 2159–80; Anil Mathur, "Older Adults' Motivations for Gift Giving to Charitable Organizations: An Exchange Theory Perspective," *Psychology & Marketing* 13, no. 1 (1996): 107–23; Alan Radley and Marie Kennedy, "Reflections upon Charitable Giving: A Comparison of Individuals from Business, 'Manual' and Professional Backgrounds," *Journal of Community & Applied Social Psychology* 2, no. 2 (1992): 113–29; Joanne R. Smith and Andreè McSweeney, "Charitable Giving: The Effectiveness of a Revised Theory of Planned Behaviour Model in Predicting Donating Intentions and Behaviour," *Journal of Community & Applied Social Psychology* 17, no. 5 (2007): 363–86.

51. Pamala Wiepking, Kym Madden, and Katie McDonald, "Leaving a Legacy: Bequest Giving in Australia," *Australasian Marketing Journal (AMJ)* 18, no. 1 (2010): 15–22.

52. Margrit Talpalaru, "Blake Mycoskie, TOMS, and Life Narratives of Conspicuous Giving," *Biography* 37, no. 1 (2014): 168–90.

53. C. Daniel Batson and Laura L. Shaw, "Evidence for Altruism: Toward a Pluralism of Prosocial Motives," *Psychological Inquiry* 2, no. 2 (1991): 107–22.

54. James Andreoni, "Giving with Impure Altruism: Applications to Charity and Ricardian Equivalence," *Journal of Political Economy* 97, no. 6 (1989): 1447–58.

55. William T. Harbaugh, Ulrich Mayr, and Daniel R. Burghart, "Neural Responses to Taxation and Voluntary Giving Reveal Motives for Charitable Donations," *Science* 316, no. 5831 (2007): 1622–25.

56. Jorge Moll, Frank Krueger, Roland Zahn, Matteo Pardini, Ricardo de Oliveira-Souza, and Jordan Grafman, "Human Fronto–Mesolimbic Networks Guide Decisions about Charitable Donation," *Proceedings of the National Academy of Sciences* 103, no. 42 (2006): 15623–28.

57. "The One-for-One Business Model: Avoiding Unintended Consequences," Wharton School, http://knowledge.wharton.upenn.edu /article/one-one-business-model-social-impact-avoiding-unintended -consequences/.

58. Ibid.

59. Anne Landman, "A 'Humanitarian Campaign' to Sell Bottled Water," PR Watch, http://www.prwatch.org/spin/2008/03/7082/humani tarian-campaign-sell-bottled-water.

60. Anna Lenzer, "After a Mother Jones Investigation, Starbucks Says It Will Stop Bottling Water in California," *Mother Jones,* http://www .motherjones.com/blue-marble/2015/05/after-mother-jones-investiga tion-starbucks-says-it-will-stop-bottling-water-cali.

61. Ibid.

62. Megan Willett, "A Social Media Expert Explains How You Can Make Something Go Viral," Business Insider, http://www.businessinsider .com/how-do-you-go-viral-2016-5.

63. Charles Vallance, "Storytelling Is Dead. Long Live Story Doing," Campaign, http://www.campaignlive.co.uk/article/storytelling-dead-long -live-story -doing/1405760.

64. John Seaman Jr. and George Smith, "Your Company's History as a Leadership Tool," *Harvard Business Review*, https://hbr.org/2012/12 /your-companys-history-as-a-leadership-tool.

65. Aaron Chatterji and Michael Toffel, "The Power of C.E.O. Activism," *New York Times*, April 3, 2016, https://www.nytimes.com/2016/04/03 /opinion/sunday/the-power-of-ceo-activism.html?_r=0&mtrref=undefined &gwh=FB6216BC436DC3499FEC54F10B499A52&gwt=pay&assetType =opinion.

66. Vallance, "Storytelling Is Dead."

67. Weber Shandwick and KRC Research, "The Dawn of CEO Activism, 2016," http://www.webershandwick.com/uploads/news/files/the -dawn-of-ceo-activism.pdf.

68. René Richard, Joop van der Pligt, and Nanne de Vries, "Anticipated Affect and Behavioral Choice," *Basic and Applied Social Psychology* 18 (1996): 111–29.

69. Amos Tversky and Daniel Kahneman, "Judgment under Uncertainty: Heuristics and Biases," *Science* 185 (1974): 1124–31.

70. Nicole Koenig-Lewis, Adrian Palmer, Janine Dermody, and Andreas Urbye, "Consumers' Evaluations of Ecological Packaging—Rational and Emotional Approaches," *Journal of Environmental Psychology* 37 (2014): 94–105.

71. Nicola Power, Geoffrey Beattie, and Laura McGuire, "Mapping our Underlying Cognitions and Emotions about Good Environmental Behavior: Why We Fail to Act Despite the Best of Intentions," *Semiotica* (2016).

72. Ibid.

73. Olli T. Ahtola, "Hedonic and Utilitarian Aspects of Consumer Behavior: An Attitudinal Perspective," *ACR North American Advances* (1985): 7–10; Barry J. Babin, William R. Darden, and Mitch Griffin, "Work and/ or Fun: Measuring Hedonic and Utilitarian Shopping Value," *Journal of Consumer Research* 20, no. 4 (1994): 644–56; Elizabeth C. Hirschman and Morris B. Holbrook, "Hedonic Consumption: Emerging Concepts, Methods and Propositions," *The Journal of Marketing* (1982): 92–101; Mor-

ris B. Holbrook and Elizabeth C. Hirschman, "The Experiential Aspects of Consumption: Consumer Fantasies, Feelings, and Fun," *Journal of Consumer Research* 9, no. 2 (1982): 132–40; Brian Lofman, "Elements of Experiential Consumption: An Exploratory Study," *ACR North American Advances* 18 (1991).

74. Sharon Shavitt, "The Role of Attitude Objects in Attitude Functions," *Journal of Experimental Social Psychology* 26, no. 2 (1990): 124–48.

75. Shih-Chang Tseng and Shiu-Wan Hung, "A Framework Identifying the Gaps between Customers' Expectations and Their Perceptions in Green Products," *Journal of Cleaner Production* 59 (2013): 174–84.

Chapter 8

1. Guilbert Gates et al., "How Volkswagen's 'Defeat Devices' Worked," *New York Times*, 2017, https://www.nytimes.com/interactive/2015/business /international/vw-diesel-emissions-scandal-explained.html.

2. Hiroko Tabuchi and Jack Ewing, "Volkswagen to Pay $14.7 Billion to Settle Diesel Claims in U.S.," *New York Times*, June 28, 2016, https:// www.nytimes.com/2016/06/28/business/volkswagen-settlement-diesel -scandal.html.

3. Joel Stocksdale, "German State Sues Volkswagen over Diesel Scandal Fallout," AutoBlog, August 2, 2016, http://www.autoblog.com/2016 /08/02/german-state-sues-volkswagen-diesel-scandal/.

4. Mark Thompson, "Volkswagen Recalls 8.5 Million Diesel Vehicles in Europe," CNN Money, October 15, 2015, http://money.cnn.com/2015 /10/15/news/companies/volkswagen-scandal-recall-germany/.

5. Nancy E. Furlow, "Greenwashing in the New Millennium," *The Journal of Applied Business and Economics* 10, no. 6 (2010): 22; "How to Identify Greenwashing," Green Options, updated March 30, 2011, http://www .greenoptions.com/a/how-to-identify-greenwashing; Thomas P. Lyon and A. Wren Montgomery, "The Means and End of Greenwash," *Organization & Environment* 28, no. 2 (2015): 223–49.

6. Eric L. Lane, "Consumer Protection in the Eco-Mark Era: A Preliminary Survey and Assessment of Anti-Greenwashing Activity and Eco-Mark Enforcement," *SSRN eLibrary* (2010): 742–73; "Honda Headed to Court Tomorrow for False Advertising of Hyped Up Hybrid Civic Claims," Brand Geek, March 6, 2012, http://www.brandgeek.net/2012/01/02 /honda-headed-court-tomorrow-false-advertising-hyped-hybrid-civic -claims/.

7. TerraChoice Environmental Marketing, "The Six Sins of Greenwashing: A Study of Environmental Claims in North American Consumer Markets," *Greenwashing Report*, 2007, http://sinsofgreenwashing.com

/index3c24.pdf; TerraChoice Environmental Marketing, "The Seven Sins of Greenwashing," *Greenwashing Report*, 2009, http://sinsofgreenwashing .com/index3c24.pdf; TerraChoice Environmental Marketing, "The Sins of Greenwashing: Home and Family Edition," *Greenwashing Report*, 2010, http://sinsofgreenwashing.com/index35c6.pdf.

8. The Green Works Natural Products Mislabeling Class Action Lawsuit is Joseph Gregorio and Patrick Quiroz v. The Clorox Company, Case No. 3:17-cv-03824, in the US District Court for the Northern District of California.

9. Stephanie Clifford and Andrew Martin, "As Consumers Cut Spending, 'Green' Products Lose Allure," *New York Times*, April 22, 2011, http://www.nytimes.com/2011/04/22/business/energy-environment/22green .html.

10. Lane, "Consumer Protection in the Eco-Mark Era"; David Gibson, "Awash in Green: A Critical Perspective on Environmental Advertising," *Tulane Environmental Law Journal* 22 (2009); TerraChoice Environmental Marketing, "The Seven Sins of Greenwashing," *Greenwashing Report*, 2009, http://sinsofgreenwashing.com/index3c24.pdf.

11. Magali A. Delmas and Vanessa Cuerel Burbano, "The Drivers of Greenwashing," *California Management Review* 54, no. 1 (2011): 64–87. Lane defines greenwashing as "making false or misleading claims regarding environmentally friendly products, services or practices." Lane, "Consumer Protection in the Eco-Mark Era." And TerraChoice Group ("The Seven Sins of Greenwashing") defines greenwashing as "the act of misleading consumers regarding the environmental practices of a company or the environmental benefits of a product or service."

12. Lane, "Consumer Protection in the Eco-Mark Era."

13. Ed Gillespie, "Stemming the Tide of Greenwash: How an Ostensibly 'Greener' Market Could Pose Challenges for Environmentally Sustainable Consumerism," *Consumer Policy Review* 18, no. 3 (2008): 79.

14. TerraChoice Environmental Marketing, "The Seven Sins of Greenwashing: Environmental Claims in Consumer Markets," 2009, http://sinsofgreenwashing.com/findings/greenwashing-report-2009/. We report the percentages based on the 2009 report for twelve stores in the United States, accounting for 1,721 products and 3,890 claims (see page 18). Information on the frequency of sins committed in Canada for 1,331 products is provided on page 19. Information on sins committed in the United Kingdom for 787 products is provided on page 20. Information on the frequency of sins committed in Australia for 866 products is provided on page 21.

15. Mark Hays, "The Social and Environmental Impacts of Bottled

Water," Think Outside the Bottle, http://www.responsiblepurchasing.org /webinars/bottled_water_webinar_slides_082608.pdf.

16. The Green Works Natural Products Mislabeling Class Action Lawsuit is Joseph Gregorio and Patrick Quiroz v. The Clorox Company, Case No. 3:17-cv-03824, in the US District Court for the Northern District of California.

17. Andrew. J. Hoffman, *SC Johnson and the Greenlist Backlash*, Case 1-429-300 (Ann Arbor: William Davidson Institute, University of Michigan, 2013).

18. Jonathan Bardelline, "SC Johnson Settles Lawsuits over Greenlist Logo," Green Biz, July 8, 2011, https://www.greenbiz.com/news/2011/07 /08/sc-johnson-settles-lawsuits-over-greenwashing-greenlist-logo.

19. "Cigarette Litter Prevention Program: The Problems and Facts," Keep America Beautiful, https://www.kab.org/cigarette-litter-prevention /problem-and-facts.

20. Erin A. Bass, "Lululemon's Commitment to the Environment: A Tangle of Seaweed, Suppliers, and Social Responsibility," *Marketing and Management Faculty Proceedings & Presentations* 5 (2010).

21. Nancy Napier, "The Myth of Multitasking," *Psychology Today*, May 12, 2014, https://www.psychologytoday.com/blog/creativity-without -borders/201405/the-myth-multitasking.

22. See, for example, Daniel Kahneman and Dan Lovallo, "Timid Choices and Bold Forecasts: A Cognitive Perspective on Risk Taking," *Management Science* 39/1 (1993): 17–31.

23. George Ainslie and Nick Haslam, "Hyperbolic Discounting," in *Choice over Time*, ed. George Loewenstein and Jon Elster (New York: Russell Sage Foundation, 1992); George-Marios Angeletos, David Laibson, Andrea Repetto, Jeremy Tobacman, and Stephen Weinberg, "The Hyperbolic Consumption Model: Calibration, Simulation, and Empirical Evaluation," *The Journal of Economic Perspectives* 15, no. 3 (2001): 47–68.

24. Kahneman and Lovallo, "Timid Choices and Bold Forecasts."

25. Arnold C. Cooper, Carolyn Y. Woo, and William C. Dunkelberg, "Entrepreneurs' Perceived Chances for Success," *Journal of Business Venturing* 3, no. 2 (1988): 97–108.

26. Neil Patel, "90% of Startups Fail: Here's What You Need to Know About the 10%," *Forbes*, January 16, 2016, https://www.forbes.com/sites /neilpatel/2015/01/16/90-of-startups-will-fail-heres-what-you-need-to -know-about-the-10/#7a25c40a6679.

27. See, for example, Daniel Kahneman, "Maps of Bounded Rationality: Psychology for Behavioral Economics," *The American Economic Review* 93, no. 5 (2003): 1449–75.

28. Kahneman and Lovallo, "Timid Choices and Bold Forecasts."

29. Martin B. Meznar and Douglas Nigh, "Buffer or Bridge? Environmental and Organizational Determinants of Public Affairs Activities in American Firms," *Academy of Management Journal* 38, no. 4 (1995): 975–96.

30. James C. Wimbush, Jon M. Shepard, and Steven E. Markham, "An Empirical Examination of the Relationship between Ethical Climate and Ethical Behavior from Multiple Levels of Analysis," *Journal of Business Ethics* 16, no. 16 (1997): 1705–16.

31. LaRue T. Hosmer, "The Institutionalization of Unethical Behavior," *Journal of Business Ethics* 6, no. 6 (1987): 439–47.

32. David P. Baron, *Business and Its Environment* (Upper Saddle River, NJ: Prentice Hall, 2003).

33. Eric Weiner, "Eastern Airlines Indicted in Scheme over Maintenance," *New York Times*, July 26, 1990, http://www.nytimes.com/1990/07/26/business/eastern-airlines-indicted-in-scheme-over-maintenance.html?pagewanted=all.

34. John B. Cullen, K. Praveen Parboteeah, and Bart Victor, "The Effects of Ethical Climates on Organizational Commitment: A Two-Study Analysis," *Journal of Business Ethics* 46, no. 2 (2003): 127–41.

35. Ibid.

36. For a review of the literature, see Kelly Martin and John Cullen, "Continuities and Extensions of Ethical Climate Theory: A Meta-Analytic Review," *Journal of Business Ethics* 69, no. 2 (2006): 175–94.

37. Richard P. Rumelt, "Inertia and Transformation," in *Resource-Based and Evolutionary Theories of the Firm: Towards a Synthesis*, ed. Cynthia A. Montgomery (Boston: Kluwer Academic, 1995): 101–32.

38. Michael T. Hannan and John Freeman, "Structural Inertia and Organizational Change," *American Sociological Review* 49, no. 2 (1984): 149–64.

39. James Maxwell, Sandra Rothenberg, Forrest Briscoe, and Alfred Marcus, "Green Schemes: Corporate Environmental Strategies and Their Implementation," *California Management Review* 39, no. 3 (1997): 118–34.

40. James Herron, "BP CEO Shies Away from Radical Change," *Wall Street Journal*, October 19, 2019, blogs.wsj.com/source/2010/10/19/bp-ceo-shies-away-from-radical-change.

41. Gabriel Szulanski, "Exploring Internal Stickiness: Impediments to the Transfer of Best Practice within the Firm," *Strategic Management Journal* 17, no. S2 (1996): 27–43.

42. Morten T. Hansen, "The Search-Transfer Problem: The Role of Weak Ties in Sharing Knowledge Across Organization Subunits," *Administrative Science Quarterly* 44, no. 1 (1999): 82–111.

43. David Gibson, "Awash in Green: A Critical Perspective on Environmental Advertising," *Tulane Environmental Law Journal* 22 (2009).

44. Federal Trade Commission, www.ftc.gov.

45. "Green Guides," Federal Trade Commission, https://www.ftc.gov/news-events/media-resources/truth-advertising/green-guides.

46. Kate Galbraith, "Search Green Search F.T.C. Sends Stern Warning on 'Biodegradable' Marketing Claims," *New York Times*, June 11, 2009, https://green.blogs.nytimes.com/2009/06/11/ftc-sends-stern-warning-on-biodegradable-marketing-claims/.

47. David P. Baron, *Business and its Environment* (Upper Saddle River, NJ: Prentice Hall, 2003).

48. Jacob Vos, "Actions Speak Louder than Words: Greenwashing in Corporate America," *Notre Dame Journal of Law, Ethics & Public Policy* 23 (2009): 673.

49. Magali A. Delmas and Michael W. Toffel, "Organizational Responses to Environmental Demands: Opening the Black Box," *Strategic Management Journal* 29, no. 10 (2008): 1027–55.

50. Felix Oberholzer-Gee, Forest Reinhardt, and Elizabeth Raabe, "UBS and Climate Change–Warming Up to Global Action?," *Harvard Business School Case* (2007): 707–11.

51. Magali A. Delmas and Vered Doctori Blass, "Measuring Corporate Environmental Performance: The Trade-Offs of Sustainability Ratings," *Business Strategy and the Environment* 19, no. 4 (2010): 245–60.

Chapter 9

1. "The Activist Company," http://www.patagonia.com/the-activist-company.html.

2. Amanda Little, "An Interview with Patagonia Founder Yvon Chouinard," *Grist*, October 23, 2004, http://grist.org/article/little-chouinard/.

3. "Company History," http://www.patagonia.com/company-history.html.

4. Lon Koontz, "Patagonia Wants You to Stop Buying Its Clothes," Newco Shift, September 19, 2016, https://shift.newco.co/patagonia-wants-you-to-stop-buying-its-clothes-9075460a23ce#.20tjtkd5t.

5. Kate Gibson, "Patagonia Stops Buying Wool Due to Mistreated Lambs," CBS News, August 17, 2015, http://www.cbsnews.com/news/patagonia-stops-buying-wool-due-to-mistreated-lambs/.

6. J. B. MacKinnon, "Patagonia's Anti-Growth Strategy," *The New Yorker*, May 21, 2015, http://www.newyorker.com/business/currency/patagonias-anti-growth-strategy.

7. Koontz, "Patagonia Wants You."

8. Ibid.

9. Thomas P. Lyon and A. Wren Montgomery, "The Means and End of Greenwash," *Organization & Environment* 28, no. 2 (2015): 223–49.

10. Vijay Kanal, "Just How Important Is the CEO to Sustainability?," *GreenBiz* (blog), January 31, 2011, https://www.greenbiz.com/blog/2011 /01/31/just-how-important-ceo-sustainability.

11. Andrew Winston, "A New Tool for Avoiding Greenwash," Sustainable Life Media, http://www.sustainablebrands.com/news_and_views /articles/new-tool-avoiding-greenwash.

12. Richard Fry, "Millennials Overtake Baby Boomers as America's Largest Generation," Pew Research Center, April 25, 2016, http://www .pewresearch.org/fact-tank/2016/04/25/millennials-overtake-baby -boomers/; Karl Moore, "Authenticity: The Way to the Millennial's Heart," *Forbes*, August 14, 2014, https://www.forbes.com/sites/karlmoore /2014/08/14/authenticity-the-way-to-the-millennials-heart/#6f49d4b9 4531; Matthew Tyson, "Millennials Want Brands to Be More Authentic. Here's Why That Matters," *Huffpost* (blog), January 21, 2016, http://www .huffingtonpost.com/matthew-tyson/millennials-want-brands-t_b_9032 718.html.

13. Don Tapscott and David Ticoll, *The Naked Corporation: How the Age of Transparency Will Revolutionalize Business* (New York: Free Press, 2003).

14. Leilani Latimer, director of sustainability initiatives at Sabre Holdings, also believes that the CEO should be the key spokesperson, at least internally. She said, "To achieve transformation inside a company, not just (potentially reversible) change, you need the CEO to be the primary advocate." Kanal, "Just How Important."

15. BU Questrom, "Timberland CEO on Green-Washing" (YouTube, 2009), https://www.youtube.com/watch?v=vyEUXq-n30I.

16. "Sustainability Disclosure Database" (Global Reporting Initiative, 2016), http://database.globalreporting.org/.

17. Jeffrey Rosenblum, Arpad Horvath, and Chris Hendrickson, "Environmental Implications of Service Industries," *Environmental Science & Technology* 34, no. 22 (2000): 4669–76.

18. Victor Luckerson, "Bangladesh Factory Collapse: Is There Blood on Your Shirt?," *Time*, May 2, 2013, http://business.time.com/2013/05/02 /bangladesh-factory-collapse-is-there-blood-on-your-shirt/.

19. Kevin B. Hendricks and Vinod R. Singhal, "An Empirical Analysis of the Effect of Supply Chain Disruptions on Long-Run Stock Price Performance and Equity Risk of the Firm," *Production and Operations Management* 14, no. 1 (2005): 35–52.

20. Magali A. Delmas, Nicholas Nairn-Birch, and Jinghui Lim, "Dy-

namics of Environmental and Financial Performance: The Case of Greenhouse Gas Emissions," *Organization & Environment* 28, no. 4 (2015): 374–93.

21. Erica L. Plambeck and L. Denend, "Wal-Mart," *Stanford Social Innovation Review* 6, no. 2 (2008): 53–59.

22. Magali A. Delmas and Ivan Montiel, "Greening the Supply Chain: When Is Customer Pressure Effective?," *Journal of Economics & Management Strategy* 18, no. 1 (2009): 171–201.

23. Nicole Darnall, G. Jason Jolley, and Robert Handfield, "Environmental Management Systems and Green Supply Chain Management: Complements for Sustainability?," *Business Strategy and the Environment* 17, no. 1 (2008): 30–45.

24. Anne Marie Mohan, "P&G Launches Supplier Environmental Sustainability Scorecard," Greener Package, June 15, 2010, https://www.greenerpackage.com/metrics_standards_and_lca/pg_launches_supplier_environmental_sustainability_scorecard.

25. Delmas and Montiel, "Greening the Supply Chain."

26. Angeloantonio Russo and Francesco Perrini, "Investigating Stakeholder Theory and Social Capital: CSR in Large Firms and SMEs," *Journal of Business Ethics* 91, no. 2 (2010): 207–21.

27. Roy C. Anderson and Eric N. Hansen, "Determining Consumer Preferences for Ecolabeled Forest Products: An Experimental Approach," *Journal of Forestry* 102, no. 4 (2004): 28–32; Mario F. Teisl, Brian Roe, and Robert L. Hicks, "Can Eco-Labels Tune a Market? Evidence from Dolphin-Safe Labeling," *Journal of Environmental Economics and Management* 43, no. 3 (2002): 339–59.

28. "Greenhouse Gas Emissions from a Typical Passenger Vehicle," EPA, November 17, 2017, https://www.epa.gov/greenvehicles/greenhouse-gas-emissions-typical-passenger-vehicle.

29. Corinne Le Quéré, Robbie M. Andrew, Josep G. Canadell, Stephen Sitch, Jan Ivar Korsbakken, Glen P. Peters, Andrew C. Manning et al., "Global Carbon Budget 2016," *Earth System Science Data* 8, no. 2 (2016): 605.

30. Eric J. Johnson, Suzanne B. Shu, Benedict G. C. Dellaert, Craig Fox, Daniel G. Goldstein, Gerald Häubl, Richard P. Larrick et al., "Beyond Nudges: Tools of a Choice Architecture," *Marketing Letters* 23, no. 2 (2012): 487–504.

31. GWPs determine the ratio of heat trapped by one unit mass of the specific greenhouse gas to that of one unit mass of carbon dioxide over a specified time period. These GWP factors were developed by the International Panel on Climate Change (IPCC), http://info.era

-environmental.com/blog/bid/58087/GHG-Emissions-Demystifying
-Carbon-Dioxide-Equivalent-CO2e.

32. "What Are Co2e and Global Warming Potential (GWP)?," The
Guardian, April 27, 2011, https://www.theguardian.com/environment
/2011/apr/27/co2e-global-warming-potential.

33. Erez Yoeli et al., "Behavioral Science Tools to Strengthen Energy & Environmental Policy," Behavioral Science and Policy Association,
2017.

34. Pablo J. Barrio, Daniel G. Goldstein, and Jake M. Hofman, "Improving Comprehension of Numbers in the News," in *Proceedings of the
2016 CHI Conference on Human Factors in Computing Systems* (New York:
ACM, 2016), pp. 2729–39.

35. Bluebulb Projects, "Measure of Things," 2017, http://www.blue
bulbprojects.com/MeasureOfThings/.

36. Jennifer Chiodo, "What Does a Ton of CO2 Look Like?," Building
Energy, June 13, 2012, https://buildingenergy.cx-associates.com/2012/06
/what-does-a-ton-of-co2-look-like/.

37. Holly Johnson, "Light Bulb Showdown: LED vs. CFL vs. Incandescent," The Simple Dollar, October 16, 2017, https://www.thesimpledollar
.com/the-light-bulb-showdown-leds-vs-cfls-vs-incandescent-bulbs-whats
-the-best-deal-now-and-in-the-future/.

38. Katherine A. Burson, Richard P. Larrick, and John G. Lynch Jr.,
"Six of One, Half Dozen of the Other: Expanding and Contracting Nu-
merical Dimensions Produces Preference Reversals," *Psychological Science*
20, no. 9 (2009): 1074–78.

39. Ian Quinn, "'Frustrated' Tesco Ditches Eco-Labels," The Grocer,
January 28, 2012, http://www.thegrocer.co.uk/channels/supermarkets
/tesco/frustrated-tesco-ditches-eco-labels/225502.article?redirCanon=1.

40. James Murray, "Exclusive: Ecover Shuns EU Eco-Label," Business-
Green, August 20, 2009, http://www.businessgreen.com/bg/news/180
6659/exclusive-ecover-shuns-eu-eco-label.

41. Magali A. Delmas, Nicholas Nairn-Birch, and Michaela Balzarova, "Choosing the Right Eco-Label for Your Product," *MIT Sloan Management Review* 54, no. 4 (2013): 10–12.

42. Abhijit Banerjee and Barry D. Solomon, "Eco-Labeling for Energy Efficiency and Sustainability: A Meta-Evaluation of US Programs,"
Energy Policy 31, no. 2 (2003): 109–23.

43. Ibid.

44. "Media Center," Trip Advisor, https://tripadvisor.mediaroom.com
/us.

45. "New Research Reveals Increasing Consumer Support for the MSC

Ecolabel," Marine Stewardship Council, September 4, 2012, https://www.msc.org/newsroom/news/new-research-reveals-increasing-consumer-support-for-the-msc-ecolabel.

46. "Media Centre," Marine Stewardship Council, https://www.msc.org/newsroom/media-centre.

47. Magali A. Delmas, "Perception of Eco-Labels: Organic and Biodynamic Wines," *UCLA Institute of the Environment* (2010): 9–10.

48. "Ecolabel Index," Big Room Inc., 2017. http://www.ecolabelindex.com/ecolabels/.

49. EPA Office of Air and Radiation, Climate Protection Partnerships Division, *National Awareness of ENERGY STAR® for 2016: Analysis of 2016 CEE Household Survey* (Washington, DC: US Environmental Protection Agency, 2017), https://library.cee1.org/content/national-awareness-energy-star%C2%AE-2016.

50. Banerjee and Solomon, "Eco-Labeling for Energy Efficiency."

51. C. Dennis Anderson and John D. Claxton, "Barriers to Consumer Choice of Energy Efficient Products," *Journal of Consumer Research* 9, no. 2 (1982): 163–70.

52. Magali A. Delmas and Ann K. Terlaak, "A Framework for Analyzing Environmental Voluntary Agreements," *California Management Review* 43, no. 3 (2001): 44–63.

53. Richard B. Howarth, Brent M. Haddad, and Bruce Paton, "The Economics of Energy Efficiency: Insights from Voluntary Participation Programs," *Energy Policy* 28, no. 6 (2000): 477–86; Banerjee and Solomon, "Eco-Labeling for Energy Efficiency."

54. Benjamin Cashore, Graeme Auld, and Deanna Newsom, "Legitimizing Political Consumerism: The Case of Forest Certification in North America and Europe," in *Politics, Products, and Markets: Exploring Political Consumerism Past and Present*, ed. Michele Micheletti, Andreas Follesdal, and Dietlind Stolle (New Brunswick, NJ: Transaction Publishers, 2004), 181–99.

55. Charlotte Leire and Åke Thidell, "Product-Related Environmental Information to Guide Consumer Purchases—A Review and Analysis of Research on Perceptions, Understanding and Use among Nordic Consumers," *Journal of Cleaner Production* 13, no. 10 (2005): 1061–70.

56. "FSC Policies & Standards," Forest Stewardship Council, https://nz.fsc.org/en-nz/policies.

57. P. Gerez-Fernández and E. Alatorre-Guzmán, "Challenges for Forest Certification and Community Forestry in Mexico," in *The Community Forests of Mexico* (Austin: University of Texas Press, 2005): 71–87.

58. Simon Counsell and K. Terje Loraas, "Trading in Credibility: The Myth and Reality of the Forest Stewardship Council," (2002); Nicole Freris and Klemens Laschefski, "Seeing the Wood from the Trees," *The Ecologist* 31, no. 6 (2001): 40–43.

59. Douglas H. Constance and Alessandro Bonanno, "Regulating the Global Fisheries: The World Wildlife Fund, Unilever, and the Marine Stewardship Council," *Agriculture and Human Values* 17, no. 2 (2000): 125–39.

60. Alexia Cummins, "The Marine Stewardship Council: A Multi-Stakeholder Approach to Sustainable Fishing," *Corporate Social Responsibility and Environmental Management* 11, no. 2 (2004): 85–94.

61. "Scgh Greencheck," SCGH, http://www.scgh.com/scgh-green check/.

62. "Our Partners," SCGH, http://www.scgh.com/our-partners/.

63. Nancy Kong, Oliver Salzmann, Ulrich Steger, and Aileen Ionescu-Somers, "Moving Business/Industry Towards Sustainable Consumption: The Role of NGOs," *European Management Journal* 20, no. 2 (2002): 109–27.

64. Ibid.

65. Marc Gunther, "Who's Peddling Pulp Fiction in the SFI vs. FSC Forestry Wars?," *GreenBiz* (blog), March 30, 2011, https://www.greenbiz.com/blog/2011/03/30/whos-peddling-pulp-fiction-sfi-vs-fsc-forestry-wars.

66. Benjamin Cashore, "What Is the Evidence for Changes in Eco-Labeling Requirements? Comparing the Dynamic Nature of Forest Stewardship Council and Sustainable Forestry Initiative Standards in the United States," in *2015 Fall Conference: The Golden Age of Evidence-Based Policy* (Washington, DC: Appam, 2015).

67. Angeloantonio Russo and Francesco Perrini, "Investigating Stakeholder Theory and Social Capital: CSR in Large Firms and SMEs," *Journal of Business Ethics* 91, no. 2 (2010): 207–21.

68. Louise Story, "'Seaweed' Clothing Has None, Tests Show," *New York Times*, November 14, 2007, http://www.nytimes.com/2007/11/14/business/14seaweed.html?pagewanted=all.

69. A. Erin Bass, "Lululemon's Commitment to the Environment: A Tangle of Seaweed, Suppliers, and Social Responsibility," in *Case Studies in Sustainability Management: The Oikos Collection*, vol. 3, ed. Jordi Vives Gabriel (New York: Routledge, 2010).

70. Lars H. Gulbrandsen, "Mark of Sustainability? Challenges for Fishery and Forestry Eco-Labeling," *Environment: Science and Policy for Sustainable Development* 47, no. 5 (2005): 8–23.

71. Lars H. Gulbrandsen, "Creating Markets for Eco-Labelling: Are

Consumers Insignificant?," *International Journal of Consumer Studies* 30, no. 5 (2006): 477–89.

72. Stephen Bass, *Certification's Impacts on Forests, Stakeholders and Supply Chains* (London: Iied, 2001).

73. Tavis Potts and Marcus Haward, "International Trade, Eco-Labelling, and Sustainable Fisheries—Recent Issues, Concepts and Practices," *Environment, Development and Sustainability* 9, no. 1 (2007): 91–106.

74. Allen Blackman and Jorge Rivera, "Producer-Level Benefits of Sustainability Certification," *Conservation Biology* 25, no. 6 (2011): 1176–85.

75. Charlotte Leire and Åke Thidell, "Product-Related Environmental Information to Guide Consumer Purchases—A Review and Analysis of Research on Perceptions, Understanding and Use among Nordic Consumers," *Journal of Cleaner Production* 13, no. 10 (2005): 1061–70.

76. Graeme Auld and Lars H. Gulbrandsen, "Transparency in Non-state Certification: Consequences for Accountability and Legitimacy," *Global Environmental Politics* 10, no. 3 (2010): 97–119.

77. Castka Pavel and Charles J. Corbett, "Governance of Eco-Labels: Expert Opinion and Media Coverage," *Journal of Business Ethics* 135, no. 2 (2016): 309–26.

Conclusion

1. Omar Isaac Asensio and Magali A. Delmas, "The Dynamics of Behavior Change: Evidence from Energy Conservation," *Journal of Economic Behavior & Organization* 126 (2016): 196–212.

2. Piers MacNaughton, John Spengler, Jose Vallarino, Suresh Santanam, Usha Satish, and Joseph Allen, "Environmental Perceptions and Health Before and After Relocation to a Green Building," *Building and Environment* 104 (2016): 138–44.

3. Victor L. Chen, Magali A. Delmas, Stephen L. Locke, and Amarjeet Singh, "Information Strategies for Energy Conservation: A Field Experiment in India," *Energy Economics* 68 (2017): 215–27.

4. Ibid.

5. Omar Isaac Asensio and Magali A. Delmas, "The Dynamics of Behavior Change: Evidence from Energy Conservation," *Journal of Economic Behavior & Organization* 126 (2016): 196–212.

6. Monifa Porter, Magali A. Delmas, and Erica Plambeck, "Environmental Product Differentiation by the Hayward Lumber Company," in *Environmental Management: Readings and Cases*, ed. Michael V. Russo (Thousand Oaks, CA: Sage, 2008).

7. Tracy Bhamra, Debra Lilley, and Tang Tang, "Design for Sustain-

able Behaviour: Using Products to Change Consumer Behaviour," *The Design Journal* 14, no. 4 (2011): 427–45; Ronald Jeurissen, "John Elkington, Cannibals with Forks: The Triple Bottom Line of 21st Century Business," *Journal of Business Ethics* 23, no. 2 (2000): 229–31.

8. Bhamra, "Design for Sustainable Behaviour."

9. Victor L. Chen, Magali A. Delmas, William J. Kaiser, and Stephen L. Locke. "What can we learn from high-frequency appliance-level energy metering? Results from a field experiment." *Energy Policy* 77 (2015): 164–175. Gill and colleagues also found that energy-efficiency behaviors account for 51%, 37%, and 11% of the variance in heat, electricity, and water consumption, respectively, between dwellings in the UK. Zachary M. Gill, Michael J. Tierney, Ian M. Pegg, and Neil Allan. "Low-energy dwellings: the contribution of behaviours to actual performance." *Building Research & Information* 38, no. 5 (2010): 491–508.

10. For example, households in the 75th percentile of HVAC usage consume over four times as much electricity as a user in the 25th percentile.

11. Renee Wever, Jasper Van Kuijk, and Casper Boks, "User-Centred Design for Sustainable Behaviour," International Journal of Sustainable Engineering 1, no. 1 (2008): 9–20.

12. Jaap Jelsma and Marjolijn Knot, "Designing Environmentally Efficient Services; a 'Script' Approach," *The Journal of Sustainable Product Design* 2, no. 3 (2002): 119–30; Dan Lockton, David Harrison, and Neville Stanton, "Making the User More Efficient: Design for Sustainable Behaviour," *International Journal of Sustainable Engineering* 1, no. 1 (2008): 3–8; Ida Nilstad Pettersen and Casper Boks, "The Ethics in Balancing Control and Freedom When Engineering Solutions for Sustainable Behaviour," *International Journal of Sustainable Engineering* 1, no. 4 (2008): 287–97; Debra Lilley, "Design for Sustainable Behaviour: Strategies and Perceptions," *Design Studies* 30, no. 6 (2009): 704–20; Bhamra, Lilley, and Tang, "Design for Sustainable Behaviour: Using Products to Change Consumer Behaviour."

13. Tang Tang and Tracy Bhamra, "Putting Consumers First in Design for Sustainable Behaviour: A Case Study of Reducing Environmental Impacts of Cold Appliance Use," *International Journal of Sustainable Engineering* 5, no. 4 (2012): 288–303.

14. Jelsma and Knot, "Designing Environmentally Efficient Services."; Wever, Van Kuijk, and Boks, "User-Centred Design."

15. Pettersen and Boks, "The Ethics in Balancing"; Lilley, "Design for Sustainable Behaviour: Strategies and Perceptions."

16. Tang and Bhamra, "Putting Consumers First in Design."

17. Timothy M. Devinney, "Is the Socially Responsible Corporation a Myth? The Good, the Bad, and the Ugly of Corporate Social Responsibility," *The Academy of Management Perspectives* 23, no. 2 (2009): 44–56.

18. Magali A. Delmas, Maria J. Montes-Sancho, and Jay P. Shimshack, "Information Disclosure Policies: Evidence from the Electricity Industry," *Economic Inquiry* 48, no. 2 (2010): 483–98.

19. Magali A. Delmas, Jinghui Lim, and Nicholas Nairn-Birch, "Corporate Environmental Performance and Lobbying," *Academy of Management Discoveries* 2, no. 2 (2016): 175–97. For example, one of the greenest utilities in the nation, Pacific Gas and Electric (PG&E) spent the second highest amount (an estimated $27 million) of all firms lobbying on climate change in 2008—just behind ExxonMobil, which spent $29 million lobbying and produced an estimated 306 million tons of greenhouse-gas emissions. PG&E openly supported a cap-and-trade system for carbon emissions and even left the US Chamber of Commerce over the organization's vociferous opposition to carbon regulation.

INDEX